The American
Southwest

Edited by Nancy Zimmerman and Kit Duane
Photography by Kerrick James

COMPASS AMERICAN GUIDES
An Imprint of Fodor's Travel Publications, Inc.

Southwest
Second Edition

Copyright © 1996, 1997, 1998 Fodor's Travel Publications, Inc.
Maps Copyright © 1996, 1997, 1998 Fodor's Travel Publications, Inc.

LIBRARY OF CONGRESS CATALOGING-IN-PUBLICATION DATA
Southwest/edited by Nancy Zimmerman and Kit Duane; photography by Kerrick James.
    p. cm. -(Compass American Guides)
Includes bibliographical references and index
ISBN 0-679-00035-6 (paper): $18.95
1. Southwest-Guidebooks. I. Title II. Series: Compass American Guides.   (Series)
F785.3 A45 1998   97-42215
917.904'33--dc 21   CIP

Compass American Guides, 5332 College Avenue, Suite 201, Oakland, CA 94618

Editors: Nancy Zimmerman, Kit Duane,   Designer: Christopher Burt, Debi Dunn
    Lawrence Cheek, Barry Parr, Debi Dunn   Map Design: Mark Stroud, Moon Street
Managing Editor: Kit Duane   Cartography
Photography Editor: Christopher Burt

Production House: Twin Age Ltd., Hong Kong   Printed in Hong Kong
10 9 8 7 6 5 4 3 2 1

The Publisher gratefully acknowledges the following institutions and individuals for the use of their photographs and/or illustrations on the following pages: **George H. H. Huey** pp. 152–153, 170–171; **Eduardo Fuss** pp. 75, 85, 103, 118, 119; **Underwood Photo Archives**, San Francisco pp. 26, 40, 45, 46, 58, 172, 244, 259; **Library of Congress** pp. 21, 193, 232-233, 344; **Museum of New Mexico** pp. 28, 54, 74, 90, 319 (middle); **Rell Francis, Springfield, Utah** pp. 41, 191; **New York Public Library** p. 27; **Fine Arts Museum of new Mexico, Santa Fe** p. 99; **Nevada State Historical Society** p. 239; **The Southwest Museum, Los Angeles** N.20135 p. 139; **Center for Southwest Studies, Fort Lewis College, Durango;** p. 157 **Church of Latter-day Saints Archives** p. 235; **Oakland Museum Kahn Collection** p. 322; **U.S. Forest Service** p. 329; **Western History Collection, Univ. of Oklahoma** p. 318 (bottom); **Arizona Historical Society Library** p. 319 (top, bottom); **Eiteljorg Museum of American Indian and Western Art** pp. 136–137. The Publisher is especially grateful to **Lawrence Cheek** for his many contributions and to **Nancy Falk** for proofreading.
    The Photographer wishes to thank **Madelaine Cassidy** and **Brian Tepp** of the Pentax Corporation for their technical support, equipment loans, and most of all for their friendship.

There is something infectious about the magic of the Southwest. Some are immune to it, but there are others who have no resistance and who must spend the rest of their lives dreaming of the incredible sweep of the desert, of great golden mesas with purple shadows, and tremendous stars appearing at dusk in a turquoise sky.

—H. M. Wormington

CONTENTS

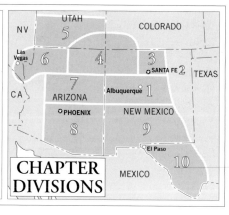

1 Central New Mexico
2 Santa Fe
3 Northern New Mexico
4 Four Corners
5 Utah Canyonlands
6 Grand Canyon and Las Vegas
7 Central Arizona
8 Southeastern Arizona
9 Southern New Mexico
10 Trans-Pecos

CHAPTER
DIVISIONS

Literary Extracts

Paul Horgan *on a Spanish colonial wedding* 86
F. Scott Momaday *on a Navajo girl* 161
Zane Grey *on a stone bridge in a storm* 211
John Wesley Powell *on river rafting* 231

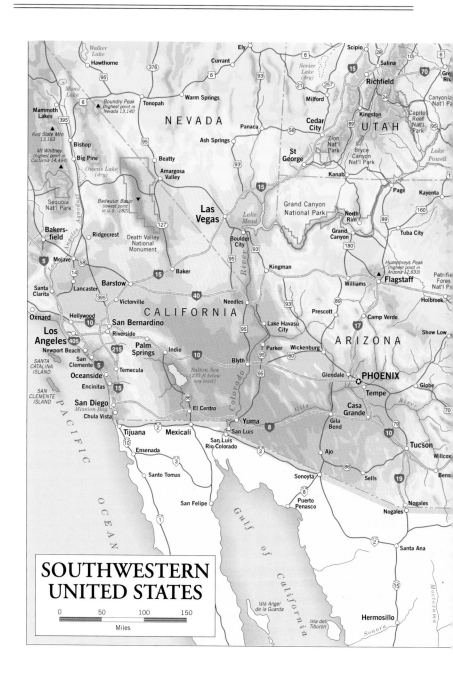

SOUTHWESTERN
UNITED STATES

0   50   100   150

Miles

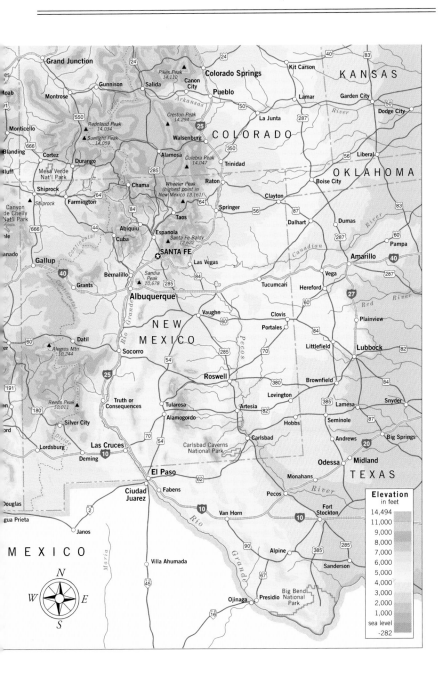

Elevation
in feet

14,494
11,000
9,000
8,000
7,000
6,000
5,000
4,000
3,000
2,000
1,000
sea level
-282

O V E R V I E W

THE AMERICAN SOUTHWEST'S windswept mesas and storied rivers, its ancient ruins, and innovative cuisine attract artists, dreamers, curmudgeons, and an ever-increasing number of visitors. Many of the latter come to the Southwest in the hope of experiencing something unique and authentic. To do so, we suggest the following:

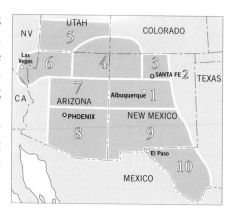

1 CENTRAL NEW MEXICO
Here lie the Zuñi and Ácoma mesa-top villages, first visited by Spanish conquistadors in 1540. Fascinating road trips from Albuquerque wind through the Manzano Mountains and along the Turquoise Trail.

2 SANTA FE
The most beautiful city in the Southwest, Santa Fe is famous for its adobe houses, fine cuisine, and dynamic art scene. Sit for a long afternoon under the cottonwoods of Sena Plaza, tour the Palace of the Governors, and visit the art galleries on Canyon Road.

3 NORTHERN NEW MEXICO

Eight pueblos line the route from Santa Fe to Taos along the Rio Grande. This is magnificent, high-desert country, famous for the quality of its light, snow-capped peaks, and small mountain towns where descendants of early Spanish colonists farm and produce traditional crafts.

4 FOUR CORNERS

Wild and remote, the Four Corners is named for the spot where four states meet—Utah, Colorado, Arizona, and New Mexico. In its many cliff dwellings and ruined cities, deserted even before the Spanish arrived, the ancient Anasazi once designed fine masonry buildings, fashioned pottery, listened to flute music, and drew pictographs on canyon walls. Today, the Navajo, Ute, and Hopi reservations stretch across its horizons.

5 UTAH CANYONLANDS

The vast canyons, arches, pinnacles, "reefs" and bizarre shapes carved into the red-rock mesas of the Colorado Plateau have earned this region the name of "standing-up country." Faced with such astounding geological wonders, the Mormon settlers bestowed upon them names that invoke both the holy and the outlandish: the Virgin River, Great White Throne, Angel's Landing, and Zion, for instance; but also the Alligator and the Chinese Wall of Bryce National Park. The great outback embraces sweeps of wilderness, such as Paria Canyon, where flash floods and quicksand are ever-present dangers. The Colorado River backs up behind Glen Canyon Dam to form Lake Powell, where the visitor can rent a boat and retreat to quiet shores and isolated red-rock canyons.

6 GRAND CANYON AND LAS VEGAS

One to 18 miles wide, 277 miles long, and one mile deep, the Colorado River's greatest piece of work is the most magnificent and incomprehensible canyon in the world. Walk along its north or south rims, descend to the bottom by mule or foot, or run its wild rapids. Just to the north of its tallest dam lies the ultimate mirage, Las Vegas, with its fantasy architecture, slots, showgirls, white tigers, erupting "volcanoes," and jousting "knights." The hotels are bargains, but the registration desk can be hard to locate: you may have to walk through a casino to find it.

7 CENTRAL ARIZONA

Set high on the edge of the dry Colorado Plateau, the Petrified Forest and the Painted Desert are splashed with colors so vibrant, it's easy to imagine they're the work of some giant, playful three-year-old. The small, inviting Oak Creek Canyon town of Sedona offers fine resorts, good restaurants, and New Age shops, set amidst spectacular red-rock walls.

8 SOUTHEASTERN ARIZONA

The Sonoran Desert's most famous denizen is the saguaro, the looming, almost humanoid cactus that has come to symbolize the desert Southwest. Yet, within this desert also lie Phoenix and Tucson, known for golf courses, fancy resorts, and baseball's spring training. Farther south is Tombstone, where Wyatt Earp and Doc Holliday shot it out with the Clanton gang at the OK Corral.

9 SOUTHERN NEW MEXICO

Here are Carlsbad Caverns; the old mining town of Silver City; the Gila Cliff Dwellings; the only town in the United States to be invaded by a foreign army since 1812; and the ghostly white sea of sand dunes laid down by a prehistoric lake.

10 TEXAS TRANS-PECOS

This far-west corner of Texas is one that few Texans have visited, yet it is the Texas most often depicted in Western movies. El Paso is its major city, the crossing point in the mountains astride the Rio Grande, followed by Indian traders in antiquity and later the Spanish conquistadors. The isolated and dry country of the Chihuahuan Desert embraces both the verdant Guadalupe Mountains and Big Bend National Park.

LANDSCAPE AND HISTORY

THE SOUTHWEST IS A TREMENDOUSLY VARIED STRETCH of geography, encompassing much more than the towering bluffs, sheer canyons, and saguaro-studded deserts that symbolize the region in the minds of most of us. Deep canyons, red buttes, and giant cacti certainly are integral parts of the Southwest; but so are lofty mountains, vast forests, and sprawling metropolitan areas.

The arrangement of these physical features has dictated the state's human settlement and economic development throughout history, and still shapes its future. Consequently, the Southwest's history is every bit as complex as its geography. Ancient cliff dwellings, Pueblo villages, Santa Fe's Palace of the Governors, dusty mine shafts, lonely army posts, Mormon pioneers, and hard-working cowboys are as "Southwest" as golf courses, blue corn tortillas, and dried chile wreaths.

■ ANCIENT LANDSCAPE

The Southwest is an open-air laboratory for geologists, a land where the earth's frame, foundation, and structure are exposed for all to see. Not only is vegetation often sparse, laying open vast tracts of naked earth and rock, but canyons cut deep through the mesas, exposing geologic time in a succession of rock layers. From rim to river, the famed Grand Canyon exposes fully seven periods of geologic time, from the Triassic (about 200 million years ago) to the Precambrian (more than 600 million years ago). More recent epochs are exposed in other parts of the Southwest. Utah, for instance, is particularly noteworthy for the exposed shelves of the Morrison Formation, whose last layer was deposited at the height of the dinosaur age, more than 65 million years ago. These upper strata are what makes Utah so rich in dinosaur fossils; the rocks of the Grand Canyon, however, are just too old for them.

Sedimentary, metamorphic, and igneous specimens make the Southwest a treasure-house for rock hounds, as do isolated curiosities like petrified wood and fossilized brachiopods, trilobites, corals, and crinoid stems. Such rich finds, hundreds of miles inland from the ocean, barely hint at the extraordinary geologic past that created the Southwest as it looks today.

Shallow seas covered much of the area for most of the Paleozoic Era, about 600

Banded sandstone in a slickrock desert area of Utah.

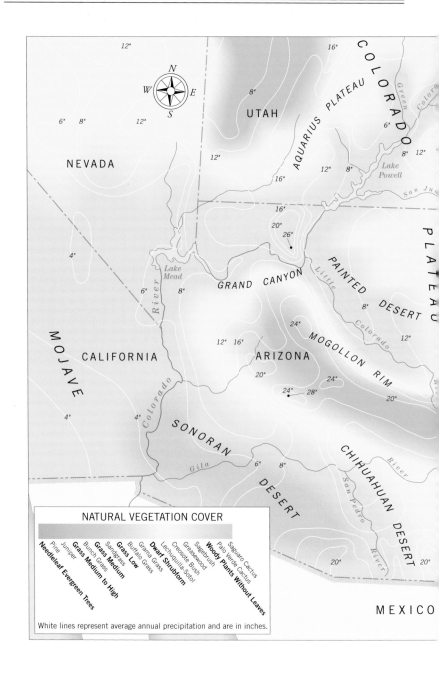

12"   16"   COLORADO

8"

UTAH   AQUARIUS PLATEAU   Green   Colo

6"   8"   12"   6"

8"   12"

NEVADA   12"   12"   8"   Lake
                                                          Powell

                    16"   San Jua

                    16"
                    20"
                    26"   PAINTED

4"   P
                                                                  L
                    Lake   GRAND CANYON   Little   A
                    Mead   DESERT T
6"   8"   8"   E
                                                                 A
                                          24"   12"
                    12"   16"   MOGOLLON RIM

MOJAVE   CALIFORNIA   ARIZONA   24"

                              20"   24"   28"   20"
                    Colorado   24" 28"

4"   4"   SONORAN   River   CHIHUAHUAN

                    Gila   6"   8"   San Pedro   DESERT

                              DESERT   River

                                                  20"   20"

NATURAL VEGETATION COVER

Saguaro Cactus
Palo Verde Cactus
Woody Plants Without Leaves
Greasewood
Sagebrush
Creosote Bush
Lechuguilla-Sotol
Dwarf Shrubform
Grama Grass
Buffalo Grass
Grass Low
Sandgrass
Grass Medium
Bunch Grass
Grass Medium to High
Juniper
Pine
Needleleaf Evergreen Trees

White lines represent average annual precipitation and are in inches.

MEXICO

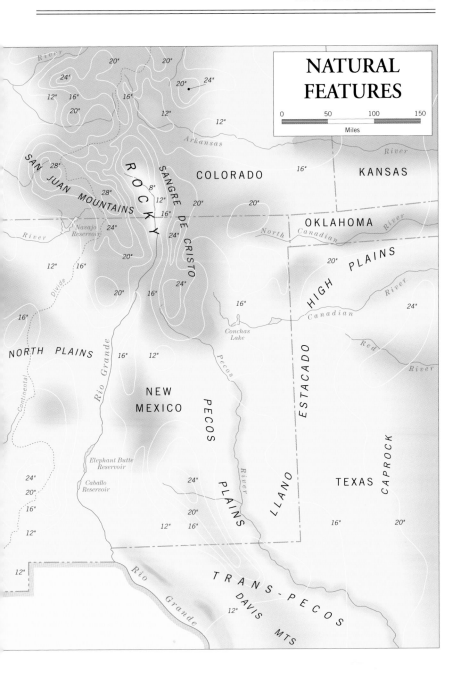

NATURAL FEATURES

0   50   100   150
Miles

River

24°
12° 16°   16°
20°

20°   20°
20°   24°
12°

Arkansas

16°   KANSAS

COLORADO

28°
San Juan   28°
Mountains   12°   20°   20°
8°
16°

OKLAHOMA   River

24°   North   Canadian
Navajo
Reservoir

River   20°   12°   20°   HIGH   PLAINS   20°

12°   16°   20°   River

24°   16°   24°

16°   ROCKY
Canadian

SANGRE DE CRISTO   Conchas
Lake

16°
NORTH   PLAINS   16°   12°   Pecos   Red   River

Continental   Rio Grande   NEW   River   24°
Divide   MEXICO   PECOS

LLANO ESTACADO   CAPROCK

Elephant Butte
Reservoir   PLAINS   TEXAS

24°   Caballo   24°
20°   Reservoir   16°
16°   12°   16°   16°   20°

12°

12°
Rio   TRANS-PECOS

Grande   DAVIS
12°   MTS

million to 225 million years ago, depositing sand and shell that in time hardened into rock. Eighty million years ago, the forces of continental drift crumpled and raised the western half of the continent, thrusting up the Rocky Mountains, and rolling back the seas. Rain falling in the mountains, flowing into rivulets and torrents, carved the rock.

The Colorado River and its many tributaries cut their canyons somewhere between five and 20 million years ago, and not entirely by the downward force of their flow. In fact, the plateau has risen, and continues to rise, challenging the obliging rivers to cut ever deeper courses.

The other great river of the Southwest—the Rio Grande—cut its 1,885-mile path from the Colorado Rockies to the Gulf of Mexico along the Rio Grande Rift, dropped by earthquakes some 25 million years ago. As the earth's crust heaved and stretched, the ruptured land erupted with violent vulcanism, creating mountain ranges and layers of lava that hardened into jagged black landscapes. Fractures in New Mexico created the Jémez Mountains, the Capulin cinder cone, and the lava flows (El Malpaís) south of Grants. Vulcanism also gave rise to the San Francisco Peaks and surrounding cinder cones of northern Arizona, as well as the Henry, La Sal, and Abajo ranges of Utah. Widespread volcanic activity scattered rich mineral deposits around the Southwest, the copper, lead, zinc, silver, and gold that would later hasten the region's human development.

Starting two or three million years ago, glaciers formed in the highest mountains, carving localized peaks and valleys. None of the large glacial sheets that covered much of the Midwest and Canada reached anywhere near the Southwest. Lakes formed as glacial ice melted, some mere mountain tarns, and others filling large, lowland basins. One of these bodies of water was New Mexico's prehistoric Lake Lucero: when it evaporated, the winds blew its gypsum sediments into 50-foot drifts, now protected in White Sands National Monument.

The glaciers receded when the climate changed again, about 10,000 years ago. Soon after, great inland deserts were forming in the Southwest. These vast, arid regions, punctuated by lofty and often well-watered mountain ranges, did not develop uniformly. Differing climates and elevations contribute to make the four distinct deserts that we know today in the Southwest.

Hallmark of Western movies and lore is the Sonoran Desert of southern Arizona, the world's wettest and most lush desert thanks to the summer "monsoon" rains that water its signature plant, the giant saguaro cactus. Higher and cooler is

Twelve years before John Wesley Powell thoroughly explored the Grand Canyon, Lieutenant Joseph Christmas Ives traveled up the Colorado River from the Gulf of California to Black Canyon—near the present site of Hoover Dam. He and his party were shipwrecked here as depicted in this engraving done in 1861 by German artist Friedrich W. Eglofstein. Lieutenant Ives was unimpressed by what he saw: "Ours has been first and will doubtless be the last party of whites to visit this profitless locality."

the Chihuahuan Desert, running north from Mexico into west Texas, southern New Mexico, and southeast Arizona, and characterized by creosote bush and sporadic grasslands. The Colorado Plateau, though heavily cut with rivers and ranges, embraces vast stretches of sere desolation, like the Painted Desert and spectacular Monument Valley. The driest of all Southwestern deserts is the Mojave Desert, along the Colorado River of the Nevada and Arizona border and sprawling west into California. Its signature plant is the Joshua tree.

■ ANCIENT CULTURES

Hunters traversed the Southwest for perhaps 12,000 years before more settled farming cultures began to develop around 300 B.C. Linked by trading routes, these cultures formed several distinct civilizations: the Hohokam of Arizona's low desert, the mountain-dwelling Mogollon, the Sinagua of the Verde Valley and southern Colorado Plateau, and—most fascinating of all—the high-desert Anasazi of

Mesa Verde in southwestern Colorado was built by the Anasazi between A.D. 1000 and 1200 before being abandoned shortly thereafter.

Petroglyphs may be found in hundreds of locations etched in sandstone walls throughout the Southwest.

the Colorado Plateau. In every case, their art, architecture, and perseverance astonish us.

In southwestern New Mexico, the Mogollon learned from their southern neighbors in present-day Mexico how to cultivate corn, squash, and beans, and how to fashion pottery. The Mogollon continued to hunt and farm in the mountains and valleys of southwestern New Mexico until the early 1300s, when they left the Gila to resettle along the Rio Grande and other drainages of the region. One of their cave settlements has been preserved at the Gila Cliff Dwellings National Monument, 44 miles north of Silver City, New Mexico.

Around A.D. 600, the Sinagua settled in northern Arizona, an area encompassing the San Francisco Peaks, and in the Verde River drainages south of Flagstaff. These farmers built the pueblos at today's Wupatki National Monument and maintained close relations with their Anasazi neighbors. They began to abandon their settlements in the 13th century, leaving behind fantastic ruins, the best known of which was (mistakenly) called Montezuma Castle by later Anglo settlers.

Most archaeologists think the Hohokam migrated up from Mexico, bringing the knowledge of irrigated desert farming with them. Eventually the Hohokam world sprawled across a third of Arizona. Around what is now Phoenix, where the Salt River provided a reliable year-round water source, they engineered and constructed canals to irrigate their corn, beans, and squash. In the Tucson basin, which probably received more rain but had no major river, they farmed the flood plains of the arroyos and built small check dams on slopes to manage runoff.

At first they lived in pit houses, constructed by digging a pit one to two feet deep, then raising a wood frame above the pit and filling in the walls with brush and sticks and a plaster of mud. About 1,200 years ago, they began to build platform mounds, some as large as football fields and 10 to 20 feet high, with storage rooms inside and free-standing houses on top. Around the year 1350, they began to build highrise adobe buildings. The ruin of just one four-story building remains outside the modern town of Coolidge. Called Casa Grande, or Big House, its purpose is still in dispute.

Hohokam arts were as sophisticated as their architecture and engineering. Depictions of scorpions, fish, lizards, turtles, snakes, birds, rabbits, and deer were painted in tight formation around their ceramic vessels. They made primitive trumpets by cutting off the spires of large conch shells. They turned other shells into jewelry by etching patterns on them, probably by using the mild acid of fermented saguaro cactus fruit.

On the Colorado Plateau, the Anasazi culture developed more or less in parallel with their neighbors, the Mogollon. At their peak, however, the Anasazi displayed a sophistication beyond any of their contemporaries.

Like the Hohokam, the Anasazi cultivated corn and squash, although their cold and arid land may have given reluctant nourishment. To supplement their diet, they devised remarkably inventive hunting techniques. Nets as long as 200 feet were woven from yucca fiber and human hair, then stretched across gulches by a few people while others chased rabbits toward them.

The first Anasazi people, known to archaeologists as the Basketmakers, lived in saucer-shaped dwellings half above ground and half underground, walled and roofed with a combination of logs and mud mortar. The later Anasazi apparently had frequent contact with other peoples, and their dramatic cultural advancement from A.D. 700 to 1300 shows them to have been extremely adaptive and dynamic. Sometime before A.D. 700, the bow and arrow made its appearance, replacing the less efficient spear and *atlatl* (wooden spear-thrower). Cotton weaving was introduced, and dogs and turkeys were domesticated.

By A.D. 1100, the Anasazi were beginning to build dramatic cliff dwellings of sandstone masonry, usually in alcoves naturally eroded out of the sides of canyon walls, high above the canyon floor. Some were extremely inaccessible and were usually reached by ladders or handholds and footholds chipped into the rock. These alcoves offered improved shelter from wind, snow, and rain and also helped preserve this incredible architecture for the national parks and monuments throughout the Four Corners region (see pages 146–185).

Their ground-level cities were equally as impressive. At Chaco Canyon, the Anasazi designed a system of dams and ditches that directed the flow of water into fields. Roads connected far-flung pueblos. Men wore ornamental jewelry made of shell, turquoise, and other gemstones, and women wove textiles from cotton they grew in their fields. Their complex architecture and the richness of their relics suggest that an entire pueblo of hundreds of people functioned as an extended family.

The peak of Anasazi civilization, the period of its most ambitious building and most industrious trade with other cultures, spanned only two centuries—from about 1100 to 1300. Then they abandoned their canyon cities and drifted away, gradually mingling with the Pueblo peoples occupying the high mesas of northern Arizona and the Rio Grande Valley of New Mexico. The Hohokam, the Mogollon, and the Sinagua all followed suit. These early peoples appear to have left their lands because of prolonged drought, overpopulation, and environmental degradation. Much controversy exists as to whether marauding tribes may have moved into this area as early as the year 1100 and raided already meager stored-food supplies. Whatever occurred, there is little doubt that the modern Hopi, the Pueblo tribes, the Pima, and the Tohono O'odham are the descendants of those ancient peoples.

■ "NEW" TRIBES

The Ute, Shoshone, Paiute, Goshute, Apache, Navajo, and other tribes were latecomers to the Southwest. Cliff dwellings remain as alien in the Navajo's homelands as the Greek ruins at Syracuse do to contemporary Sicilians.

In the 1500s, Athapaskan-speaking tribes, including the Navajo and Apache, made their way down from Canada into the Southwest. Decidedly different from the agrarian natives of the Southwest, the nomadic Navajo were adept traders, offering baskets, animal hides, and jerky in exchange for corn, cotton cloth, and turquoise.

The Navajo claim as their ancestral origin the headwaters of the San Juan River in New Mexico and called it Dinetah, but they were expelled from this region by the Utes and began moving south and east into Anasazi lands. They built hogans—circular mud-plastered dwellings—and learned from the Pueblo Indians how to farm. They never completely gave up their wandering ways, and took naturally to a pastoral life of herding small bands of sheep and goats after these were introduced by the Spanish. Only in modern times have they developed villages.

Like their relatives the Athapaskan Navajo, the Apache hunted bison and deer and gathered roots, nuts, and berries. Broad-faced with high cheekbones, aquiline noses, and muscular physiques, the handsome Apache lived in thatched wickiups and animal-skin teepees. When the Apache arrived in the Southwest, they

The Utes were nomadic hunter-gatherers that roamed the Colorado Plateau. Above is a hand-tinted portrait of Ute Chief Severa and his family taken in 1899. (Underwood Archives, San Francisco)

A photograph taken by frontier lensman Edward Curtis in 1907 shows Hopi women grinding corn. Unlike the nomadic Utes, the Hopi were town dwellers. (New York Public Library)

separated into bands, staked out their territories, and never considered themselves a single tribe. Among the bands were (and are) the Jicarilla, the Mescalero, and the Chiricahua—the last of whom achieved notoriety for their long guerrilla war against the Spanish, the Mexicans, and the Americans.

The Utes were hunter-gatherers who lived nomadically in the high, inter-mountain region north of the Four Corners. Of Shoshone stock and therefore culturally different from the Navajo, the Utes probably raided the northern frontier of the Anasazi world during a period of drought, contributing to the collapse of their predecessors' more urbane culture. The Utes looked to the Plains Indians for much of their culture, living in teepees and pulling their goods in travois as they migrated between camps. They acquired horses around 1800 and were famous for their bravery in battle. As raiders they continually plundered the Spanish and Indian villages of northern New Mexico, often causing them to relocate. Today, their descendants live on four reservations, including the large Ute Mountain Indian Reservation, adjacent to Colorado's Mesa Verde National Park.

■ ARRIVAL OF THE SPANISH

The Catholic kingdom of Spain entered the New World at the end of the 15th century to reap both riches and souls. Inspired by the wild successes of Cortez and Pizarro in plundering the Aztec and Inca empires, Spanish explorers kept pushing into new territories, hoping to strike mineral wealth. The great prize of northern explorers was a land called Cíbola, or the "Seven Cities of Gold," a well-stoked myth of European origin, and one with the power to set armies in motion.

Following encouraging reports from a Spanish exploratory expedition led in 1539 by Fray Marcos de Niza, the Viceroy of New Spain planned a new, more ambitious venture, appointing a 30-year-old friend, Francisco Vásquez de Coronado, to lead it the next year. His army of 336 soldiers, four priests, several hundred Mexican Indians, and large herds of horses and stock animals probably entered modern-day Arizona along the San Pedro River, pushing northeast to Ácoma and the Rio Grande Valley, and eventually pursuing their pipe dreams to the plains of

Coronado's party, searching for the fabled cities of gold, arrives in New Mexico in 1540 and claims the territory for the Spanish Empire. From a mural by Gerald Cassidy, 1921. (Museum of New Mexico.)

Kansas. They found no golden cities, only pueblos of sun-dried mud; but members of his party did put the Grand Canyon, the Rio Grande, and nearly 80 native pueblos on the Spanish map. They also unwittingly brought a renaissance to the Plains Indian cultures, when expedition horses escaped and ran wild.

Without the pressing hope for gold, nearly a century passed before the Spanish mounted other expeditions to the region. Juan de Oñate's expedition of 1598 established New Mexico's first capital of San Gabriel near the confluence of the Rio Grande and Chama River. That done, Oñate left to continue his explorations, claiming vast territories for Spain at a cost of much bloodshed in the native Pueblos. In his absence, the San Gabriel colony failed, largely because colonists spent more time searching for precious metals than farming. Oñate was ignominiously recalled to Mexico for trial.

A more lasting capital was established between 1607 and 1610 by Oñate's successor, Pedro de Peralta, in a high valley below the Sangre de Cristo Mountains. Peralta named the new capital La Villa de Santa Fe (the City of Holy Faith), ultimately shortened to Santa Fe. From there, Catholic priests ventured out into the surrounding pueblos to spread the virtues of the faith, and colonists settled into remote haciendas.

Santa Fe today is a thriving, beautiful city, but in the 17th century it was a small, fortified town meant to protect the Spanish settlers of northern New Mexico from hostile Indian tribes. In 1680, the Puebloans revolted under the leadership of Popé, a shaman-warrior from San Juan Pueblo. They burned mission churches, destroyed farms, and killed priests and colonists. Spanish farmers and ranchers retreated to Santa Fe, where they held out for nine days in the Palace of the Governors before fighting their way out. Colonists, priests, and Christianized Indians retreated down the Rio Grande to what is now Ciudad Juárez in Mexico, across the river from El Paso. Of the 2,500 settlers who joined in the retreat, 1,946 were recorded as having arrived.

Twelve years passed before the Spanish reconquered New Mexico, and when the settlers returned to Santa Fe, a battle ensued. Twenty-one Spaniards and 81 Puebloans died. Four more years were needed to reclaim the outlying pueblos, thus ending the longest and most successful rebellion against European colonists of any Native American tribe.

(following pages) The church of San Geronimo de Taos reflects the early Spanish influence in the region.

The dispirited Puebloans fell on harder times. By the end of the 1700s, only 19 pueblos remained, and these had lost half their population to European diseases. By contrast, the Spanish thrived and grew in number, lured north from Mexico by new tracts of land. Most traveled in caravans on the Camino Real, also known as the Chihuahua Trail, a 533-mile trade route that connected Chihuahua in northern Mexico with Santa Fe. (The fabled Santa Fe Trail from Missouri was not blazed until 1821, for the Spanish Crown prohibited Santa Fe from trading with the United States.)

Life was hard in the small settlements and ranches of New Mexico, but as years passed, relations between the Pueblo Indians and Spanish became more cordial. The Spanish brought to Indian culture domesticated animals, *horno* ovens, and new crops, among them onions, barley, wheat, peas, and, from Mexico, tomatoes and chocolate. Indian women shared their traditional methods for cooking corn, beans, and chile. The different cultures traded herbs and healing plants, and pottery and weaving methods. With the introduction of sheep, the Indians became experts in weaving wool rugs and cloth. The Spanish adopted the flat-roofed architecture of the pueblos, and the two peoples intermarried. Both suffered from raids by Comanches and so came together for defense.

In Arizona, Jesuit missionaries led by the tireless Italian-born Father Eusebio Kino were at first welcomed by the Pimas and Papagos (now called by their original name, Tohono O'odham) when they established missions in 1701 at Guevavi, near modern Nogales, and at Bac, eight miles south of today's downtown Tucson. These were the northernmost outposts in a chain of 22 missions Kino stretched across the deserts and grasslands of northern Mexico. The normally peaceful Pimas rebelled in 1751, killing more than 100 Spanish ranchers, miners, and priests in an uprising that ranged from Bac to the Sonoran coast. The Spanish government responded with a show of force, beginning by building a presidio (fort) at Tubac, 40 miles south of Bac. Another fort was built at Tucson in 1775 to discourage Apache raids.

Wardrobe of a Spanish Colonial Lady

In 1598, Mexican-born explorer Juan de Oñate led an expedition of settlers and missionaries into northern New Mexico. Twelve years later several more Mexican families were sent to the settlement including Capt. Antonio Conde de Herrera and his wife, Doña Francisca Galindo. Doña Francisca's wardrobe and household goods, listed below, represent the type of objects an upper-class colonial woman would have had during the early 17th century.

Doña Francisca's Dresses
- Two of brown and green cloth, trimmed
- One velvet adorned with velvet belts and gold clasps
- One black satin with silk gimps
- One black taffeta, trimmed
- One green coarse cloth with sashes embroidered in gold
- One crimson satin embroidered in gold
- One red satin with sashes and gold trimmings
- One tawny color with a white China embroidered skirt
- (Additionally) four ruffs

Doña Francisca's Household Goods
- Two pitchers
- Small pot and saltcellar of silver
- Six small and one large spoon
- One bedspread of crimson taffeta trimmed with lace
- Eight sheets
- Six pillows
- Three bolsters
- Two additional new pillows embroidered in silk of various colors

(Courtesy, The Palace of the Governors)

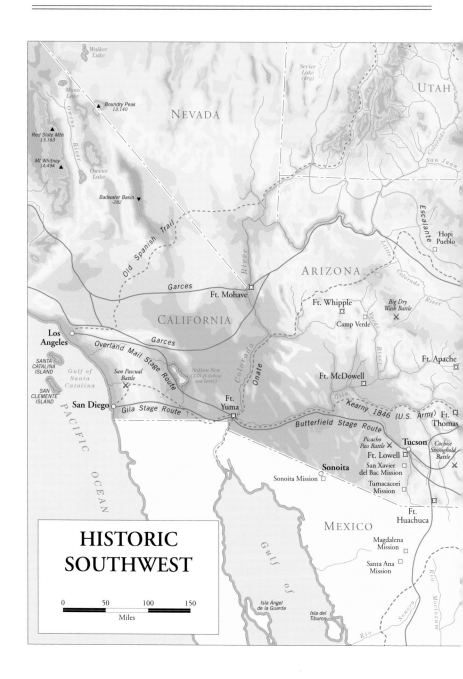

Walker Lake

Mono Lake

Sevier Lake (dry)

UTAH

NEVADA

Boundry Peak 13,140

Red Slate Mtn 13,163

Owens River

Colorado

San Juan

Mt Whitney 14,494

Owens Lake

Badwater Basin -282

Old Spanish Trail

Escalante

Hopi Pueblo

ARIZONA

Little Colorado River

River

Garces

Ft. Mohave

Ft. Whipple

Big Dry Wash Battle

CALIFORNIA

Camp Verde

Los Angeles

Garces

Overland Mail Stage Route

Colorado

Onate

River

Ft. Apache

SANTA CATALINA ISLAND

Gulf of Santa Catalina

San Pascual Battle

Salton Sea (235 ft below sea level)

Ft. McDowell

SAN CLEMENTE ISLAND

San Diego

Gila Stage Route

Ft. Yuma

Gila

Kearny 1846 (U.S. Army) Ft. Thomas

PACIFIC

Butterfield Stage Route

Picacho Pass Battle

Tucson

Cochise Stronghold Battle

Ft. Lowell

OCEAN

Sonoita

San Xavier del Bac Mission

Sonoita Mission

Tumacacori Mission

Ft. Huachuca

MEXICO

Magdalena Mission

Gulf

Santa Ana Mission

Rio Moctezuma

of

Rio Sonora

Isla Angel de la Guarda

Isla del Tiburon

Rio

HISTORIC SOUTHWEST

0   50   100   150

Miles

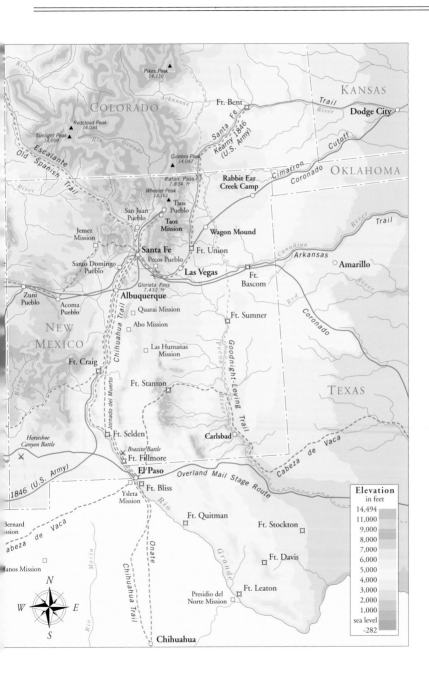

SOUTHWEST HISTORY TIMELINE

1000–1275 Ancient Anasazi Indian culture flourishes. Stone cities are built in the overhangs of cliffs, crops are irrigated, and the arts—music, pottery, petroglyphs, architecture—flourish.

1300 Anasazi cities fall silent, their buildings abandoned, and the Anasazi people vanish. Pueblo Indian culture begins to develop at Taos on the upper Rio Grande, and at Zuñi, Ácoma, and Hopi mesas.

1500 Nomadic Utes, Navajos, and Apaches have arrived in the Southwest. They have little in common with the Puebloans.

1540 Rumor reaches pueblos on the Rio Grande that strange men have arrived to the west, wearing shining clothes that make them impervious to arrows, and riding enormous animals, never before seen. They are Spanish conquistador Francisco Vásquez de Coronado and his band of soldiers and adventurers, looking for gold.

1607–1610 Spanish settlers continue to make the arduous journey across Mexico's northern deserts and the fearsome Jornada del Muerto to settle northern New Mexico. They establish the town of Santa Fe, and build haciendas along the Rio Grande, while Franciscan missionaries set out to build churches and convert the Indians.

1680 Puebloans chafe as the Spanish take over their land, outlaw their religion, and utilize techniques of the Inquisition (like burning people alive) to save Indian souls. Under the leadership of Popé of San Juan Pueblo, they drive the Spanish settlers back to the southern side of the Rio Grande.

1691 The Spanish return to New Mexico and flourish. Pueblo culture falters, and more than half of their people die of smallpox and other introduced diseases. Utes and Apaches acquire the horse and become adept riders and raiders.

1751 Spanish settlers in Arizona are driven back to Mexico by the Pima and Papago (Tohono O'odham), but within a year the settlers return.

1776 Father Francisco Tomás Garces, a missionary to Arizona, seeks a northerly route from Santa Fe to Monterey in California, and sees the Grand Canyon.

1821 Mexico revolts against Spain, and its northern territories begin to trade with the United States for the first time. The Santa Fe Trail is opened, and Anglos begin to move into the Southwest.

1836–1848	Texas becomes a republic; the U.S. goes to war with Mexico, and the Southwest becomes part of the United States.
1847	Brigham Young arrives in Utah with his Mormon followers, who later filter down into the Utah Canyonlands, there to establish flourishing communities and polygamous families.
1860–1865	The United States is engulfed in the Civil War, and skirmishes are fought on the borders of the Southwest. Texas, a slave state, secedes; New Mexico is briefly captured by the South, and the last battle of the war is fought on the Gulf Coast of Texas, *after* the South has surrendered at Appomattox.
1869	John Wesley Powell leads a rafting expedition on the Colorado River through the Grand Canyon. Despite the terrifying rapids, all survive the trip except three men who decide to hike out rather than run Separation Rapid and they are later killed by Paiutes.
1875	Billy the Kid, 5' 7" and 15 years old, begins his outlaw career by shooting his first man. A non-smoker who plays the piano, he raises cain in Arizona and New Mexico—killing, robbing, and riding around for six more years, until he's shot by Sheriff Pat Garrett.
1881	In Tombstone, Arizona, Wyatt Earp and Doc Holliday shoot it out with the notorious Clanton gang at the OK Corral.
1916	Pancho Villa, Mexican revolutionary and part-time desperado, invades an American town—Columbus, New Mexico. He burns it down and kills 18 people. General Pershing takes off in hot pursuit across the desert, but never catches up with Villa.
1930	Painter Georgia O'Keeffe steps off a train in New Mexico and is captured by its beauty. Soon after, she settles near Abiquiú and ever after paints the flowers, hills, colors, and shapes of the desert.
1944	Gambling town Las Vegas, darling of the Mob, roars to life in the Mojave Desert. Mobster Bugsy Siegel gains notoriety as he builds the Flamingo, but in 1947, 14 days after it opens, the Flamingo flops. In June, Siegel is "offed" in Beverly Hills.
1968	Edward Abbey, working for the park service at Arches National Monument in Utah, writes *Desert Solitaire*.
1971	London Bridge is moved from the Thames River in London, England, to Lake Havasu in the Arizona desert. Almost overnight, savvy locals erect Tudor storefronts and organize Shakespeare festivals.

■ AMERICAN ERA

In 1821, Mexico gained its independence from Spain, taking New Mexico, Arizona, and Texas along with it. In one of the new government's most far-reaching policy changes, the ban on trade between New Mexico and the United States was lifted. Perhaps the Spanish ban had been wise, for Mexican rule survived the opening of the Santa Fe Trail by only 25 years.

American mountain men had been trading at the edge of the Rockies and along the Spanish frontier since Thomas Jefferson completed the Louisiana Purchase in 1803, adding huge chunks of the South and Midwest to the fledgling United States. When William Becknell, a frontier trader and Indian fighter, decided to push on southwest with a wagonload of goods, he had the good fortune to pull into Santa Fe as the town was celebrating independence. Becknell was laden with brightly colored cloth, kettles, knives, and looking glasses he had expected to exchange with Indians. Instead, he found Spanish settlers eager to buy his wares, and he quickly returned to Missouri for more. Thus the Santa Fe Trail was born.

At first, the trail was used by daring tradesmen who hauled tools, cloth, shoes, and nails across the prairie. Mountain men also used the route, coming to Colorado and New Mexico to trap beaver and hunt deer. Tiny mountain villages in the Sangre de Cristo range still bear names recalling French fur-trapper founders, such as Le Doux and Pendaries, and an annual Mountain Man Rendezvous trade fair is still celebrated in Taos each fall.

Trade was not all that came down from the United States. The nation was in an expansionist mood, and increasing numbers of its people were inspired by Manifest Destiny to move west. In 1836, American settlers under Sam Houston defeated the Mexican army at the San Jacinto River, and declared themselves the Republic of Texas. In time, drovers escorted thousands of longhorn cattle up from Texas through the Pecos River Valley on into Colorado, establishing the Goodnight-Loving Trail.

❖

When the United States annexed Texas in 1845 and set its western border at the Rio Grande instead of the Rio Nueces, Mexico resisted. In the ensuing Mexican War, Gen. Stephen Watts Kearny crossed the Mountain Branch of the Santa Fe Trail at the head of 1,600 troops, passing through Colorado into New Mexico. Kearny met no resistance at Las Vegas, New Mexico, where he announced from a rooftop that the land was now part of the United States. On August 18, the

The cowboy, his horse, and saguaro cactus are the enduring images of the American Southwest.

general peaceably claimed the capital of Santa Fe for his homeland, promising its citizens that their property rights and religion would be respected and that their new country would protect them from hostile Indians.

Meanwhile, forces under generals Winfield Scott and Zachary Taylor pushed south, invading the heart of Mexico. When Scott's army marched on Mexico City, they wrenched away an American victory. The ensuing Treaty of Guadalupe Hidalgo of 1848 officially ceded the Southwest, from Texas to California, to the United States.

Five years later, the Americans completed their continental map with the Gadsden Purchase from Mexico for $10 million. The purchase included a section of southern Arizona and New Mexico where the Gila Trail crossed the Chihuahuan and Sonoran deserts.

The change to American rule did not immediately attract a large influx of settlers. From West Texas to California's Mojave Desert, the land was considered too dry, too mountainous, and too vulnerable to Indian attack to be of much interest to homesteaders. Wagon trains along the Santa Fe Trail were still subject to attack by Comanche and Kiowa raiders. Most travelers considered the central portion of the American Continent—especially the Southwest and the Rockies—a wasteland to be endured while making the crossing to California and Oregon.

The mule was the greatest traction factor in the development of the Southwest. Camels, oxen, and horses were tried, but only a mule could endure the conditions of the country and the rigors of heavy-teaming. (Underwood Archives, San Francisco)

In the 1840s Mormons brought irrigation and farming to the dry desert regions of Utah for the first time since the disappearance of the Anasazi. (Courtesy Rell G. Francis)

Not all Americans shunned the high, dry western lands, however. With a party of 148 members of the Church of Latter-day Saints, church leader Brigham Young settled Utah's Great Salt Lake Valley in 1847, embracing this region largely because it was so remote from American interference. The Mormons soon proved that western lands could be made to bloom through irrigation. Over the following decade, thousands joined the Mormons in their new State of Deseret, fanning out on Young's orders through what is now Utah and northern Arizona, and to remote oases like Las Vegas, Nevada, to settle and secure a larger Mormon homeland.

❖

The Civil War brought increased attention to the Southwest from Washington. Texas joined the Confederacy in 1861 at the instigation of pro-slavery forces, mainly consisting of residents of eastern Texas, a prime cotton-growing area adjoining Louisiana. Though far from the cotton plantations of East Texas, the Texas desert region west of the Pecos River had to follow suit. In February 1862, Brig. Gen. Henry Sibley led a small Confederate army of 2,600 men up the Rio Grande. The soldiers met little resistance until they reached Valverde, a tree-shaded ford on the Rio Grande. There, on February 21, Sibley was greeted by 3,800 Union troops led by Col. Edward Canby, commander of federal forces in New Mexico. Brandishing squirrel rifles, double-barrel shotguns, pistols, and bowie knives, the Rebels charged across the river, overrunning the inexperienced Union troops. By day's end, Canby's troops were retreating south toward Fort Craig. Sibley led his men northward, where they hoisted the Confederate flag above defenseless Albuquerque and Santa Fe. Both cities were devoid of troops, who had shifted north to join forces with Fort Union soldiers and a group of Colorado Volunteers.

A month later, at Glorieta Pass, a wide swath of grassland bordered at either end by steep cliffs, Sibley's army was outsmarted. Major John Chivington and a group of Colorado Volunteers crept behind Confederate lines, destroyed ammunition supplies, burned 73 wagons, and killed 600 horses and mules. Often referred to as the Gettysburg of the West, this battle marked the beginning of New Mexico's expulsion of Confederate troops. Sibley retreated, pursued by Canby and his regrouped army, until the Texans slipped out of the territory for good.

To reward the Pueblo Indians for remaining neutral throughout the Civil War, President Abraham Lincoln in 1863 presented each of the 19 pueblos with a black ebony cane crowned with silver and inscribed with his signature. These symbols of the pueblos' dominion, along with silver-tipped staffs given to the pueblos in 1620 by the Spanish government, are brought out every January and ceremoniously conferred upon a new pueblo governor as he takes office.

■ TAMING THE SOUTHWEST

While U.S. soldiers were preoccupied with the Civil War, the Apache and Navajo stepped up their raids on settlers, driving off sheep and cattle. The Indians met little resistance until Gen. James Carlton and his California Column arrived in 1862, following the withdrawal of Confederate troops from New Mexico. After enlisting the help of Col. Kit Carson in negotiating with the Navajo, the general rounded up 400 Mescalero Apache in southern New Mexico and moved them to the new Bosque Redondo Reservation. The reservation spread alongside the cottonwood-shaded banks of the Pecos River near Fort Sumner, a new installation built to supervise the Indians' relocation. Carlton's idea was for the Apache—nomadic warriors and hunters—to settle down as farmers.

Kit Carson offered peace with the semi-nomadic Navajo by offering them exile to Bosque Redondo. When they refused, Carson's men relentlessly burned hogans, butchered sheep, chopped down peach trees, and destroyed fields of corn. Weakened and demoralized, the Indians surrendered in 1864 and agreed to relocate to Bosque Redondo. What followed was the "Long Walk," in which thousands of Navajos trudged across 300 miles

A portrait of Kit Carson in the Kit Carson Home and Museum of Taos.

of desert covered with yucca, cholla cactus, and hardened lava beds. Those who failed to keep up were shot. This brutal march so affected the Indians that they date historical events by referring to whether the events occurred before or after the Long Walk.

At the reservation, the 8,500 Navajos failed to mix with the Apache. Both tribes resented their imprisonment. Disease ravaged their ranks, and the crops were destroyed by parasites. A few years later, Carlton admitted failure. In 1868, the Navajo were given 3.5 million acres amid the red-rock canyons and piñon mesas of their homeland, now the largest Indian reservation in the country. In 1873, the Mescalero Apache received 460,177 acres among the forested slopes of the Sacramento Mountains.

The Chiricahua Apache had never accepted foreign encroachment on their native lands. Over past centuries, they had harried the Spanish, the Mexicans, and other tribes, and they continued to raid American settlements along the southern Rio Grande and in Arizona under charismatic leaders like Cochise and Geronimo until well into the 19th century. Finally President Grant appointed Gen. George Crook, a brilliant military strategist who came to understand and respect the

Apache, to put down the troubles. By building a network of 16 army forts in Arizona, hiring "tame" Apaches who knew the land to work as scouts, and fighting for well over a decade, he was able to persuade the great Indian warrior Geronimo to surrender in 1886.

Similar struggles took place all over the West as white settlers supplanted Indians on their lands. As one band of Indians was forced from its traditional land, it entered the lands of another band. They often fought among themselves before joining against the common invader.

In the end, the clash between the Indian and non-Indian cultures resulted in the near destruction of the Indians' way of life. Native Americans were moved to reservations, there to become ranchers and farmers. Those who chose not to live on the reservations, where the conditions were never very good, had to fit into a society that did not accept their culture. Most Indians adopted non-Indian clothes and homes. Children were sent away to school to learn "civilized" ways.

Between 1869 and 1872, the last blank space on the map of the continental United States was filled in after two courageous expeditions down the Colorado River by Major John Wesley Powell. A detachment of Powell's 1872 expedition, led by his chief topographer, A. H. Thompson, discovered and named the last major river added to the U.S. map. They called it Escalante in honor of the Spanish explorer and priest who stumbled upon the Grand Canyon in 1776, only the second Spanish party to behold that amazing sight.

Unfortunately, neither herding the Indians onto reservations nor filling in blank spaces on maps brought peace to the Southwest. During the late 1800s, saloons outnumbered churches in many towns, and the law of the smoking gun often prevailed over that of men with badges. Range wars erupted, along with violent struggles for power. Cattle rustlers operated freely, and Anglo lawyers who received their fees in property benefited most in disputes over land-grant boundaries. The worst of the range disputes came to be known as the Lincoln County War of July 1878, when the U.S. Cavalry had to be called in to put down five days of killing between different factions. The "war" is also noteworthy as Billy the Kid's first job.

The pattern of settlement was inexorable, however. Southwest towns began to grow, supplementing their Spanish-adobe and Indian-pueblo architecture with Yankee wood-frame houses. In some towns, social divisions among Anglo, Indian, and Hispanic residents were sharply drawn, but in many others, such as Tucson and Santa Fe, the different cultures mingled and formed what would later be called a distinctive Southwest culture.

Prospectors took more than a passing interest in the arid lands of the Southwest. Gold and silver strikes in the Colorado Rockies, Utah, Nevada, Arizona, and even parts of New Mexico brought men willing to endure any hardship in order to strike it rich. Mines usually played out in very short order, but some lived long enough to generate small towns, like Tombstone, and large legends, like the Lost Dutchman's Mine of Arizona's Superstition Mountains. As the 19th century progressed, miners came to work in the coal mines near the New Mexican towns of Gallup, Raton, and Madrid, as well as the silver and copper mines near Silver City, New Mexico, and Bisbee and Jerome, Arizona. In the end it was copper—not gold or silver—that transformed the Southwest from a frontier of far-flung, economically independent settlements into an economy largely controlled by outsiders.

An important role in Americanizing the Southwest went to the railroad, which reached Santa Fe in 1880. With trains to bring in settlers and the amenities of life, and to haul out cattle and ore, railroad camps and old Spanish settlements readily expanded into thriving towns, while rural settlers were able to make their enormous sheep and cattle ranches more prosperous.

Fortune seekers from around the world flocked to the mines of the Southwest. The three miners photographed in this early Arizona copper mine were from Austria, Mexico, and England. (Underwood Archives, San Francisco)

The Old West and the New West meet at Phoenix Airport in the 1950s.
(Underwood Archives, San Francisco)

■ TWENTIETH CENTURY

The territories of the Southwest were among the last to become states of the Union. Colorado and Utah joined in 1896. New Mexico and Arizona didn't become states until 1912; only Hawaii and Alaska joined later. And still, for many decades thereafter, the Southwest economy continued to revolve around its 19th-century mainstays of mining, ranching, and agriculture.

The southern border with Mexico was briefly caught up in international politics in 1916, when Mexican revolutionary Pancho Villa attacked Columbus, New Mexico, killing and looting, apparently in retaliation for American recognition of Mexico's new president, Villa's sworn enemy. The cavalry pursued and killed most of his men, but President Wilson ordered an additional punitive expedition, led by Gen. John "Blackjack" Pershing, to pursue Villa into Mexico. Though they never captured Pancho Villa, his troops were decimated. He himself was assassinated in 1923.

The advent of the automobile age brought more travelers than ever across the vast landscapes of the Southwest. Along the routes of new highways, towns that had hitherto been of secondary importance—Albuquerque and Flagstaff, to name but two—suddenly became centers of commerce. The most famous highway of all, old Route 66, inspired novels, music, and a television show; it still attracts a cult following of road-trippers.

New roads also brought tourists to admire the stunning natural and historical wealth of the Southwest. Congress established Grand Canyon National Park in 1919, followed soon after by Mesa Verde and Zion national parks, and a plethora of national monuments preserving the ruins of ancient civilizations. Artists, writers, and film producers "discovered" the Southwest in the early decades of the century, attracted by its brilliant natural light, the rich colors and stunning shapes of its landscapes, and its exotic ambiance. The works of Georgia O'Keeffe, D. H. Lawrence, Peter Hurd, John Steinbeck, Ansel Adams, and other creative people did as much to redefine the image of the Southwest among readers and gallery patrons as John Ford's Western film visions of Monument Valley did for the much larger movie-going public.

Get your kicks on Route 66: the trans-national highway was immortalized in Jack Kerouac's book On the Road *and Nat King Cole's song "Route 66."*

More notorious publicity followed development of the first atomic bomb in Los Alamos, New Mexico, in 1945. World War II also brought new army bases and other wartime industries to the Southwest, particularly aerospace and other defense industries, which took advantage of the wide open spaces and warm winters.

Increasing population brought greater demands for water, both for growing towns and agriculture. Water rights for the Colorado River became a source of bickering between states, especially Arizona and California. All was settled, at least officially, by the Colorado River Compact, which sought to divide the water according to predetermined scales of usage among the states. The construction of great dams along the river, such as Hoover Dam in 1935, provided dependable sources of water and hydroelectricity, permitting a growth boom in cities like Las Vegas, Nevada. Their vast reservoirs also flooded areas of great natural beauty, much of which also had religious importance to the Native Americans. In the early 1960s, Glen Canyon Dam drowned the extraordinary Glen Canyon beneath a 186-mile-long reservoir, Lake Powell. Though unsuccessful at stopping the dam, the rallied forces of conservation were able to salvage some victories by prompting the establishment of Canyonlands National Park and an expansion of Grand Canyon National Park.

For the Southwest, however, probably the most long-reaching change of the 20th century was the development of air conditioning. Though Northerners had been flocking south for the winters since the late 19th century, air conditioning rendered the summers suddenly more bearable. With cheaper electricity and water from the reservoirs, settlements like Phoenix, Tucson, Las Vegas, and El Paso were able to grow far beyond the limitations dictated by a desert environment, setting reckless precedents that many other desert cities still seem only too willing to follow.

When completed in 1935, Hoover Dam paved the way for the development of Las Vegas.

CENTRAL NEW MEXICO

■ HIGHLIGHTS
Zuñi Pueblo
Ácoma Pueblo
El Morro
El Malpaís
Albuquerque Old Town
Manzano Mountains
Coronado State Park
Turquoise Trail

■ LANDSCAPE
From its western border near Gallup to Albuquerque, central New Mexico is a landscape of lightly forested mountains, piñon-covered hills, red-rock mesas, and black volcanic badlands. The badlands are lava flows from ancient volcanoes, and there's an oceanic feel to their vastness. Beyond the black lava, the land is colored in subtle shades of brown and green, bright with light, shadowed during summer afternoons by passing thunderheads. The vegetation and the light create a soothing tableau, stark but not desolate.

The city of Albuquerque sprawls across a large valley along the Rio Grande, in the shadow of the Sandía Mountains. Because it lies at the intersection of two highways and was built with little planning or attention to public spaces, its setting has been swamped in a sea of asphalt and mini-malls.

■ TRAVELERS ORIENTATION
Interstate 40 crosses central New Mexico midway as it traverses the continent from California to the North Carolina coast. Three hundred and twenty-five long miles yawn between Flagstaff, Arizona, and Albuquerque, New Mexico, and another 284 miles east to Amarillo, Texas.

Just to the south of I-40, along NM 53, lie two places of almost unearthly bleakness and magic: the Zuñi Indian reservation and El Malpaís lava flow.

Southeast of Grants, spur roads drop through dry arroyos to Sky City, the ancient pueblo home of the Ácoma Indians. As with Zuñi, Ácoma is the site of great and tragic stories of the Spanish conquest, and the setting is one of high-desert vistas and vastness. Albuquerque is New Mexico's biggest city, a multi-ethnic, burgeoning town, whose airport is a major point of access to central and northern New Mexico. Good motels and an eclectic variety of restaurants are available, and its historic Old Town is worth a visit.

Several of the routes north from Albuquerque toward Santa Fe and southeast through the Manzano Mountains cover areas of great scenic beauty and historic interest. These regions are the subject of this chapter.

Food & lodging appears on page 78.

The elevation is higher and the weather is cooler than most people expect who travel into central New Mexico. For instance, the town of Gallup stands at 6,510 feet above sea level, and during the winter, nighttime temperatures often drop to well below freezing. The best time of the year to visit is in late spring (April–May) and early fall (September–October) when the air is warm and dry. In July and August, afternoon thunderstorms may occur, especially over the higher mountains. Winters are cold and sometimes snowy above 6,500 feet. At any time of the year extreme fluctuations of daily temperature, as much as 50° F (28° C), are common due to the dryness of the air and intensity of sunshine. Precautions should be taken to protect oneself from the sun's rays year round, as the high-altitude sun is strong even in winter. The climate of this region is best represented by weather stations in Albuquerque (elevation 4,950) and the town of Zuñi (elevation 6,300).

TEMPS (F°)	AVG. JAN. HIGH	AVG. JAN. LOW	AVG. APRIL HIGH	AVG. APRIL LOW	AVG. JULY HIGH	AVG. JULY LOW	AVG. OCT. HIGH	AVG. OCT. LOW	RECORD HIGH	RECORD LOW
Albuquerque	47	22	71	40	93	65	70	43	105	-17
Zuñi	44	17	67	36	85	56	66	38	101	-26

PRECIPITATION (INCHES)	AVG. JAN.	AVG. APRIL	AVG. JULY	AVG. OCT.	ANNUAL	SNOW
Albuquerque	0.4	0.5	1.3	0.9	8.1	11
Zuñi	1.0	0.6	1.9	1.3	11.8	30

■ HISTORY

The story of central New Mexico begins with a colossally bogus rumor that inspired bloodshed, arrogance, and unbridled greed. In 1536, four half-starved survivors of the Narváez Expedition that had tried to colonize Florida for Spain stumbled into Mexico. They hadn't learned much about Florida, but during their flight westward they had heard fables about a wealthy people to the north of Mexico who lived in great houses and traded in valuable minerals. The eager viceroy of New Spain commissioned a mini-expedition headed by Fray Marcos de Niza to reconnoiter. In 1539 the band reached the Zuñi pueblo of Hawikuh, where two notable events occurred: the black slave Estebanico, sent ahead as a scout, was murdered by the natives. Meanwhile, Fray Marcos stood on a nearby hill where the mischievous New Mexico sunlight bewitched him; he later reported to the viceroy that "it appears to be a very beautiful city; the houses are . . . all of stone, with their stories and terraces . . ." He was convinced he had found the fabled Seven Cities of Cíbola.

The friar's report triggered the vastly more ambitious Coronado expedition of 1540–41. Hawikuh, of course, turned out to be an adobe village worthless to the Spaniards, who nevertheless invaded and killed a number of Indians. The entourage surged on to the Rio Grande, where they seized the Tiwa village of Alcanfor to provide winter shelter for their 336 soldiers, 100 Indians, assorted slaves, and thousands of horses and mules. During the two winters and one summer that the army encamped at the pueblo, Francisco Vásquez de Coronado searched for gold as far north as Kansas. He found nothing. His band of *conquistadores* crept back to Mexico City empty-handed and humiliated.

Spaniards from Mexico tried at least five other forays into central New Mexico during the 16th century but made no permanent settlements and few willing Christian converts among the Pueblo Indians. Their luck began to change with the dawn of the 17th century and Don Juan de Oñate's first permanent colony and capital near the confluence of the Rio Grande and the Chama River. It was named San Gabriel. In 1607, the colony turned against Oñate and he was recalled to Mexico. That year his successor, Pedro de Peralta, began building a new capital, Santa Fe, some 30 miles to the south.

Ninety-nine years later, Francisco Cuervo de Valdés, provisional governor of New Mexico, shuttled 30 families from the trading center of Bernalillo 17 miles

WEST-CENTRAL NEW MEXICO

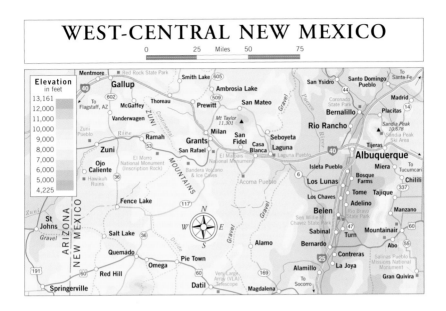

south to the middle Rio Grande Valley. To flatter the Duke of Alburquerque, then the Viceroy of New Spain, Valdés named the community after him. (The first "r" was later dropped.)

For more than a hundred years this area prospered and slumbered as a distant outpost of the Spanish empire. Then, in 1821, it suddenly found itself part of the rebellious nation of Mexico. Twenty-seven years later, Albuquerque was ceded to the United States in treaties following the Mexican War. Mid-century discoveries of gold and silver in the mountains to the east of Albuquerque sparked a bonanza that quickly ran out. Today, the small towns of central New Mexico seem suspended in time, while Albuquerque has become an industrial and distribution center for the Southwest.

■ ZUÑI PUEBLO

As it cuts south from I-40 toward Zuñi, NM 53 traverses a landscape of pale cliffs, finger mesas, and a deep turquoise sky. The views are of stark land formations, soaring raptors, and a gentle palette of light greens, grays, and earth tones.

Mountains seem distant, and there is stillness all around. The dramatic skies are like a constantly shifting painting.

Dwellings in this area are, for the most part, small and plain. An extremely modest standard of living here coexists with an enviable simplicity, and a lonely setting with an embracing tranquillity.

❖

The Zuñis had farmed along the Zuñi River in the shadows of surrounding mesas for hundreds of years before the first Spanish explorers arrived. The tribe domesticated and raised turkeys and kept eagles in captivity for their feathers. Traders exchanged turquoise and salt with Plains Indians for buffalo hides, and with Mexican tribes for parrot plumes. Well connected to surrounding pueblos, they were accustomed to running 20 miles round-trip to carry messages.

Although the Zuñis grudgingly accepted the Spanish presence, allowing them to build churches and erect crosses, they never fully embraced the Christianity that was forced upon them. Even today, Christianity takes a back seat to their own ancient religion, and the Zuñis maintain an elaborate ceremonial organization.

Shalako dancers at Zuñi Pueblo in 1897. (Museum of New Mexico)

Because the Hopi believe the sun is the source of life, the most revered man in the tribe is the Sun Priest, who oversees solstice ceremonies.

Zuñi craftsmen are famous for their jewelry, in particular silver pieces inlaid with turquoise, shell, and jet. They have also made a craft of animal fetishes fashioned out of carved minerals, glass, and stones, embellished with gemstones, as well as "Zuñi needlepoint," intricate patterns of tiny gemstones (most often turquoise) set in silver.

Zuñi Pueblo has 8,000 members, making it the largest in New Mexico. It appears much like any other small New Mexican town, as a maze of low, flat-roofed houses, small vegetable patches, and dusty, unpaved streets. A few craft shops are mixed in among stores and businesses. In the morning the delicious smell of baking bread wafts forth from *hornos,* beehive-shaped clay ovens built at the side of nearly every home.

Tribal permission is required if you wish to visit two nearby places of interest —the crumbling ruins at Hawikuh (the site of Coronado's visit) and the unexcavated Village of the Great Kivas, three ancient pueblos located 18 miles north of Zuñi.

Visitors will notice that the Indian people of New Mexico are inherently friendly, but reserved and self-contained. Outsiders should take care to respect their privacy. In particular, ask permission before photographing an individual or a ceremony. *To reach Zuñi, take NM 602 29 miles south from I-40 at Gallup, then travel 10 miles west on NM 53.*

■ EL MORRO

To the east of Zuñi Pueblo, NM 53 follows an ancient Indian trade route past a massive 200-foot-high sandstone mesa visible for miles, on top of which sits an 875-room pueblo of Anasazi-Mogollon origin, abandoned about 1350. It has been preserved as El Morro (The Bluff) National Monument.

At the base of the pale cliff is a natural basin filled with water, replenished by summer rains and winter snows—a natural rest stop. Travelers have been unable to resist leaving their marks on the smooth sandstone surface for nearly a thousand years. Indian petroglyphs were first, followed by signatures and messages written by Spanish explorers, and later Anglo settlers. Two years before Jamestown, Virginia, was founded in 1607, Juan de Oñate left an inscription: "Passed by here the

Inscription Rock at El Morro National Monument has supplied a surface for graffiti artists since Diego de Vargas passed along the way in 1692.

Adelantado Don Juan de Oñate, from the discovery of the Sea of the South on the 16th of April 1605." The "Sea of the South" was the Gulf of California.

When Don Diego de Vargas was on his way to reclaim Zuñi after the Pueblo Revolt, he too left his mark: "Here was the General Don Diego de Vargas who conquered for our Holy Faith, and for the Royal Crown, all of New Mexico at his own expense, year of 1692." Through the centuries, explorers, traders, soldiers, surveyors, and settlers carved messages as they passed by. Thus the name **Inscription Rock** seems most appropriate.

El Morro National Monument's fine visitors center, with its museum featuring tools and pottery from the pueblo, is open year-round. *Located 56 miles southeast of Gallup on NM 53; or about 33 miles east of Zuñi. Call (505) 783-4226.*

■ EL MALPAIS

Further east lies a massive lava flow (the remains of five major eruptions from nearby volcanoes) that sprawls between Zuñi and Ácoma pueblos south of the present-day town of Grants. As recently as 700 years ago, rivers of molten rock and flying cinders oozed across the sandstone and limestone valley. Indian legends tell of rivers of "fire rock."

Early Spanish and American travelers rarely ventured across the hardened lava. Leading their horses around it, they called the 114,000-acre lava-rock valley El Malpaís (the Badlands). In 1988, the federal government recognized the unique geological features of the area and established El Malpaís National Monument and Conservation Area and opened up a visitors center in Grants, 10 miles to the north.

The valley's violent past can be seen along a portion of the trade route marked by the Indians. Aptly called the Zuñi-Ácoma Trail, the 7.5-mile path crosses all five of the major lava flows that blanket the broad valley, with a sharp, chunky lava called *a'a,* and ropy lava known as *pahoehoe.* A network of four-by-four wooden posts acts as trail markers connecting the ancient cairns. If you walk this way, wear thick-soled shoes.

At the eastern edge of the flow and visible from NM 117 is a magnificent natural arch called **La Ventana** (The Window). Years of wind pounding against the soft sandstone and water seeping into cracks have left a 125-foot-high opening in the rock. Black and red striations of color called "desert varnish" play on the underside of the 165-foot span. *Located east of Zuñi and south of Grants, El Malpaís can be approached on NM 53 or NM 117; (505) 285-5406.*

La Ventana Arch has a span of 165 feet and rises 125 feet above the desert floor.

■ ÁCOMA PUEBLO

Ácoma Pueblo is romantically but not inaccurately termed the "Sky City" for its dramatic pose atop a 367-foot-high mesa that soars above a dry country sculpted with mesas, arroyos, and sandstone cliffs. In the distance rises 11,000-foot Mount Taylor; to the south is the Rio San José, used by both Ácoma and Laguna to irrigate crops.

Ácoma also is sometimes called the oldest continuously occupied settlement in America, a distinction challenged by the Hopi village of Old Oraibi in Arizona. Actually, neither village can be dated to the precise year of its founding; published dates for Ácoma range from A.D. 1150 to the late 1200s. Venerable enough, at any rate.

The Ácomas claim their ancestors arrived from Mesa Verde in what today is southern Colorado. According to legend, the Indians were told by Ia'atik, mother of all Indians, to see a mesa resembling an ear of corn. They found Enchanted

View of Ácoma Pueblo in the 1890s. (Underwood Archives, San Francisco)

Mesa and built a rock-walled village atop the mountain. Only one route led up the precipitous 430-foot cliffs of the desert monolith. Another legend has it that one day, when most of the tribe was tending fields on the plains, a violent storm moved in, wiping out the path to the top. A young girl and her grandmother, stranded on the mountain, leaped to their deaths rather than remain there to starve. The tribe then moved to the nearby Acuco Mesa.

In 1541 one of Coronado's parties came across it and reported that "The natives . . . came down to meet us peacefully, although they might have spared themselves the trouble and remained on their rock, for we would not have been able to disturb them in the least." Ironic words, because half a century later the Spaniards were to disturb these pueblo people in a shockingly cruel fashion.

Juan de Oñate's party marched up the mesa in 1598 and extracted the usual pledge of allegiance to the king from the residents. Later that year, as another Spanish party camped below the Sky City, a battle ensued and the Ácomas prevailed. A furious Oñate dispatched a larger force to teach the Indians a lesson. They did. Hundreds of Indians were killed and hundreds more were taken prisoners. The Spaniards then cut off one foot of each captive man to serve as a "deterrent" to any future rebelliousness, and sentenced all the prisoners, male and female, to 20 years as slaves to Oñate's soldiers.

There are 465 houses atop the mesa, but only 13 families still live there—most Ácomas occupy more convenient houses in nearby villages.

The architectural centerpiece of the town is the mission church of **San Estéban del Rey,** completed in 1640. It's one of several wonderful New Mexican missions that are almost more sculpture than architecture: pure, bold, unadorned form —the adobe Parthenon of this Acropolis. Inside, the church walls feature not only the traditional Stations of the Cross, but also symbolic native art, such as an ear of corn growing under a benevolent rainbow.

Village houses lack electricity, plumbing, and phones, but they have screen doors, milled casement windows, and a few second stories of concrete block set over adobe. There are seven square *kivas* (or ceremonial chambers) all built above ground—which one guide says was a ruse to fool the Spaniards into thinking they were mere houses so the Ácomas could carry on their religion in secret.

Ácomas have long been known for their fine pottery, produced from a local clay of exceptional whiteness. Ácoma potters will often speak of ceramics as having their own spirits and their own lives.

Visitors are allowed only on guided tours. There is a charge for tours, and an additional charge for taking still pictures. No video cameras are allowed. Because of recent controversies about their traditional "rooster pull" (when horsemen gallop past a rooster buried up to its neck in the sand and try to pull it up) they may close feast days to the public. *Located south of I-40, about 60 miles west of Albuquerque; call the Ácoma Tourist Visitor Center in advance. Guided tours leave every half hour, every day year-round. (505) 470-4966.*

■ LAGUNA PUEBLO

Named for a nearby lake that has since become a meadow, this pueblo was established in 1699 by the Spanish governor Pedro Rodríguez Cubero. Later that year, the San José de Laguna Church was completed, making it the last of the early mission churches in New Mexico. The people of Laguna Pueblo have much in common with those of Ácoma. Both speak Keresan, a language related to no other known language family; both grow crops near the Rio San José, and both make excellent, and quite similar, pottery.

Today Laguna Pueblo is divided into six villages, with Old Laguna Village as its longtime capital. The church still stands on a hill overlooking simple pueblo

Ácoma Indian pottery (above) is known for its exquisite detail and fine craftsmanship.

San Estéban del Rey mission church (opposite) is the essence of pure, bold, unadorned form.

New Mexico Festivals & Events

J A N U A R Y

All Kings Day. Various dances at most northern pueblos. (800) 793-4955

F E B R U A R Y

Grants: Mt. Taylor Winter Quadrathlon
Grueling 75-km race up the 11,000-foot mountain and back to town. Contestants bike, run, ski, and snowshoe. (505) 287-4802

Red River: Mardi Gras in the Mountains
Bead throwing, parades, face painting, and lots of parties. (505) 754-2366

M A R C H

Albuquerque: Fiery Foods Show
Try out the latest and hottest products on the market. (505) 842-9918 or (800) 284-2282

A P R I L

Alamogordo: Rattlesnake Roundup
Scores of the poisonous snakes are displayed. (505) 434-0788

Los Ojos: Tierra Wools Spring Harvest Festival
A community celebrates new lambs and new fleece. Last weekend in April. (505) 588-7231

Silver City: Gila Bird & Nature Festival
Guided hikes, talks, and birdwatching outings. (800) 548-9378

M A Y

Statewide: Cinco de Mayo celebrations.
Albuquerque: Albuquerque Festival of the Arts

A two-week celebration of the visual, literary, performing, and culinary arts of the city. (505) 842-9918

Carlsbad: Mescal Roast
Traditional Mescalero Apache ceremonies: dances, craft demonstrations, blessings, and mescal tasting. (505) 887-5516

Taos: Art Festival
Two weeks of events celebrating the arts, from festivals to major openings. (800) 732-8267 or (505) 758-3873

J U N E

Albuquerque: Festival Flamenco
Two weeks of flamenco workshops and concerts. (505) 842-9918

Albuquerque: New Mexico Arts and Crafts Fair
Juried show featuring the works of 200 artists; music and food. (505) 884-9043

Albuquerque: Summerfest
Every Saturday in summer a different nationality is celebrated on Civic Plaza. Food, entertainment, crafts. (505) 768-3483

Chama: Chama Valley Music Festival
A different lineup entertains on every weekend in June. (505) 756-2836

Farmington: Anasazi, the Ancient Ones Pageant
Outdoor summer theater chronicles the culture that once thrived in the area. Pageant runs July through August. (800) 448-1240

Santa Fe: El Rancho de las Golondrinas Spring Festival
Open house at the living-history ranch. (505) 471-2261

JULY
Capitán: Smokey Bear Stampede
Rodeo, parade, Western dances. (505) 354-2273
Santa Fe: Chamber Music Festival
Six weeks of concerts. (505) 983-2075
Santa Fe: Santa Fe Opera
World-class productions nightly July through mid-August. (505) 986-5900
Santa Fe: Spanish Market
Artisans display woodwork, tinwork, sculpture, painting in prestigious fair on Plaza. (505) 983-4038

AUGUST
Bernalillo: Fiesta de San Lorenzo
Parade and matachine dances honoring town's patron saint. (505) 867-3311
Deming: Great American Duck Race
Waddlers compete for $2,000 purse in spirited competition across dryland course. (800) 848-4955
Lincoln: Old Lincoln Days
Billy the Kid pageant, music, food, and a Pony Express ride. (505) 653-4025
Santa Fe: Frontier Market and Summer Festival
At El Rancho de las Golondrinas, La Cienega. Trade goods by mountain men, Indians, and traders from the Santa Fe Trail and Camino Real. (505) 471-2261

Santa Fe: Indian Market
Largest showing of Native American artwork in the country. Traditional and contemporary art. (505) 983-5220

SEPTEMBER
Ruidoso Downs: All American Quarter Horse Futurity
World's richest quarter horse race. (505) 378-4431
Santa Fe: Fiesta de Santa Fe
Longest running community celebration in the country, celebrates the Spanish retaking of the city in 1692. Pet parade, arts and crafts, burning of Zozobra. (505) 988-7575
Taos: Old Taos Trade Fair
Demonstrations in traditional skills; performances at Martínez Hacienda. (505) 758-3873 or (800) 732-8267
Taos: Arts Festival
Two-week festival showcasing local artists. (505) 758-3873 or (800) 732-8267

OCTOBER
Albuquerque: Kodak Albuquerque International Balloon Fiesta
Food, music. (800) 733-9918
Santa Fe: Harvest Festival
At El Rancho de las Golondrinas, La Cienega. Costumed villagers demonstrate the working farm's operation. Hand-pressed apple cider. (505) 471-2261

DECEMBER
Statewide: Las Posadas
Re-enactment of Joseph and Mary's search for shelter in Bethlehem.

dwellings. Its imposing, if plain, exterior belies the rich decorations within. The ornate and colorfully painted pine altar carved by Indian craftsmen is flanked by paintings of St. Barbara and St. John Nepomucene, and an animal hide attached to the ceiling is colored with Indian symbols of the rainbow, sun, moon, and stars. All this reverent beauty sits uncomfortably close to the freeway. *Visible along I-40 near exit 114, about 45 miles to the west of Albuquerque; (505) 552-6654.*

■ ALBUQUERQUE

The Rio Grande, shaded by leafy cottonwoods, cuts a north-south swath through the city of Albuquerque. Five dormant volcanic cones, the Sleeping Sisters, mark the city's western edge, and a shrub-covered mesa spreads out under their shadow.

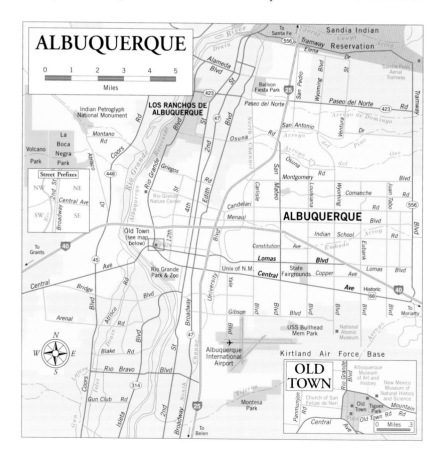

Between this mesa and the cactus-covered foothills of the Sandía and Manzano mountains, Albuquerque stretches forth in a sea of asphalt and flat rooftops. The city has grown out instead of up and now encompasses 125 square miles of high desert and straddles two interstate highways.

Albuquerque's 400,000 citizens are a mix of Indians, Yankees, families of long standing, Hispanic immigrants, and an increasingly cosmopolitan mélange of scientists, academics, techies, and yuppies. The city still maintains an easygoing pace and small-town friendliness despite being on the verge of becoming swamped by smog, traffic, and a growing crime rate. Downtown has recently received a facelift, and flaunts gleaming skyscrapers. The most interesting district is Old Town.

Old Town. Through most of the 18th century, Albuquerque was just a loose string of farms and ranches flanking the Rio Grande, but in 1779 Santa Fe ordered the residents to form a compact community, defensible against Apache attacks, around the church of San Felipe de Neri. This was the genesis of Old Town. It has gone through its ups and downs since, and most recently has been "spruced up." Is it authentic? Well, a few buildings have suffered "Puebloization" for the sake of tourism. For instance, the *vigas,* or ceiling beams, protruding from intersecting walls of the 1879 **Antonio Vigil House** at 413 Romero Street would, if real, collide at right angles inside the house. They're fake. Real vigas jut north and south, or east and west, but never intersect.

Facing the plaza is Old Town's centerpiece, the 1793 **church of San Felipe de Neri** (which replaced an earlier structure). Its style is best described as French Carpenter Gothic—executed, amazingly, in adobe. It claims to be the third oldest church in the United States that has continued to hold services since its founding. (There are 800 families in the parish today). The adjacent plaza, refreshingly, still serves its ancient civic function. Neighborhood residents relax on the benches, read newspapers, and feed pigeons. This feels like the spiritual center of Albuquerque, much more than its anonymous downtown.

There are about two dozen galleries in Old Town, along with many more boutiques, jewelry stores, and restaurants. Recommendation: **Agape Southwest Pueblo Pottery,** 414 Romero Street, one of the most comprehensive Indian pottery galleries in the Southwest.

While Old Town receives most of its visitors during the summer months, December is an especially magical time. On Christmas Eve the neighborhood is transformed into a world of shimmering light when, in traditional Hispanic style,

Old Town's citizens set out more than 15,000 *luminarias* (referred to as *farolitos* in Santa Fe and points north). These are votive candles placed with a handful of dirt in a small brown paper bag, and set along sidewalks and rooftops, symbolically illuminating the way for Mary and Joseph as they search for lodging in Bethlehem. *To visit Old Town, exit I-40 at Rio Grande Boulevard and drive about a half mile south. Street parking is available, and there are municipal lots to the north and east.*

Albuquerque Museum of Art and History. Adjacent to Old Town and decidedly worth a visit, this huge museum focuses mainly on New Mexico art, culture, and history. Walking tours of Old Town start from the museum Tuesday through Sunday from mid-April through October. *2000 Mountain Road NW; (505) 243-7255.*

New Mexico Museum of Natural History and Science. Across the road from the Albuquerque Museum, at the northern edge of Old Town. The life-size *Triceratops* that stands guard in front is a clue to what's inside: 4.6 billion years of New Mexico's geologically tumultuous past. *Mountain Road at 19th; (505) 841-2802.*

Luminarias *(candle lanterns) decorate the plaza in front of San Felipe de Neri Church during Chrismastime. At Albuquerque's Old Town plaza (opposite) craftsmen from around the region sell their goods.*

Albuquerque Parks. More than 145 city parks help break up the urban sprawl. The finest of them is the Albuquerque Biological Park, which includes the long-established **Rio Grande Zoological Park**, the **Albuquerque Aquarium**, and **Rio Grande Botanic Garden**. *2601 Central NW Avenue.* A few blocks north is the **Rio Grande Nature Center**, two miles of trails along the river lead through a riparian environment or bosque (woodlands) that attracts pheasants, roadrunners, toads, beavers, and skunks. The visitors center is built partially underground, and the unobtrusive design enables visitors to watch bird life both above and below the surface of a three-acre pond. During the migration months of May and October, Canada and snow geese, sandhill cranes, and an occasional whooping crane stop at the center to rest. Free guided walks along the park's trails are conducted every weekend. *Candelaria Road west of Rio Grande Boulevard (see map on page 64).*

Petroglyph National Monument. Preserved here are 15,000 images, believed to be 2,000 to 3,000 years old, pecked into a lava escarpment by early Indian residents. The most vivid ones are startlingly clear and refined images of birds, animals, humans, and abstractions left by late-arriving Puebloans after A.D. 1300. Interpreting prehistoric art is a risky enterprise. Some signs almost surely track clan migrations, some might have been engraved prayers or curses, some may have served as solar calendars, some could be abstract art or casual graffiti. A visit here resolves no mysteries, but it is like touring a prehistoric art museum. Three easy, self-guided trails lead to the best rock art in the monument. *Located west of I-25, a few miles north of Albuquerque. From I-25 take I-40 west to Coors Road exit north. Turn left on Atrisco Drive, which becomes Unser Boulevard. The monument is at 6900 Unser Boulevard; (505) 839-4429.*

Sandía Peak. Rising above the desert foothills at the eastern edge of Albuquerque, this is a lush, forested mountainscape with spectacular views of the city below. An all-weather road leads to the summit, where visitors can set out along 80 miles of hiking trails or simply take in the view from the observation deck.

Another way to reach the top is by riding the **Sandía Peak Aerial Tramway,** an 18-minute, 2.7-mile journey that leaves behind clusters of cholla cactus and ascends above jagged granite outcroppings until it reaches the windy, pine-covered summit. From the top, the city and surrounding desert stretch to the horizon, sliced by the greenbelt of the Rio Grande. In the winter, skiers glide along cross-country trails or schuss the groomed slopes of **Sandía Peak Ski Area,** carved from the forest on the mountain's eastern flank. Dusk is the most dramatic time to be atop the 10,678-foot peak, when the disappearing sun casts a rosy glow as it sets behind the West Mesa. At the summit of Sandía Peak, warm up with hot chocolate at the High Finance Restaurant. *To reach Sandía Peak by car, drive east on I-40 to NM 14 (north), then six miles to NM 536 and continue west; Sandía Ranger Station (505) 281-3304. To reach the tramway's base take I-25 north of Albuquerque to Tramway Blvd. exit 234, then turn left on Tramway Rd.; (505) 856-6419.*

■ MANZANO MOUNTAINS

East of Albuquerque, I-40 bisects the Sandía and Manzano mountain ranges through Tijeras (Scissors) Canyon on its way to the eastern plains. One of the state's more interesting drives curves along the eastern foothills of the Manzano Mountains on NM 337. Leaving Tijeras Canyon, the road climbs and dips, sometimes hugging lichen-covered granite outcroppings and other times passing through wide-open meadows of yellow wildflowers. Interspersed along this route are villages with intriguing names such as Chilili, Tajique, Torreon, and Manzano. In 1829, at the mountain range's southern end, Spanish settlers built a small fort for protection from Apache attacks. They named their community **Manzano,** after an apple orchard established there in 1800. Still bearing fruit today, this orchard is one of the oldest in the country.

Manzano remains a sleepy community of tin-roofed adobe homes, some with horses in the yard, and a stuccoed adobe church. South of Manzano, the rolling slopes of junipers and piñons give way to the meadows of the **Estancia Basin,** traveled by prehistoric nomadic hunters who camped on the shores of a huge lake that filled the basin 12,000 years ago. Settlement came in the 10th century, when Mogollon Indians established villages alongside dependable streams and springs. Conquistador Juan de Oñate visited the area in 1598, but Spaniards didn't move in until Franciscan priests settled alongside Indians in the early 1600s.

Three of these pueblos, Quarai, Abo, and Gran Quivira, separately situated in a 25-mile radius of the ranching center of Mountainair, have been preserved as **Salinas Pueblo Missions National Monument.** At Punta de Agua, a hamlet on NM 55, a gravel road veers off to the west, leading to the mission ruins at **Quarai.** Sandstone walls still loom 40 feet above a grassy plain, much as they did in 1630 when the church of La Purísima Concepción de Cuarac was completed. A well-marked trail passes by the unexcavated mounds of pueblo dwellings, covered with

(following pages) The ruins of Quarai in Salinas Pueblo Missions National Monument.

patches of grass. Close by the settlement, a grove of towering cottonwoods indicates the springs that were so vital to Quarai's survival.

Seventeen miles southwest (via NM 55 and US 60) at **Abo,** Indians erected their mission church in the late 1620s atop a rise in a wide valley surrounded by hillsides covered with piñon and juniper trees. Built of bright red sandstone, the **Abo church** is 30 feet high. Stone buttresses support two-foot-thick walls. The narrow Abo River flows gently nearby the Indians' three-storied rock-walled homes, now covered with red soil and patches of pale green desert grass. Only partial walls show above the earth.

South of the town of Mountainair, NM 55 crosses vast fields of cholla cactus and brilliant, orange-red Indian paintbrush. An occasional hawk soars in silence overhead. Looking up, you can see the partial walls of the **mission church at Gran Quivira** rise majestically atop a distant mesa. Once 1,500 people lived at Gran Quivira, although no water source is known within 30 miles. Historians believe the Indians irrigated their fields with rainwater captured in natural limestone cisterns, or they may have tapped a spring that has since dried up. The Indians here also hunted bison and fashioned pottery that they painted with black and white stripes.

In the 1670s, besieged by Apache and drought, the Indians of the Salinas Valley left their homes to take refuge at pueblos along the Rio Grande.

A visitors center for these three restored pueblos is in Mountainair on Main Street, two blocks from the **Shaffer Hotel**—itself worth a visit. The Shaffer is a fine example of Pueblo Deco architecture, with orange and black squares and black swastikas (Indian symbols for happiness) adorning the exterior. Clem "Pop" Shaffer's place has recently been restored as a bed-and-breakfast, and you can get a good Mexican meal or a piece of homemade apple pie in the Historic Shaffer Hotel Dining Room.

To return to Albuquerque take NM 60 to NM 47 and turn north on I-25. Just off the interstate, about 18 miles south of Albuquerque in Isleta Pueblo, is one of the oldest missions in the United States: **St. Augustine Church.** Surrounded by adobe homes and rough shacks, the church has an other-worldly quality. Outside, the walls are high, white, and irregular; inside, a sense of mystery lingers amid paintings of saints.

The pueblo itself dates from the 16th century and is one of the oldest and largest in New Mexico. Its history followed the generally tragic course of most

Southwest Indian villages. Although its population acquiesced fairly amicably to the imposition of the Catholic faith and Spanish culture, this didn't protect them from being decimated by disease, conflict, and forced relocation. Isleta was a thriving town when the Spanish first arrived, but by 1692 it was home to only a handful of Indians, many of them refugees from other pueblos. Today, the pueblo has a population of 3,000.

■ CORONADO STATE MONUMENT

The first major town north of Albuquerque is Bernalillo, one of the oldest European towns in the United States. Once a farming and ranching village, it has become a bedroom community for its nearby metropolis.

Long ago the area was home to Tiwa Indians who had drifted down from Chaco Canyon around A.D. 1150. At the 1,200-room pueblo built along the banks of the Rio Grande, these Indians farmed and built several underground ceremonial *kivas,* which they entered by ladder through an opening in the roof. On the walls of one *kiva* they painted black fish, masked kachinas dressed in yellow shirts with black skirts and white sashes, white rabbits, white clouds, seeds and corn, and white-tipped red arrows. Near the end of the 17th century, the Indians abandoned the pueblo, probably moving south. Sands drifted over Kuaua's mud walls, burying it for the next 250 years.

When archaeologists excavated the pueblo in 1935, they discovered 85 layers of adobe plaster inside the *kiva,* 17 of which contained painted symbols of the Indians' complex relationship with the earth and the heavens. Some of these original murals are encased in glass inside the visitor center at Coronado State Monument, which was created in 1940 to preserve the pueblo ruins. Reproductions of the paintings line the walls of a reconstructed *kiva,* which you can enter by climbing down a solid wooden ladder into the cool subterranean interior.

It was here, at **Kuaua Pueblo,** that Spanish conquistador Francisco Vásquez de Coronado wintered his exploratory expedition in 1540. Adjacent to the monument is **Coronado State Park,** a collection of picnic shelters and campsites set atop additional ruins, some older and some newer than Kuaua, and the charred remains of a Spanish hacienda that was burned during the Pueblo Revolt in 1680 when the Pueblo Indians chased the Spanish settlers out of New Mexico. *Off NM 44, one mile northwest of Bernalillo; (505) 867-5351.*

■ THREE RIO GRANDE PUEBLOS

North of Bernalillo, the Rio Grande courses alongside three Keresan-speaking pueblos: San Felipe, Santo Domingo, and Cochití (use a good map in trying to locate these sites). While these pueblos share a language, each has its own dialect and is known for a special tradition: San Felipe for its ceremonial dances, Santo Domingo for its jewelry and August Corn Dance, and Cochití for its pottery. San Felipe and Santo Domingo are both very conservative pueblos, forbidding cameras and tape recorders. Remember to ask permission at the governor's office before walking around the communities and striking up conversations with residents.

San Felipe Pueblo, one of the most traditional pueblos in New Mexico, is known for its beautiful ceremonials. The most colorful is the Green Corn Dance on May 1st when hundreds of costumed Puebloans participate in day-long dancing and singing rituals.

Though many of **Santo Domingo's ceremonies** are closed to the public, on August 4th visitors are welcome to the elaborate Corn Dance. It begins in mid-morning when the comic Koshare appears painted in black and gray stripes to

Koshare clowns play an important role in the Corn Dance. Above they perform at San Juan Pueblo in 1935. (Museum of New Mexico)

CLASSIC SOUTHWEST JEWELRY

COCHITI PUEBLO
SILVER SQUASH BLOSSOM NECKLACE

Traditional squash blossom necklaces feature side pendants in the shape of a squash or pumpkin flower. In this necklace from Cochiti Pueblo, 25 miles west of Santa Fe, the squash blossoms have been replaced with crosses; this particular design has a double-barred cross with a heartlike bottom, resembling the Catholic sacred heart and the Indian dragonfly that in many Pueblo cultures was the symbol for water.

ZUÑI BRACELET

The Zuñi Pueblo, the largest pueblo in New Mexico, is located due west of Albuquerque near the Arizona border. For centuries, Zuñis traded turquoise to Plains Indians for buffalo hides and to Mexican tribes for parrot plumes. Over the years the Zuñi have become famous for their extraordinary work in turquoise and silver as exemplified above in this huge, sunburst-design, cluster bracelet. Circa 1930.

NAVAJO CONCHA BELTS

The idea for concha belts derived from disk-shaped hair ornaments sold to Plains Indians by white traders as early as 1750. Navajos linked hair ornaments to form decorative belts, impressing into the silver Mexican designs. Circa 1885.

warn the pueblo of attackers who are on their way to the village. Having done that, the dancers pantomime the ensuing battle, in which the Indians defeat the invaders.

At **Cochití Pueblo**, outsiders are welcome to view the Church of San Buenaventura, its interior displaying tin candlesticks brought from Chihuahua and a larger-than-life painting of the patron saint that adorns the center wall above the altar. The pueblo also is recognized for its pottery, especially red-and-black "storyteller" dolls that depict little children clinging to an open-mouthed grandmother or grandfather figure.

All three pueblos are located west of I-25, between Albuquerque and Santa Fe, about 10–20 miles north of Bernalillo. See map on page 114. Watch for signs on the interstate leading to individual pueblos. Call for hours: San Felipe; (505) 867-3381. Santo Domingo; (505) 465-2214. Cochití Pueblo; (505) 465-2244.

Just north of Cochití Pueblo's water tanks (painted to look like animal-skin drums), the Rio Grande backs up behind **Cochití Dam,** creating a swimming hole and a haven for windsurfers. Motorboats are prohibited because they create wakes, leaving the waters to small sailboats and fishermen trolling for bass, crappie, and pike. *(505) 465-2300.*

■ TURQUOISE TRAIL

East of the Sandía Mountains, NM 14 travels through the old mining towns of Golden, Madrid, and Cerrillos. More than a thousand years ago Pueblo Indians in the Cerrillos Hills south of Santa Fe were using stone hammers to mine for turquoise—highly prized for its beauty, as well as its purported ability to ensure good fortune and a long, healthy life. Apparently, this turquoise found its way to Canada and Mexico where, according to legend, Montezuma II, the powerful Aztec emperor, proudly displayed his pendants and necklaces of Cerrillos turquoise.

North of I-40, NM Highway 14 passes the communities of Cedar Crest and Sandía Park, which sprawl on the eastern flanks of the Sandía Mountains. But finally the two-lane road leaves the suburbs behind, and the land opens up. Tall yellow-green grasses mix with an occasional cholla cactus, the air is scented with juniper berries, and hills are dotted with piñons and junipers. The snowcapped peaks of the Sangre de Cristo Mountains appear behind corners as the road winds its way to **Golden,** once a bustling goldmining district on the northern edge of the San Pedro Mountains.

A general store and gift shop sit on the highway along with a few homes constructed of adobe, rock, and galvanized iron. Piñons sprout from the ruins of rock homes that proliferated in the mid-1800s when the town was booming with 22 stores and 100 houses. Still, nobody got rich because there wasn't enough water to wash the gold dust from the sand.

Golden's only really impressive building is a little mission church atop a hill at the northern edge of town. Built in the late 1830s soon after the gold rush began, the adobe church honored **St. Francis of Assisi.**

The slate-blue swell of the Sandía Mountains rises to the southwest, the ski runs of Sandía Peak Ski Area appearing from the distance like fairways divided by the deeper green pine trees. Pale-green lichen covers rock outcroppings as the road penetrates the Ortiz Mountains, then descends into the once-thriving coal mining district of **Madrid** (pronounced "MAD-rid"). Charcoal-gray and pinkish-red tailings pile up underneath bare slopes, reminders of an era that began in 1889, when the mines produced 500 tons of coal a day, two-story wooden cabins lined the main street, and white picket fences protected groomed lawns and well-tended flower gardens. Company-owned Madrid boasted tennis courts, a seven-hole golf course, a shooting range, and a 30-piece brass band that marched in an annual Fourth of July parade. Nowadays the historic but ramshackle wooden structures house galleries, boutiques, and restaurants.

A few more bends in the road and **Los Cerrillos** (often called just "Cerrillos") appears beneath leafy cottonwoods. Its boom days long over, this sleepy hamlet often is used as a western movie set because of its few faded storefronts, dirt streets, and rundown exteriors. In the late 1800s, when Los Cerrillos still had hotels and saloons filled with miners seeking their fortunes in gold, Thomas Edison paid a visit. He tried to extract gold from sand and gravel using static electricity, but wasn't able to.

Today the **Turquoise Trail Trading Post** sells locally mined gemstones, herbs, tie-dyed T-shirts, petrified shark's teeth, and miniature adobe bricks, and features a homespun petting zoo of goats, sheep, and burros. The Clear Light Opera House is now a recording studio.

From Cerrillos, NM 14 continues northward until it hooks up with I-25 for the final few miles into Santa Fe. NM 14 goes to Santa Fe as well, but it penetrates the heart of a commercial district. The interstate is faster and prettier. See map, page 114.

Central New Mexico Food & Lodging

■ FOOD & LODGING

> *Restaurant prices:*
> Per person, not including drinks, tax, and tips:
> $ = under $10; $$ = $10–20; $$$ = over $20
>
> *Room rates:*
> Per night, per room, double occupancy:
> $ = under $50; $$ = $50–100; $$$ = over $100

Albuquerque

population 385,000   elevation 5,311

✕ **Acapulco Tacos & Burritos.** 840 San Mateo SE; (505) 268-9865 $
Painted in bright colors reminiscent of its namesake, this New Mexican taqueria offers a wide variety of burritos. Get one to go, or eat outside at the picnic tables.

✕ **Alvarado Brewing Co.** 515 Central NW; (505) 242-6800 $-$$
Great beers made on the premises and contemporary Southwestern cuisine. Informal but sophisticated.

✕ **Artichoke Cafe.** 424 Central Ave. SE; (505) 243-0200 $$-$$$
The decor is "upscale storefront," the food is innovative without being over the top. They describe it as "French American," which means lots of fresh fish dishes. A good place to mingle with Albuquerque yuppies.

✕ **Barelas Coffee House.** 1502 4th SW; (505) 843-7577 $
Bustling neighborhood landmark where politicians brainstorm and every-one else enjoys the green chile.

✕ **Casa Chaco.** In the Albuquerque Hilton, 1901 University Blvd. NE; (505) 884-2500 $
Breakfast and lunch menu features standard, but high quality, coffee shop fare. A particular favorite is the corn bread baked with New Mexico's indigenous chile. Every evening Casa Chaco reopens for dinner with candlelit tables, linen tablecloths, and upscale Southwestern cuisine.

✕ **Dion's Pizza.** Three of the 7 locations: 8010 Academy NE; (505) 821-3911 10401 Montgomery NE; 293-7183 4200 Coors NW; 898-1161 $
The best pizzas in town, and good salads to complement them. Lively atmosphere at each location.

✕ **Duran Central Pharmacy.** 1815 Central NW; (505) 247-4141 $
A local favorite where the waitresses are friendly and the chiles are hot.

✕ **El Patio.** 142 Harvard SE; (505) 268-4245 $
A favorite with the nearby university students and faculty. Among the top-rated favorites are the green-chile chick-

en enchiladas, carne adovada, vegetarian avocado burritos, and honey-laden sopaipillas. Outdoor patio.

X **Garcia's Kitchen.** Four locations:
1113 Forest NW; (505) 247-9149
1736 Central SW; (505) 842-0273
2525 Pennsylvania St.; (505) 881-0086
3601 Juan Tabo St.; (505) 275-5812 $
You're in for a fun dining experience at any Garcia's Kitchen. At one location a toy clown crosses a high wire above your table; at another a colorful mural decorates the exterior. Great carne adovada.

X **Il Vicino.** 3403 Central NE; (505) 266-7855 $
This trendy Nob Hill cafe serves pizza with gourmet toppings baked in a wood-fired oven. Wonderful salads and calzones. The beer is brewed on the premises.

X **Kanome.** 3128 Central SE; (505) 265-7773 $-$$
You'll find Asian food with a twist at one of the city's most stylish eateries. There is nothing traditional here, except for chopsticks.

X **M&J Sanitary Tortilla Factory.** 403 2nd SW; (505) 242-4890 $
A local favorite where lawyers, students, and artists mingle at lunchtime over plates of enchiladas and burritos.

X **New Chinatown.** 5001 Central NE; (505) 265-8859 $-$$
Look for the red and green pagoda, where you'll find spicy Szechuan dishes along with other traditional entrees.

X **Paul's Monterrey Inn.** 1000 Juan Tabo NE; (505) 294-1461 $$-$$$
A traditional dimly lit, wood-grained

steakhouse where you'll find the best cuts of meat perfectly prepared to your liking.

X **Rio Bravo Restaurant and Brewery.** 515 Central NW; (505) 242-6800 $
Informally sophisticated cafe where you can try one of their own beers and contemporary Southwestern cuisine.

X **Sadie's Dining Room.** 6230 4th NW; (505) 345-5339 $
Strong margaritas, hot and well-seasoned chile, and generous portions make this one of Albuquerque's most popular Mexican restaurants.

X **Scalo Northern Italian Grill.** 3500 Central SE; (505) 255-8781 $$
This trendy spot offers exotically spiced homemade pasta dishes, along with creative meat, chicken, and fish entrees. Reservations are recommended.

X **Seasons Rotisserie & Grill.** 2031 Mountain NW; (505) 766-5100 $$-$$$
A wonderful new restaurant in Old Town serving generous portions of grilled and rotisseried meats, Mexican, Southwestern, and vegetarian dishes. Delightful patio.

⌂ **Adobe & Roses.** 1011 Ortega NW; (505) 897-2329 $$
This bucolic North Valley B&B is nestled among lily ponds and fruit trees.

⌂ **Casas de Suenos.** 310 Rio Grande SW; (505) 247-4560 $$$
Flower gardens separate private casitas in this rambling, Old Mexico–style compound a block from Old Town. The B&B's centerpiece is the main building designed by well-known Albuquerque architect Bart Prince.

Central New Mexico Food & Lodging

⊟ **Casita Chamisa.** 850 Chamisal NW; (505) 897-4644 $$-$$$ Cottonwoods shade the North Valley acreage which surrounds this 150-year-old farmhouse. Also the site of an archaeological dig, the B&B has an indoor pool and welcomes children and pets.

⊟ **El Vado Motel.** 2500 Central SW; (505) 243-4594 $ Route 66 devotees will enjoy a stay in this vintage tourist court dating from the national highway's heyday. Neon sign out front. Only five blocks from Old Town.

⊟ **Hyatt Regency Hotel.** 330 Tijeras NW; (505) 842-1234 or 800-233-1234 $$$ One of Albuquerque's most luxurious hotels. Rooftop swimming pool.

⊟ **La Posada de Albuquerque.** 125 Second NW; (505) 242-9090 $$$ Uniquely restored 50-year-old downtown hotel designed by New Mexico native son Conrad Hilton.

⊟ **Sarabande.** (B&B), 5637 Rio Grande NW; (505)345-4923 $$$ Flower-filled courtyards accent this territorial-style home in pastoral North Valley. Swim in heated 50-foot lap pool or explore the valley's irrigation ditches via mountain bike.

Albuquerque Environs

✕ **Cafe de las Placitas.** 664 NM 165, Placitas; (505) 867-1610 $-$$$ Menu changes regularly at this nicely designed adobe restaurant in the foothills of the Sandía Mountains.

✕ **Prairie Star.** 255 Prairie Star Rd., (off Hwy. 44); Bernalillo.; (505) 867-3327 $$ Enjoy a sunset view of the Sandia Mountains at this elegant hacienda about 20 minutes from Albuquerque.

✕ **The Range Cafe and Bakery.** 925 Camino del Pueblo, Bernalillo; (505) 867-1700 $-$$ Homecooking has never been this good, especially the turkey pot pie and morning muffins.

✕ **Teofilo's Restaurant.** 144 Main St., Los Lunas; (505) 865-5511 $ Light and airy atmosphere where you'll find tasty traditional New Mexican fare.

⊟ **Apache Canyon Ranch.** #4 Canyon Dr.,Canoncito; (505) 836-7220 $$-$$$ Surrounded by Indian reservations, this isolated ranch 30 minutes west of town offers unobstructed vistas and a telescope for magnificent celestial displays. Rates include breakfast and dinner.

⊟ **Elaine's.** 72 Snowline Estates, 30 minutes east of Albuquerque in Cedar Crest; (505) 281-2467 $$ European antiques fill this three-story, log B&B situated in the mountains.

⊟ **Hacienda de Placitas.** 491 NM 165, Placitas; (505) 867-3775 $$$ A windmill that once serviced the Santa Fe Railroad marks the spot for this romantic inn. Good breakfasts and views of the Jémez Mountains.

⊟ **Hacienda Vargas.** NM 313, Algodones; (505) 867-9115 $$–$$$

Once a stagecoach stop on the Camino Real, this beautifully kept horseshoe-shaped adobe inn offers rural quiet. Each room in the B&B has a kiva fireplace and French doors. Relax under a 200-year-old cottonwood tree in the courtyard, then visit the original chapel.

⊞ **The Sandhill Crane.** 389 Camino Hermosa, Corrales; (505) 898-2445' (800) 375-2445 $$-$$$
Wisteria, honeysuckle, and trumpet vines drape the walls of this recently renovated adobe hacienda that offers views of the Sandia Mountains.

Gallup

population 19,000   elevation 6,600

✕ **Genaro's.** 600 W. Hill; (505) 863-6761 $
Patrons fill the vinyl booths at this cafe to eat the house specialties—stuffed sopaipillas and posole.

✕ **Jerry's Cafe.** 406 W. Coal; (505) 722-6775 $
You'll find great bean burritos at this no-frills eatery.

⊞ **El Rancho Hotel.** 1000 E. US 66; (505) 863-9311 or (800) 543-6351 $-$$
Stay in rooms once occupied by Hollywood stars who came to the area to star in period Westerns. Their photos line the walls of lobby balcony. This historic, centrally located hotel retains an ambiance of yesteryear.

⊞ **Holiday Inn.** 2915 W. US 66; (505) 722-2201 or (800) 432-2211 $$
Full-service motel west of town.

Grants

population 8,600   elevation 6,460

✕ **La Ventana Steakhouse.** 110½ Geis; (505) 287-9393 $-$$
This steakhouse is named after a giant rock arch south of town.

✕ **Uranium Cafe.** 519 W. Santa Fe Ave.; (505) 287-7540 $
Homecooking is the forte here, where if you're lucky, you can sit in the booth that used to be a car. Lunch only.

⊞ **Holiday Inn Express.** I-40 East Interchange; (505) 285-4676 $$
Quiet roadside motel east of town.

Madrid

population 300   elevation 6,000

✕ **Mine Shaft Tavern.** On NM 14; (505) 473-0743 $-$$
Steaks and burgers, served alongside beers and margaritas, in a popular locals tavern.

Mountainair

population 930   elevation 6,499

✕ **Historic Shaffer Hotel Dining Room.** 103 Main Street; (505) 847-2888 $
Burgers and New Mexican food in fun Pueblo Deco setting. The homemade desserts are delicious.

⊞ **Historic Shaffer Hotel.** 102 Main St.; (505) 847-2888 $$
Recently restored bed-and-breakfast in a historic Pueblo Deco building.

Central New Mexico Food & Lodging

S A N T A   F E

■ HIGHLIGHTS
Santa Fe Plaza
Palace of the Governors
St. Francis Cathedral
Loretto Chapel
Indian Pottery
Arts
Adobe Architecture
Cuisine

■ SETTING
Santa Fe is the quintessential Southwestern city, with unique adobe architecture, marvelous Indian and Hispanic art work, and a low-key if affluent lifestyle. The town itself is set on a high-desert plateau, with mountain ranges visible on every side—in particular the Sangre de Cristos, which glow red in the sunset. The air is fine and pure, and the temperature moderate. Santa Fe's magic has to do with the quality of light under the blazing high-desert sun. During the day the colors on the mountains shift from slate gray to indigo to terra cotta, becoming a shade of deep pink that darkens to violet as the sun descends. The adobe buildings glow and radiate the light in the morning and at dusk. It's this light that has drawn artists, mystics, poets, and lovers of beauty for centuries.

■ TRAVELERS ORIENTATION
Plane service into Santa Fe is limited, and most people who arrive by air come into Albuquerque, rent a car, and drive north 60 miles on Interstate 25. Commuter plane service to Santa Fe is available from Denver. If you come into town this way, don't expect to find shuttle vans into Santa Fe, taxis waiting out front, or information desks. This is a very quiet airport.

The drive north from Albuquerque along I-25 passes through gently rolling hills with finger mesas visible in the distance and mountain ranges on all sides: the Sandía, Ortiz, and Jémez. Once you climb to the crest of La Bajada hill, about 20 miles south of Santa Fe, you see a plateau sprawled out before you with Santa Fe in the distance, looking larger than it is across unobstructed desert. In the distance lie the Sangre de Cristos.

The approach to the city itself can be a disappointment, for the road into town is the same unplanned commercial sprawl you'll see everywhere else in the West, even if it is toned down and pseudo-adobe. But don't despair. In the center of town and on back roads, a beauty remains that is unique.

You will find Santa Fe's extraordinary regional cuisine one important reason to come here. At the end of this chapter you will find a long list of restaurants, many of which are nationally recognized for combining originality with tradition. As for places to stay, Santa Fe once again offers a range of choices for the traveler from small, in-town, adobe bed-and-breakfasts to elegant historic hotels and resorts. **Food & Lodging** appears on page 106.

Clean air, low humidity, and abundant sunshine (300 sunny days a year on average) are the ingredients of Santa Fe's extraordinarily appealing climate. The best time to visit is between April and October, when even summertime temperatures are comfortable due to the altitude (7,200) and the dry air. Occasional afternoon thunderstorms occur in July and August, and a handful of winter storms blanket the town in snow. The Santa Fe Ski Area, only a 30-minute drive north of town in the Sangre de Cristo Mountains, is snow-covered continuously from late November until mid-April.

| TEMPS (F°) | AVG. JAN. | | AVG. APRIL | | AVG. JULY | | AVG. OCT. | | RECORD | RECORD |
	HIGH	LOW	HIGH	LOW	HIGH	LOW	HIGH	LOW	HIGH	LOW
Santa Fe	42	18	67	34	85	56	64	35	99	-18

PRECIPITATION (INCHES)	AVG. JAN.	AVG. APRIL	AVG. JULY	AVG. OCT.	ANNUAL	SNOW
Santa Fe	0.7	1.1	2.3	1.1	13.8	36

■ HISTORY AND CULTURE

The first group of European settlers to arrive in northern New Mexico came in 1598 under the leadership of Spanish governor Juan de Oñate. They were 130 families, 270 single men, and 11 Franciscan friars, along with 7,000 head of cattle and 83 wagons and carts. After enduring incredible hardships in the Chihuahuan Desert as they traveled north from Mexico, they settled along the Rio Grande near San Juan Pueblo. During the next decade the settlement was embroiled in disputes, and Oñate, after his notorious encounter with the Ácomas when he cut off one foot of every man in the pueblo, returned to find that most of his settlers had deserted him.

In 1607, under the leadership of a new governor, Pedro de Peralta, the original settlers regrouped and, joined by a new group of families brought north by Peralta, set about to build a capital at Santa Fe. Six districts were marked out for the town and a square block for government buildings. Residents were directed to elect four councilmen, two of whom were to be empowered as judges.

By 1612, Santa Fe was a fortress-like compound, with arsenals, a jail, a chapel, and governor's offices. Two interior plazas were joined by outer walls, and entry was gained through a single gate before which had been dug a defensive trench. Settlers who agreed to live in the area for 10 consecutive years were given two lots for house and garden; fields in which to plant vegetable gardens, vineyards, and olive groves; and another 133 acres of land.

In 1680, Pueblo Indians rose in revolt and drove the Spanish out. When they returned in 1692, led by a Spanish nobleman, Diego de Vargas, the Indians surrendered, and Santa Fe was refurbished. For 130 years little changed; then Mexico gained its independence from Spain and allowed the opening of the Santa Fe Trail. Anglos brought in a plethora of new goods: calico, pots and pans, tools. In 1848, after the United States settled its war with Mexico, Santa Fe officially became a part of the United States.

In 1851, Santa Fe's famous Bishop Lamy arrived in Santa Fe with a mission to revitalize the Catholic Church. Born to a peasant family in France, Jean Baptiste Lamy came to the United States from seminary and spent 11 years building churches and schools in Ohio and Kentucky. Idealized by Willa Cather in *Death Comes for the Archbishop,* reviled by others for his cultural arrogance, Lamy was responsible for building beautiful St. Francis Cathedral a block from the Plaza.

Screen depicting the Virgin of Guadalupe in the Santuario de Guadalupe. (Photo by Eduardo Fuss)

SPANISH COLONIAL WEDDING

*A*t last all was ready, and the engaged youth and maiden, who though under the same roof since their betrothal had kept away from one another, now met again and before the altar in the evening, accompanied by their godparents. They were married in candlelight, with the handshaped earthen walls of their family about them, and a burden upon them of solemn commitment. Tensions broke when the vows were done. All gathered in the sala for the wedding feast. Now a river house had put forth another reach of growth and promise of the future, all in proper observance of ways that were as old as memory. In her white silk wedding dress the bride went on the arm of her husband in his rich silver-braided suit and his lace-ruffled shirt. Everyone came past to embrace them, and then the feast began. Roast chickens basted in spiced wine and stuffed with meat; piñons and raisins; baked hams; ribs of beef; fresh bread of blue meal; cookies, cakes, sweets; beakers of chocolate and flasks of wine; bowls of hot chile; platters of tortillas, all stood upon extra tables draped to the floor with lace curtains. All feasted.

Then came music, and dark eyes fired up. The sala was cleared, while the musicians tuned up on two or three violins, a guitar and a guitarron, or bass guitar. Servants came to spread clean wheat straw on the earth floor to keep dust from rising, or stood by with jars of water from which to sprinkle the floor between dances. In the candlelight the faces of the woman, heavily powdered with Mexican white lead, looked an ashen violet, in which their eyes were dark caves deeply harboring the ardent emotion of the occasion. The orchestra struck up . . .

Before midnight the bride retired not to reappear. Her maiden friends and her godmother went with her. The groom drank with the men in whose company he now belonged, while boys watched and nudged. The dancing continued, and humor went around. The groom's father calling above the noise in the hot, hard-plastered room, urged everyone to keep right on enjoying themselves. Presently the groom managed to slip away. In the bridal chamber the ladies admitted him and left him with his bride. Across the patio the merriment continued. Voices were singing. Someone shouted a refrain. The violins jigged along in a remote monotonous sing, and the gulping throb of the guitarron was like a pulse of mindless life in the night.

—Paul Horgan, *Great River: the Rio Grande in North American History*

Santa Fe was captured by the Confederacy briefly in 1862, but was retaken by the Union a month later, and in 1912 it became the capital of the 47th state of the Union.

Santa Fe is dominated by its Spanish colonial traditions, and its art and architecture are among the most exciting and beautiful in the United States. The town's oldest families are of Spanish descent, and many visitors meet museum docents, shopkeepers, or innkeepers proud to say that their families have been in this area for 300 years. Many places and things are referred to by their Spanish names: *arroyos* for gullies, *acequias* for ditches. The bright blue trim, so popular for adobe houses, is considered a good-luck color (the Spanish got this from the Arabs, who believe turquoise wards off the "evil eye"). Indians too, credit turquoise and its color with positive qualities.

Anglos, of course, have been a part of Santa Fe for 150 years, and this is reflected in the architecture of older buildings that reflect a New England sensibility. More recently, a number of "gated" communities have sprung up outside the city. Their almost completely Anglo population has, in some cases, enforced a perception of Anglos as rich outsiders.

Indians in Santa Fe are of mostly Puebloan extraction. Some work in business or the state government; others are craftsmen and artists who bring their wares to the Plaza.

Santa Fe is a city large numbers of people are eager to live in. They visit it once, can't get it out of their minds, and begin thinking of ways to return, permanently. Excessive development threatens to eliminate the very qualities that spurred the development in the first place. Santa Fe is bulging outward, not always prettily, and the old Plaza area is now lined with galleries and restaurants catering to the tourist trade. Hardware stores, barber shops, and drug stores have moved to strip malls on Cerrillos Road.

❖

Santa Fe means "Holy Faith;" consciously or not, many people are drawn to the spirituality of Santa Fe and its surrounding region, where every major religion of the world and many obscure ones are represented within a 50-mile radius. Visitors are constantly commenting on the strong spiritual essence, the tranquillity, the timelessness they sense here.

■ POINTS OF INTEREST

Santa Fe is a walker's city, and not only because it is compact and fairly flat. More importantly, Santa Fe has a visual and tactile romance that can't be fully appreciated through a car window.

An arched niche cut in an adobe wall, a vine or flower spilling color through it. An early 19th-century house wrapped around an all-but-hidden courtyard. A whimsical sculpture planted in a patio or vacant lot. A private shrine dedicated to St. Francis or the Virgin Mary. The ethereal auburn-to-gold glow of adobe walls in the early evening sun.

Streets are narrow, traffic befuddling, and there's hardly ever a place to park, so walking Santa Fe makes practical sense. Strolling at random, getting off the beaten track, stopping at one or another of the city's excellent restaurants, are easily available pleasures.

Plaza. Dating back to the founding of Santa Fe, the Plaza has been the focus of a host of momentous events in Santa Fe history. In the 1680 Pueblo Revolt, an army of furious Indians camped in the Plaza and besieged more than a thousand

Santa Fe Plaza is the heart of the town's tourist district, offering sidewalk crafts, boutiques, restaurants, and several of the region's best hotels.

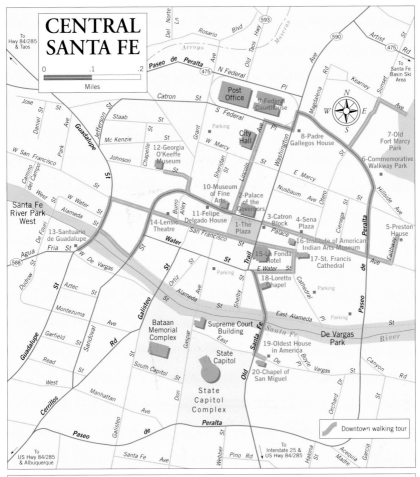

CENTRAL SANTA FE

0   .1   .2
Miles

Map labels:
To Hwy 84/285 & Taos
Del Norte Ln
Rosario Blvd
Arroyo
Paseo de Peralta
Catron St
Post Office
9-Federal Courthouse
Maseras Hwy
Artist St
To Santa Fe Basin Ski Area
Kearney
Sunset Ave
Jose St
Daniel St
Staab St
Grant St
S Federal Pl
Parking
City Hall
W Marcy St
8-Padre Gallegos House
7-Old Fort Marcy Park
6-Commemorative Walkway Park
Guadalupe
Jefferson St
Mc Kenzie St
12-Georgia O'Keeffe Museum
Johnson St
Chapelle St
Sheridan St
Lincoln St
Washington
E Marcy St
Nusbaum
Otero St
Hillside Ave
W San Francisco
Park Ave
Camino del Campo
West St
W Water St
Alameda St
10-Museum of Fine Arts
2-Palace of the Governors
3-Catron Block
4-Sena Plaza
Cienega St
Peralta
5-Preston House
Santa Fe River Park West
Burro Alley
11-Felipe Delgado House
14-Lensic Theatre
1-The Plaza
Palace
16-Institute of American Indian Arts Museum
13-Santuario de Guadalupe
De Four
San Francisco St
Water St
Agua Fria St
W De Vargas
St Trail
15-La Fonda Hotel
17-St. Francis Cathedral
de
Faithway
Dudrow
Aztec St
Ortiz St
Alameda Ave
E Water St
Parking
18-Loretto Chapel
Cathedral
Parking
Paseo
Montezuma Ave
Galisteo St
Shelby St
East Alameda
Parking
Sandoval St
Garfield St
Rd
Bataan Memorial Complex
Gaspar
Supreme Court Building
East
Santa Fe
De Vargas Park
Santa Fe River
Read St
South Capitol St
State Capitol
19-Oldest House in America
Boyle Pl
De Vargas St
Canyon Rd
West
Manhattan
Don
Ave
State Capitol Complex
20-Chapel of San Miguel
Orchard Dr
Cerrillos
Galisteo St
Paseo de
Peralta
St
Downtown walking tour
To US Hwy 84/285 & Albuquerque
Santa Fe Ave
Webber St
Pino Rd
To Interstate 25 & US Hwy 84/285
Halona St
Acequia Madre
Garcia

Catron Block 3
Chapel of San Miguel 20
Commemorative Walkway Park 6
Federal Courthouse 9
Felipe Delgado House 11
Georgia O'Keeffe Museum 12
Institute of American Indian Arts Museum 16
La Fonda Hotel 15
Lensic Theatre 14
Loretto Chapel 18

Museum of Fine Arts 10
Old Fort Marcy Park 7
Oldest House in America 19
Padre Gallegos House 8
Palace of the Governors 2
The Plaza 1
Preston House 5
St. Francis Cathedral 17
Santuario de Guadalupe 13
Sena Plaza 4

Museum of Indian Arts & Culture, Museum of International Folk Art, Wheelwright Museum, and the Center for Contemporary Arts see Greater Santa Fe Map.

Spanish refugees huddled in the Palace of the Governors. In 1846, Gen. Stephen Watts Kearny led his army into the Plaza, proclaimed New Mexico a United States territory, and raised the Stars and Stripes over the Palace. In 1962, the Plaza became a National Historic Landmark.

The Plaza's obelisk honors heroes of the Civil War and Indian wars. On its north side, an inscription commemorated the bravery of those who had "fallen in the various battles with savage Indians in the territory of New Mexico." Recently, the word "savage" has been chiseled out by an anonymous editor.

The grassy Plaza, shaded with lovely blue pine, American elm, spruce, cottonwood, and ornamental plum trees, remains Santa Fe's spiritual heart. People pass the time reading newspapers on benches; tourists stroll through wondering why every American city doesn't have such a gracious centerpiece. And in the evenings teens congregate in groups, flirting, smoking, and looking both cool and bored.

Palace of the Governors. Flanking the north side of the Plaza is the Palace of the Governors. Built in 1610, it is the oldest government building in the United States. Like the Plaza, it has seen remarkable events in New World history. When

The De Vargas Pageant proceeds down Palace Avenue during the Santa Fe Fiesta of 1919. (Museum of New Mexico, photo by Jesse L. Nusbaum)

Spanish governor Don Diego de Vargas recaptured Santa Fe from Indian revolutionaries in 1693, he and his men were astounded to find that the Indians had, in essence, remodeled it into a pueblo, even converting a defensive tower on the east end into a *kiva.* Except for the 13 years of Pueblo occupation, the palace served as apartments for Spanish and then Mexican governors, and in 1862, Confederate soldiers borrowed it for their temporary headquarters. In the 1870s, Territorial Governor Lew Wallace wrote part of *Ben-Hur* while living in it.

Over the centuries the Palace has undergone much remodeling. The towers are gone, and the *portal,* a wide, covered porch that extends around the building, is a 1913 addition. Indians have been selling their jewelry and pottery in front of what is now the museum for hundreds of years. In recent times, vendors have been required to register with a museum program that ensures crafts are handmade by those who sell them, or by their immediate families.

Today you can see the interior of the Palace, now part of the **Museum of New Mexico,** and get a visual sense of the world in which the early Spanish officials lived: its thick adobe walls are painted white. Inside, a collection of artifacts —wooden wagons or *carretas,* gowns, vestments, spurs, and pottery—evoke the mood of Spanish colonial life. Some of the museum docents are from colonial Spanish families, and they relish retelling the story of *la Entrada* (the Entry). *100 Palace Street; (505) 827-6474.*

Sena Plaza. One block east of the Palace lies a block-long row of contiguous adobe buildings (beginning with 107 East Palace) that includes Sena Plaza. Governor de Vargas granted one of his lieutenants, Arias de Quiros, a building site here for his help in the 1693 reconquest. Quiros planted wheat and built a two-room house—now long gone. Don José Sena, scion of a prominent 19th-century Santa Fe family, later constructed the adjacent 33-room adobe mansion around a courtyard. Parts of these buildings date from the late 18th, others from the early 20th century, but sorting them out would be impossible. Many old Santa Fe houses grew like this, by accretion over generations and centuries.

The courtyard is comfortable and shady, dominated by a mammoth cottonwood tree and surrounded by shops. There are benches for relaxing here, along with a fountain, a biodegrading old wagon, and devil-barely-cares landscaping with vines and shrubs creeping over rough stone borders. It's the polar opposite of a primly manicured formal Victorian garden, and one of the loveliest public spaces in Santa Fe.

Sena Plaza also houses some charming shops and restaurants. For example, the Montez Gallery specializes in religious art, especially *santos* and *retablos*. La Casa Sena's Cantina features waiters who sing Broadway show tunes and occasionally opera, and they are *good*. Further east of Sena Plaza at 209 East Palace is **Palace Avenue Books,** offering a generous selection of books about Santa Fe and the Southwest.

Commemorative Walkway Park. Built on a hillside overlooking Santa Fe, this park can be found by following Paseo de Peralta as it curls northwest. A paved path and staircase leads to the top of a hill, with 20 plaques outlining Santa Fe history along the way. Near the top is a tall, white steel cross commemorating the deaths of the 21 Franciscan missionaries killed in the Pueblo revolt of 1680. There is no memorial to the Pueblo Indians who died attempting to protect their own religion and culture from the Spaniards.

At the hilltop is **Old Fort Marcy Park,** site of the first United States military post in the Southwest, begun immediately after General Kearny seized New Mexico in 1846. Nothing but mounds of dirt remain of the adobe fort, but the park is the prime place to watch sunsets over Santa Fe.

Padre Gallegos House. At the bottom of the hill, below the park, Paseo de Peralta curves west, to meet Washington Avenue. To the left at 231 Washington is the Gallegos House built around 1857 by Padre José Manuel Gallegos, one of the many Spanish priests Bishop Jean Baptiste Lamy fired after his arrival in 1851. Gallegos later married and pursued a successful career in politics. The house is remarkable for its dignity, graceful proportions, and sheer size—Padre Gallegos didn't do badly after being punted out of the priesthood. Gallegos House now offers an additional attraction: SantaCafe, one of Santa Fe's finest restaurants.

Museum of Fine Arts. On the corner of Lincoln Avenue and West Palace Avenue, the Museum of Fine Arts was completed in 1917, shifting the Spanish Pueblo Revival style into high gear. The massive façade at the south end tries mightily to emulate the mission of San Estéban Rey at Ácoma.

The museum's emphasis is on 20th-century New Mexican art. On permanent display are the works of one the region's most luminous painters of the desert, Georgia O'Keeffe, along with works by Taos art colony founders, Ernest Blumenschein and Bert Geer Phillips. *107 W. Palace Avenue; (505) 827-4455.*

The spiral staircase in the Loretto Chapel has no central support: it's built like a huge, rigid wooden spring.

Georgia O'Keeffe Museum. For years visitors have searched New Mexico in vain for significant works of the famed painter, only to discover that the bulk of her oeuvre was held in private collections. This new museum, a couple of blocks west of the Museum of Fine Arts, changes all that, offering the public a look at a vast range of her work previously unavailable to the general public. *217 Johnson St., (505) 995-0785.*

Santuario de Guadalupe. South on Guadalupe Street, across the Santa Fe River, is the Santuario de Guadalupe, a late 18th-century church that has twice endured "remuddling." Originally a typical New Mexican adobe chapel, it was dressed up as a neo-Gothic New England church in the 1880s, then re-costumed yet again as a rather drab California mission in 1922. But go inside: there's a lovely and astounding baroque altar screen depicting the Virgin of Guadalupe and a Holy Trinity of three identical men. The painted screen is signed José de Alzibar, 1783.

Plaza Shops. The three blocks from the Plaza to Sandoval Street include some of Santa Fe's most intriguing shops and galleries. There are no fewer than three bookstores, including one that specializes in books and recordings from Latin America; and an excellent Indian pottery gallery (Andrea Fisher Fine Pottery).

La Fonda Hotel. This landmark sprawls over most of a block at East San Francisco, Shelby, and Old Santa Fe Trail. It was designed in the Spanish Pueblo style by Rapp & Rapp in 1922, then enlarged and remodeled in 1928 by John Gaw Meem. All through the lobby and corridors are delightful exhibitions of folk art murals painted by Ernest Martínez, who has been the hotel's in-house artist for 40 years.

Institute of American Indian Arts Museum. Across E. San Francisco Street at Cathedral Place is Santa Fe's division of IAIA, a nationally recognized college for American Indian artists. The paintings and sculpture on display here are alternatives to the more commercially appealing Indian art in the galleries. As a curator's plaque in one of the museum's exhibits notes, "An attempt has been made to stay away from the stereotypical images made of the American Indian by himself or herself. What has been selected is only a sample of an undercurrent of work that most often has been overlooked—overlooked because they have no feathers, no brave warriors on horseback, no romantic view of teepees or tall seductive women with hair fluttering in the wind." *108 Cathedral Place; (505) 988-6281.*

St. Francis Cathedral. The most impressive if not the most endearing building in Santa Fe, the cathedral closes off the east end of San Francisco Street with an architectural thunderclap, regarding the lower adobe neighborhood around it with the authority of a medieval baron.

The cathedral was designed overseas in Auvergne by the French architect, Antoine Mouly, and his son, Projectus. The Moulys journeyed to Santa Fe in 1870 to oversee construction. After a time Antoine lost his eyesight and Projectus took over. When lack of funds halted construction of the Cathedral, Projectus was contracted to build the Loretto Chapel. Before he could resume work on the Cathedral, Projectus died in 1879 and a new French architect, François Mallet, was employed. Then, in a real-life soap opera, Mallet became entwined with the wife of Lamy's nephew, and was shot dead on San Francisco Street in 1879. The architect who finally finished the cathedral was the nephew of Joseph Priest Machebeuf —who had been in seminary with Lamy in France and come with him to the United States. The younger Machebeuf revised and finished the building, which was consecrated in 1886. It is an excellent French cathedral, convincing in every respect except for its perfunctory pipe organ and the odd painted *reredos* depicting guitar-playing American saints.

Loretto Chapel. Around the corner on Old Santa Fe Trail is Bishop Lamy's other architectural monument. This was the small chapel of the Loretto nuns, the most famous of whom was Lamy's lovely young niece, Marie, who left France with her uncle when she was a child. She was educated by the Ursulines in New Orleans, then, barely in her teens, traveled to Santa Fe in 1857 along with her best friend from the convent. Marie entered the Loretto novitiate, becoming Sister Francesca. Legend has it that she played the piano beautifully, and after her own brother came to Santa Fe and became a priest under Lamy's tutelage, she always tried to have a new piano piece ready to play for him when he came to visit.

Design and construction of the Loretto Chapel were undertaken by Projectus Mouly. When his work was criticized, he resigned, took up drinking among "bad company," and died of pneumonia.

Finished in 1878, the chapel was built in a light, graceful Gothic Revival style.

Now deconsecrated and privately owned, it operates as a museum and there is a small admission charge to see inside.

A well-worn legend, impossible to verify, swirls around the graceful spiral staircase to the choir loft. The chapel was completed without one, by architects accustomed to having male novitiates ascend to choir lofts on ladders. The nuns realized this wouldn't do, because communicants could see under the skirts of anyone ascending the ladder. There was also safety to consider: long skirts trip people who try to climb ladders in them, and it seemed likely that a fair number of girls might fall off the ladder. Only a staircase would do, but there was no room to retrofit it.

The Sisters of Loretto decided to dedicate a novena to St. Joseph, patron saint of carpenters. On the ninth and last day of the novena, a man with a toolbox appeared on a donkey and built the "miraculous staircase," which has no central support—it's a rigid wooden spring, a miracle indeed of 19th-century engineering. When the staircase was finished, the sisters looked for the carpenter to offer payment. He had vanished. Some versions of the legend maintain that the miraculous carpenter was St. Joseph himself. Recently, historians have uncovered his identity —a Frenchman from southern New Mexico.

Barrio de Analco. This neighborhood along De Vargas Street, across the Santa Fe River, is one of Santa Fe's oldest. It was first occupied by Tlaxcalan Indians from Mexico who accompanied the earliest settlers and missionaries as servants, then resettled by soldiers after the 1693 reconquest. Several of the private homes on alley-like De Vargas Street date from the 18th century.

The **"Oldest House in America"** at 215 E. De Vargas allegedly incorporates part of a puddled-adobe pueblo dating from about A.D. 1250, but its *vigas* have been dendrochronologically dated from 1740 to 1767. There is an admission charge.

Across the street at 401 Old Santa Fe Trail, is the **Chapel of San Miguel,** built around 1626 and destroyed at the start of the Pueblo Revolt. The present structure, rebuilt in 1710 and much modified over the years, holds an intriguing carved and painted folk-churrigueresque *reredos* installed in 1798. When the chapel was last restored in 1955, excavators found shards of Anasazi pottery under the floor.

The Chapel of San Miguel was originally constructed in 1626, but has been rebuilt and modified considerably over the past centuries.

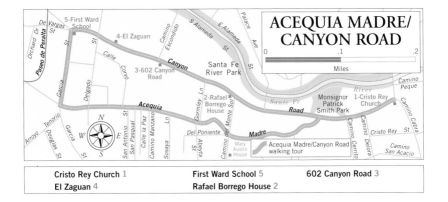

Cristo Rey Church 1	First Ward School 5	602 Canyon Road 3
El Zaguan 4	Rafael Borrego House 2	

Galleries. In a one-mile, several-hour walk along Canyon Road, Santa Fe's gallery ghetto, you could see and buy:
- 12th-century Anasazi pottery
- 19th-century Sioux ceremonial moccasins
- 20th-century American bowling pins
- Native American feather prayer fetishes
- Contemporary American impressionist painting
- Contemporary American abstract expressionist painting
- Contemporary Russian painting
- Contemporary Czech furniture
- Handmade turquoise, silver, or gold jewelry
- Kinetic sculpture with neon lighting
- Tibetan Buddha sculptures
- Moose- and mule deer-antler chandeliers
- Cowboy art
- Gay erotic nude cowboy art

And vastly more. The list could run on for pages. There are about 80 galleries on Canyon Road, said to be the most concentrated art market on Earth—and another 120 galleries sprinkled elsewhere around Santa Fe. Street parking along this route is very limited. There's a pay lot in the 800 block across from the restaurant El Farol, but walking Canyon Road is definitely the way to see it. Pop into as many galleries as time permits. Usually only two or three art works are visible through the windows, and they may not be representative of the surprises inside.

Santa Fe Mountains in October, ca. 1919–1920, by Sheldon Parsons, who was the first director of Santa Fe's Museum of Fine Arts. (Courtesy Museum of Fine Arts, Santa Fe)

■ ARTS AND ADOBE ARCHITECTURE

The modern era of Native American arts was inaugurated by the railroad, by which the first tourists arrived in Albuquerque in the 1880s. Indians had pottery to sell them, pottery the visitors quickly bought up. No one had much wanted it since the opening of the Santa Fe Trail in 1824 and the resulting influx of new cooking and storage vessels from the United States.

Early Indian pottery had been fashioned in styles that had arrived with the Anasazi, but by the 1880s, most of it was utilitarian and indifferently made. But once tourists and owners of trading posts who catered to them saw their beauty and were willing to buy it, Pueblo potters began taking their work seriously. Among the Hopis, Nampeyo was the founding genius. Born in the 1860s, living on an isolated mesa few had ever heard of, she made pots later displayed at the Smithsonian and the Boston Museum of Fine Arts. Just north of Santa Fe, a San Ildefonso potter named María Martínez became the pivotal figure in not only the revival but the new blossoming of an ancient art. A modest woman who said she "never cared about being well known or anything," María, with the help of her husband, Julian, began making pots for the tourist trade in the early 1900s. María would build the pots, not on a wheel but in the classic manner of coiling snakes of moist clay into the pot's rough shape, then scraping it smooth, and finally polishing it with a "slip" or skin of fine clay. Julian, a self-taught designer, would then apply the paint. In 1918, an experiment produced a whole new kind of pottery—matte black designs on a gloss black background—and it made both artistic and commercial history. In a few years, several potters in San Ildefonso were making a living in black-on-black ceramics, and potters at other Rio Grande pueblos, sensing at last an opportunity to sell their work, began to develop distinctive styles of their own.

Pueblo pottery today is a very highly developed art form, intricate and expressive, constantly evolving far from its utilitarian roots. Any good Pueblo pot is still formed in the laborious, time-honored coil-and-scrape fashion. This is important not merely for tradition's sake. Hand-forming a bowl or pot gives it a humane, slightly imperfect architecture (like an adobe building) that provides a welcome retreat from the anonymity of machine production; the artist's character lives in the work.

Many other Indian arts have thrived in this century, particularly painting, sculpture, and jewelry—and along with them have thrived the artists.

The annual **Indian Market,** staged in the Santa Fe Plaza every August since 1921, now draws 1,200 exhibiting artists and fills every motel room from Albuquerque to Taos with eager buyers.

The Spanish settlers of New Mexico lived hard lives on a hard land, but they were not barren of artistry. Among the earliest artistic expressions was furniture, adzed and built by hand out of soft ponderosa pine, and decorated with chiseled designs of religious icons, fruit, vines, prancing lions, and abstract geometric figures such as rosettes. As Pueblo craftsmen were employed to build some of the furniture, Indian motifs such as chevrons, cornstalks, and ziggurats cross-pollinated the Spanish traditions for a unique New Mexican style. The hand-painted modern imitations that have formed the cornerstone of "Santa Fe Style" speak of a yearning for simpler times—and a romanticization of the Spanish Colonial era in the Southwest.

More important to the perpetuation of Spanish culture were the *santos*—small wooden statues of Roman Catholic saints that held places of honor in both home and church. The carving of *santos* in northern New Mexico is an art form that has continued in an unbroken line for more than three centuries, passed along from generation to generation.

Today, contemporary Hispanic art is flourishing in the striking multimedia work and ceramics of artists like Pedro Romero and the paintings of artists like Anita Rodriguez and Federico Vigil. Vigil's work can be seen in several of Santa Fe's museums and in the county courthouse, where he was commissioned to paint a spectacular mural.

For one weekend every July the Plaza is converted into a traditional **Spanish Market.** Among the hundreds of Spanish arts and crafts sold here look for *santos,* carved and painted furniture, weavings, and embroidery. The **Contemporary Hispanic Market** is held the same weekend and is located just off the Plaza on Lincoln Avenue.

Adobe's romance abides in Santa Fe. You can begin to understand it in early morning or evening light. The old houses on Acequia Madre and Old Santa Fe Trail, made of mud bricks and bathed in mud plaster infused with wisps of straw, actually appear to glow. The low sun transmutes the mud into gold. Carefully maintained, an adobe building will weather the centuries.

New Mexico's Indians had long built with mud, puddling it up into free-form walls, but the Spanish introduced the use of adobe bricks. They had learned it centuries earlier from their own occupiers, the Moors: the word "adobe" is derived from the Arabic *al-tub*, "the brick." The technique for making and laying the brick has changed little. Mix dirt, water, and straw, then pour it into wooden forms to make bricks of a standard 10 x 14 x 4 inches and let them dry in the sun. Pry them out of the forms and let them bake, or "cure," for a few more days. Then layer them into walls with mud mortar. Contemporary infidels sometimes mix asphalt into the adobe to improve its stability, but this compromises its earthen color and texture. Traditionally, mud plaster was applied to protect the exterior walls, and it used to be the women's job to replaster them once a year. Today, stucco clads most of Santa Fe's modern adobe homes, reducing the maintenance burden.

Making adobe bricks is a craft; making them into a structure, an art. The church of San Francisco de Asís in Ranchos de Taos (left) is a magnificent example of this art. (Photo above by Eduardo Fuss)

■ CUISINE

Santa Fe is an outrageously interesting place to eat. Somewhere close to 175 restaurants are listed in the Santa Fe phone directory, not counting chain eateries. Choices are as varied as in any big city and include Spanish tapas, Chinese *dim sum*, Pacific Rim fusion, French, Italian, Thai, American Indian, Asian Indian —and especially New Mexican. Through the first three-quarters of this century, the glory of Santa Fe food was basic but delicious traditional New Mexican dishes: *enchiladas, chiles rellenos, tamales, carne asada, carne adovada*, simmered beans, *posole*. Nobody fretted about cholesterol, nor about which chile might best flavor a papaya-tangerine sauce for pheasant breast. Local sources dispute exactly when and how the nuevo New Mexican (or nouvelle Numex) era began, but Mark Miller's famous Coyote Cafe, born in 1987, certainly had something to do with it. Miller conjoined ingredients and techniques from Mexico, New Mexico, France, and Berkeley, drew a gush of national publicity and the suspicion of local traditionalists, and inspired a rash of innovation. The upshot is that Santa Fe has the most inspired cuisine and the greatest variety of any city in the Southwest.

It is declassé to refer to the traditional dishes of Santa Fe, such as *picadillo* and *carne adovada* as "Mexican food." The preferred term is *New* Mexican food. Santa Fe isn't just being snooty. There are real differences between the traditional Hispanic cooking of northern New Mexico and that elsewhere in the Southwest. The reason is that until recently, Santa Fe and its environs remained relatively isolated and culturally unique, so its cuisine developed unique characteristics.

To get an insight into the farming traditions of the Rio Grande Valley, visit the **Santa Fe Farmers' Market (Sanbusco Market Center)**, Tuesday and Saturday mornings, June through October. It's as much cultural reservoir as food market; some of the families selling produce out of pickups and campers have been working the same New Mexico land for six or seven generations. Familiar figures include a man roasting hundreds of green chiles in a rotating steel mesh drum heated by roaring propane jets made from recycled tin cans (the aroma is delectable); another selling miniature decorative corn in a mosaic of white, yellow, cherry, and purple kernels. And there are stands selling apple cider (100% organic, made last night), homemade salsas and chutneys, apples, squashes, tomatoes, lettuce, onions, and herbs. Free samples abound, and they definitely generate sales.

Santa Fe's supermarkets routinely carry ingredients that are almost impossible to find even in other Southwestern cities with large Hispanic populations. The local Albertson's carries canned *menudo* (tripe soup), *camarón* (dried and shredded shrimp), and, of course, powdered Chimayó chile. Chile is not just an ingredient here, but a passion, and Santa Feans eat it hot.

CHILES

There are more than 300 varieties of chiles and a universe of things one can do with them. They can be used fresh, pickled, dried, smoked, crushed, or powdered. A whole pod or several can be simmered all day in a stew to impart a distinctive flavor—and different varieties do have different flavors. A chipotle, which is a smoked jalapeño, will invest the pot with both smoke and fire, while an ancho has a plumlike flavor. Even greater differences exist in the fire quotient, which comes from an alkaloid chemical called capsaicin that develops naturally in the chile. Measured scientifically in Scoville Units, an everyday bell pepper will rate close to zero Scoville Units, a jalapeño typically will score about 5,000, and an habanero up to 300,000! Eating an habanero, a brilliant orange chile about the size of a stubby thumb, is like grabbing a mouthful of live killer bees. Carelessly rub your eye after fingering one, and it will put an end to productive work for the rest of the day.

Southwesterners seldom eat their chiles straight. Instead, they're commonly incorporated into salsas, or sauces.

The first thing an outlander needs to know is the meaning of the question "Red or green?" which usually follows any order of a traditional New Mexican plate. It means red or green sauce, which is slathered over burritos, chiles rellenos, enchiladas, omelets—practically everything but salmon. Red is made with dried chiles, green with fresh. Before freezers and trucks from California, green was the summer sauce, and red warmed New Mexico's palates through the winter. Both now are made year-round. Green tends to be hotter. It is made mostly or entirely with Hatch chiles, grown in southwestern New Mexico. Hatches are the same species as the familiar Anaheims from southern California, but New Mexico's cool summer nights urge the chile to develop more capsaicin.

Chiles even find their way onto New Mexican breakfast plates. Huevos rancheros is one popular staple: eggs poached in a red chile sauce, served over corn tortillas and dripping with melted cheese. Breakfast burros (burritos) are unpredictable but delicious. At El Taoseño in Taos, they can be a bacon-and-egg scramble swaddled in a flour tortilla; at Tia Sophia in Santa Fe, shredded potatoes and bacon wrapped in a flour tortilla and drenched in an eye-opening green chile sauce.

Santa Fe Food & Lodging

■ Food & Lodging

> *Restaurant prices:*
> Per person, not including drinks, tax, and tips:
> $ = under $10; $$ = $10–20; $$$ = over $20
> *Room rates:*
> Per night, per room, double occupancy:
> $ = under $50; $$ = $50–100; $$$ = over $100

Santa Fe Restaurants

✗ **Anasazi Restaurant.** 113 Washington Ave.; (505) 988-3236 $$$
Both decor and cuisine would make a prehistoric Anasazi think he'd gone to another world. Modern foodies may think they've gone to heaven. Complicated, innovative, and beautifully prepared New Southwestern dishes may mingle, for example, venison, dried cherries, and pumpkin. Elegant, but nobody demands you dress up. Santa Fe's best restaurant.

✗ **Atalaya Restaurant and Bakery.** 320 S. Guadalupe St.; (505) 982-2709 $–$$
With its warm, red-brick interior and bright blue awning, Atalaya is immensely inviting. Owner John O'Brien keeps his menu simple, but appealing. Try tortilla soup, shrimp and grits, or Jamaican jerked chicken served with sweet potato fries.

✗ **Bistro 315.** 315 Old Santa Fe Trail; (505) 986-9190 $$$
Chef Matt Yohalem prepares classic French dishes—escargot in a puff-pastry shell, steak au poivre, oven-roasted duckling in cranberry sauce—with flair at this elegant, smoke-free bistro. The flavors are strong and complex, but rarely heavy, and the wine list is superb—one of Santa Fe's more sophisticated dining spots.

✗ **The Burrito Company.** 111 Washington Ave.; (505) 982-4453 $
Authentic New Mexican food on a budget actually exists downtown, served sans fanfare on paper plates. Atmosphere comes with the sidewalk tables, set out for a view of the Palace of the Governors. Ample and fiery plates of red chile burritos or enchiladas and posole are a bargain.

✗ **Cafe Pasqual's.** 121 Don Gaspar Ave.; (505) 983-9340 $$ -$$$
Fresh ingredients always, a sunny dining room with cheerful hand-painted tiles, and an outrageously eclectic menu drawing inspiration from New Mexican, Chinese, Thai, and owner Katherine Kagel's Jewish grandmother's cooking make this one of Santa Fe's most inspired small restaurants. Smuggle all this home; buy her cookbook on your way out.

✗ **Chow's Contemporary Chinese Food.** 720 St. Michael's Dr.; (505) 471-7120

$$
"Contemporary" is the key word here, since most American Chinese food is anything but. With innovations such as scallops in jade sauce (made with ginger, green onion, cilantro, and spinach), Chow's wows.

X **Corn Dance Cafe.** 1501 Paseo de Peralta; (505) 982-1200 **$$**
Here's a fascinating concept: traditional Native American cooking dressed up with fancy contemporary techniques. Emphasis is on wood-grilled seafood and meats and healthful eating—owner Loretta Barrett Oden, a member of the Potawatomi tribe, points out that buffalo, which appears in several guises on her menu, is even lower in cholesterol than chicken.

X **Coyote Cafe.** 132 W. Water St.; (505) 983-1615 **$$$**
Very popular. Very noisy. And very controversial. Some conservative Santa Feans resent the fame Mark Miller's restaurant has drawn, because it caused the eclipse of traditional New Mexican cuisine, at least in the national consciousness. Rabbit enchiladas with molé poblano and orange-jicama salsas? Radical indeed, but Coyote's food is superb. Expensive prix fixe except for weekend brunch.

X **El Farol.** 808 Canyon Rd.; (505) 983-9912 **$$**
What could be more appropriate than Spanish cuisine in the old Spanish capital? Specialty at El Farol ("The Lantern") is tapas—plates of Spanish specialties such as shrimp sautéed with garlic, sherry, and lime juice. Good Spanish wine list, entertainment nightly.

X **Geronimo.** 724 Canyon Rd.; (505) 982-1500 **$$$**
No connection to the famed Apache warrior at this attractive, upscale eatery, but a man named Geronimo Lopez did own the house for a time around the mid-18th century. There's nothing historic about the menu, however, which changes nightly and features New Southwestern dishes such as an ostrich quesadilla appetizer or an entree of blackened red snapper tossed with pasta, and smoked tomato and chipotle chile sauce.

X **Il Piatto.** 95 W. Marcy St.; (505) 984-1091 **$$**
The decor is a thousand kitchen implements hung on the walls, which correctly focuses diners' minds on what's important in this rightly celebrated new bistro: the food. Pasta, roast chicken, grilled seafood, liberal herbal seasoning.

X **La Casa Sena.** 125 E. Palace Ave.; (505) 988-9232 **$$-$$$**
Two restaurants here: a stylish and expensive place serving northern New Mexican crossed with nuevo, and a crowded cantina with simpler and slightly cheaper food and superb young musicians who sing Broadway show tunes and wait tables. Try an alfresco lunch in the plaza; the cantina for a fun evening.

X **La Tertulia.** 416 Agua Fria; (505) 988-2769 **$$**
This pretty restaurant housed in a his-

Santa Fe Food & Lodging

Santa Fe Food & Lodging

toric adobe Dominican convent offers traditional tamales and adovada and some more modern creations, but turns back before the "nuevo" border. Lace tablecloths under all these chile sauces are an impractical but graceful touch. Reservations requested.

X **Old Mexico Grill.** 2434 Cerrillos Rd.; (505) 473-0338 $$

As the name suggests, this restaurant serves Mexican, not New Mexican food—for example, a salad of shrimp on lettuce, jicama, and oranges, or roast chicken smothered in a sauce of serrano chile, peanuts, pumpkin, and sesame seeds. Serious Mexican cuisine, not common in the United States.

X **Paul's.** 72 W. Marcy St.; (505) 982-8738 $$

Look around; you'll know you're in Santa Fe: wooden lizards and snakes roam the peach-painted walls, chickens painted like dalmatians perch in the windows. But the new American food is as serious as the decor is playful—like the salmon baked in a crust of crushed pecans and bathed in sorrel sauce. Good value.

X **Pink Adobe.** 406 Old Santa Fe Trail; (505) 983-7712 $$-$$$

Housed in a 300-year-old building, former barracks for Spanish soldiers, "the Pink" is a landmark. The menu is fairly standard, featuring enormous steaks, lamb, pork, and traditional New Mexican dishes.

X **SantaCafé.** 231 Washington Ave.; (505) 984-1788 $$-$$$

This elegant restaurant has eclipsed the Coyote Cafe in national fame, offering a fusion-style cuisine of Asian, European, and New Mexican food. (Example: ginger-cured salmon on crispy won tons with tequila-citrus aioli.) Setting is the historic Padre Gallegos House, private (and palatial) residence of one of the priests defrocked by Bishop Lamy.

X **Tia Sophia's.** 210 W. San Francisco St.; (505) 983-9880 $

Best place to eat breakfast in Santa Fe. Arrive at 7, park without fear of a ticket, and order the breakfast burrito, huevos rancheros, or cheese enchiladas. Open for breakfast and lunch, not dinner.

X **Tomasita's.** 500 S. Guadalupe; (505) 983-5721 $

"Chile is a main ingredient of our dishes and we serve it hot. If you are new to the taste please ask for a sample before ordering. . . ." So warns this traditional New Mexican restaurant's menu. Believe it: this may be the hottest New Mexican food in America. Tomasita's is hot commercially, too; it's Santa Fe's most popular restaurant. Huge crowds. No reservations.

X **Whistling Moon Cafe.** 204 N. Guadalupe St. (505) 983-3093 $-$$

The former executive chef at the renowned SantaCafé, Tracy Ritter, and partner Gabriel Hakman introduced this moderately priced Mediterranean cafe a few years ago, and it was an instant hit. Look for Greek, Italian, and north African dishes like falafels, grilled lamb, panini, pizza, and salade Nicoise—but whatever you order, save room for the cafe's most popular dish, the cumin-coriander fries.

Santa Fe Lodging

✓⊓ **Alexander's Inn.** 529 East Palace Ave.; (505) 986-1431 $$-$$$
A short walk from the Plaza, this wonderful inn has all the appealing qualities of a B&B—delicious breakfast, homemade cookies and brownies throughout the day, pretty garden and deck, and a relaxed and friendly atmosphere—without any of the drawbacks. The innkeeper doesn't live in the house, so you don't feel as if you're invading a stranger's home, and the inn itself is large enough to satisfy privacy seekers. The accommodations—all of which are charmingly decorated—include five rooms in the main house, two guesthouses on the property, and two adobe casitas up the street.

⊓ **Bishop's Lodge.** Bishop's Lodge Rd. off NM 590, 3 miles north of Santa Fe; (505) 983-6377 or (800) 732-2240 $$$
This luxury resort began as an unpretentious mountain retreat for Bishop Lamy, who bought the property for $80 sometime in the 1860s. Operated as a resort by the Thorpe family since 1918, it now features 88 rooms, a restaurant, horseback riding, tennis, and a seven-day-a-week summer children's program to keep youngsters occupied. Quiet, forested, beautiful views.

⊓ **El Paradero.** 220 W. Manhattan Ave.; (505) 988-1177 $$-$$
One of Santa Fe's first B&Bs, El Paradero remains among the most pleasant. Twelve rooms in a rambling 1800s adobe farmhouse remodeled in Territorial style. Fine breakfasts. Six

blocks to the Plaza.

✓⊓ **El Rey Inn.** 1862 Cerrillos Rd.; (505) 982-1931/ (800) 521-1349 $$-$$
More than a basic motel, rooms are beautifully decorated in Pueblo, Spanish, or Victorian styles. Many have fireplaces. A good value.

⊓ **Garrett's Desert Inn.** 311 Old Santa Fe Trail; (505) 982-1851 or (800) 888-2145 $$
The architecture is strictly Motel Deco Plain-o, but rooms are very pleasant and freshly furnished—and these are among the most affordable downtown digs you're going to find. Four blocks from the Plaza.

✓⊓ **Hotel Plaza Real.** 125 Washington Ave.; (505) 988-4900 or (800) 279-7325 $$$
This small hotel, built in 1990, features rooms that open onto a narrow brick courtyard brightened with many flowers. Most have wood-burning fireplaces.

⊓ **Hotel St. Francis.** 210 Don Gaspar Ave.; (505) 983-5700 or (800) 529-5700 $$-$$$
This gracious Victorian hotel was built in 1923, allowed to run down, and thoroughly renovated in 1986. Most rooms are still small by modern standards. Grand lobby and veranda, high tea served to guests every afternoon.

⊓ **Hotel Santa Fe.** 1501 Paseo de Peralta; (505) 982-1200 or (800) 825-9876 $$-$$$
A little farther from the Plaza (six blocks), a little less expensive. This modern 131-room Pueblo Revival hotel has large, warmly decorated rooms and a free shuttle to downtown.

Santa Fe Food & Lodging

⛌ **Inn at Loretto–Best Western.** 211 Old Santa Fe Trail; (505) 988-5531 or (800) 528-1234 $$$
Adjacent to the famous Loretto Chapel, this five-storied Pueblo-style inn is decorated with handmade furnishings and Native American artwork. Reasonably priced for the location; includes a swimming pool and restaurant.

⛌ **Inn of the Anasazi.** 113 Washington Ave.; (505) 988-3030 or (800) 688-8100 $$$
A beautiful and very expensive small hotel that opened in 1991 and met with resounding acclaim. All rooms have gas fireplaces and ceilings of vigas and latillas. Don't expect views; all 59 rooms are squeezed into a long, narrow downtown block between another hotel and a burrito shop.

⛌ **Inn of the Animal Tracks.** 707 Paseo de Peralta; (505) 988-1546 $$-$$$
Five rooms in a delightful restored adobe four blocks from the Plaza. A warm staff and an inviting, cozy atmosphere. Each room is whimsically decorated after a different animal—the "soaring eagle," the "loyal wolf," etc. Always changing, always savory breakfasts.

⛌ **Inn on the Alameda.** 303 E. Alameda St.; (505) 984-2121/ (800) 289-2122 $$$
An intimate 67-room hotel by the linear River Park four blocks east of the Plaza. "Breakfast of Enchantment" buffet included. Some fireplaces, some rooms with views.

⛌ **La Fonda.** 100 E. San Francisco St.; (505) 982-5511 or (800) 523-5002 $$$
Kennedy slept here, as did Errol Flynn and Raymond Burr. Each room and most of the public spaces have been graced with murals or painted furnishings by Ernest Martínez, La Fonda's resident artist for 40 years. A grand and comfortable hotel whose tapestry of art, architecture, and history makes it worth the price.

⛌ **La Posada de Santa Fe.** 330 E. Palace Ave.; (505) 986-0000 or (800) 727-5276 $$$
Parts of this famous inn date from the 1930s; today 119 rooms of varying styles and decor sprawl across six acres of gracious but not fussy landscaping. Some rooms feature Southwestern decor, some Victorian. Ask about views; the cheaper rooms overlook parking lots.

⛌ **Pecos Trail Inn.** 2239 Old Pecos Trail; (505) 982-1943 $$
Good location two miles from downtown but away from the visual blight of Cerrillos Road. Large rooms, some with kitchenettes. A good value.

⛌ **Ten Thousand Waves.** Hyde Park Rd., 3 1/2 miles north of Santa Fe; (505) 982-9304 $$$
A unique Japanese-style health spa offering private and communal hot tubs outdoors in the woods, massage therapy, herbal wraps, and six luxury cabins for overnighters. Especially popular with sore skiers returning from the mountains.

Baking bread the old-fashioned way at El Rancho de las Golondrinas, a living-history museum just south of Santa Fe.

NORTH-CENTRAL NEW MEXICO

■ HIGHLIGHTS
Indian Pueblos
Taos
Chimayó.
Abiquiú
Ghost Ranch
Jémez Mountains
Los Alamos
Bandelier National
   Monument
Chama

■ LANDSCAPE
North of Santa Fe the Rio Grande flows past intricate rock formations and striated cliffs, piñon-dotted hills and snowcapped peaks, and a constantly changing tableau of villages, mesas, and mountains enhanced by the play of light and shadow over the land. Pueblos and small Hispanic villages have been built along the river, but the open country is always before you—the Jémez Mountains visible to the west, the Sangre de Cristos to the north and east, and a vast, infinitely variable sky overhead. Author Willa Cather once wrote of the sky here: "Elsewhere the sky is the roof of the world; but here the earth was the floor of the sky."

The countryside near Velarde is a farming region, where roadside stands overflow with apples, pears, and peaches in the late summer; fresh chile, garlic, and *ristras* (dried chile wreaths) in the autumn.

■ TRAVELERS ORIENTATION
Sophisticated Santa Fe, described in the previous chapter, is the central city of this area. Outside of Santa Fe, life is simple and traditional. Family-owned farms, cafes, and stores are the norm.

The main route from Santa Fe to Taos is along NM Highway 68, which for the most part parallels the Rio Grande. Another is the so-called High

Road via NM 76 and 518. Along the High Road to Taos are beautiful small towns where artisans produce exquisite pottery, *santos,* woodcarvings, and weavings.

Most Indian pueblos are located off the main road, and in the case of Tesuque and Taos are near towns of the same name. If you wish to visit a pueblo, try to do so on a feast day or dance day (see page 129); the action will be infinitely more rewarding than wandering around an all-but-deserted plaza.

One of the loveliest and least-known trips through this area follows the western side of the Rio Grande south through the Jémez Mountains. Sometimes dubbed the "Thunderbird Trail" because of the bird-like shape naturally etched into a mountain overlooking the road near Zía Pueblo, this drive can be driven as a loop that passes through Los Alamos, Bandelier National Monument, and Jémez Pueblo, before curving back to I-25 and back to Santa Fe. The route from Española to Chama is also a lovely trip (see page 135), and can include a spectacular trip on the Cumbres and Toltec Scenic Railroad.

Food & Lodging appears on page 140.

The best time to visit this region is between May and October. Summertime temperatures are comfortable due to the altitude and dryness of the air, although in July and August afternoon thunderstorms are frequent. The town of Cimarron in the mountains east of Taos receives more thunderstorms than any other town in North America (110 days each year). Winters are cold and snowy especially in the high mountains, where up to 300 inches of snow fall annually. The climate of this region is best represented by weather stations in Chama (elev. 7,900), Taos (elev. 6,950), and Los Alamos (elev. 7,400).

TEMPS (F°)	AVG. JAN. HIGH	LOW	AVG. APRIL HIGH	LOW	AVG. JULY HIGH	LOW	AVG. OCT. HIGH	LOW	RECORD HIGH	RECORD LOW
Chama	35	5	59	24	81	44	61	26	99	-28
Los Alamos	42	12	61	28	84	50	65	30	95	-18
Taos	40	10	64	29	87	50	67	32	101	-27

PRECIPITATION (INCHES)	AVG. JAN.	AVG. APRIL	AVG. JULY	AVG. OCT.	ANNUAL	SNOW
Chama	2.0	1.4	2.9	1.5	22.1	102
Los Alamos	1.0	1.1	3.3	1.5	18.3	51
Taos	0.8	0.9	1.6	1.1	12.0	38

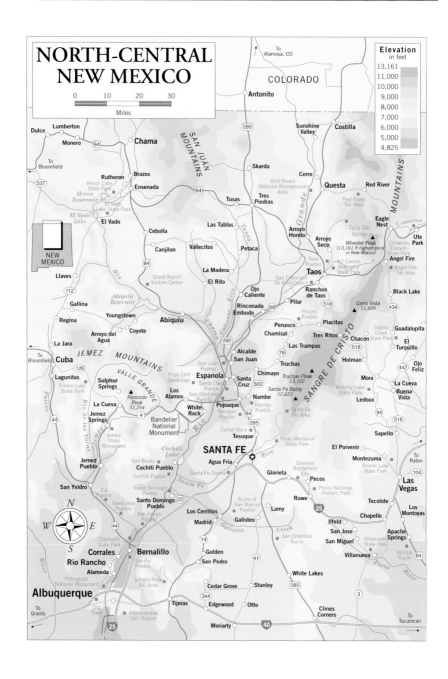

NORTH-CENTRAL NEW MEXICO

0   10   20   30
Miles

Elevation
in feet
13,161
11,000
10,000
9,000
8,000
7,000
6,000
5,000
4,825

COLORADO

To Alamosa, CO

Antonito

Dulce
Lumberton
Monero
To Bloomfield
537
Chama

SAN JUAN MOUNTAINS

285

Sunshine Valley
Costilla

Rutheron
Brazos
Ensenada
Heron Lake State Park
Heron Reservoir
El Vado Lake State Park
El Vado Lake
El Vado
64

Skarda
Cerro
Wild Rivers National Recreational Area
Questa
Red River
Red River Ski Area

MOUNTAINS

Tres Piedras
Tusas
64

Arroyo Hondo
Arroyo Seco
Eagle Nest
Cimarron Park
Ute Park

Cebolla
Canjilon
Vallecitos
Las Tablas
Petaca

Wheeler Peak (13,161 ft highest point in New Mexico)
Taos Pueblo
Kit Carson Memorial State Park

Cimarron Canyon State Park
Angel Fire
Angel Fire Ski Area

NEW MEXICO

Llaves
112
Gallina
Abiquiu Reservoir
84
Ghost Ranch Visitors Center
La Madera
El Rito
San Francisco de Asis Church
Taos

Black Lake

Regina
Youngstown
Coyote
Abiquiu
Ojo Caliente
Rinconada
Embudo
68
Pilar
Ranchos de Taos
Picuris Pueblo
518
Cerro Vista 11,939
434

Arroyo del Agua
La Jara
JEMEZ MOUNTAINS
285
Penasco
Placitas
Tres Ritos
Chacon
518
Coyote Creek State Park
Guadalupita
El Turquillo

Cuba
126
Lagunitas
Finton Lake State Park
Sulphur Springs
VALLE GRANDE
Redondo Peak 11,254
Los Alamos
San Juan Pueblo
Puye Cliff Dwellings
Santa Clara Pueblo
San Ildefonso Pueblo
Espanola
Santa Cruz
503
Chimayo
Truchas Peak 13,102
Santa Fe Baldy 12,622
Chamisal
Las Trampas
76
Truchas
Holman

Mora
Morphy Lake State Park
Ledoux
94
La Cueva
Buena Vista
518

La Cueva
Jemez Springs
Jemez State Monument
White Rock
Pojoaque
Tesuque Pueblo
Nambe
Nambe Pueblo
84
Santa Fe Ski Area
Sapello

Jemez Pueblo
Cochiti Lake
Camel Rock
Tesuque
285
Hyde Memorial State Park
El Porvenir
Montezuma
Storrie Lake State Park
To Raton
104

San Ysidro
Zia Pueblo
Tent Rocks
Cochiti Pueblo
Cochiti Pueblo
Santa Ana Pueblo
SANTA FE
Agua Fria
Santa Fe Downs
Glorieta
Glorieta Battlefield Site
Pecos
Pecos National Historic Park
Las Vegas

Santo Domingo Pueblo
San Felipe Pueblo
Santo Domingo Pueblo
22
Ruins of San Marcos Pueblo
Los Cerrillos
Madrid
Galisteo
Lamy
Rowe
25
San Cristobal Ruins
Ilfeld
Chapelle
San Jose
San Miguel
Villanueva
Villanueva State Park
Tecolote
Los Montoyas
Apache Springs
Aurupa Ruins
84

Coronado State Park
Corrales
Rio Rancho
Alameda
Bernalillo
Sandia Pueblo
14
Golden
San Pedro
41
White Lakes
Villanueva

N
W   E
S

Petroglyph National Monument
Albuquerque
To Grants
Old Town
Albuquerque Int'l Airport
25
Sandia Peak Ski Area
Tijeras
344
Cedar Grove
Edgewood
Stanley
Otto
285
Moriarty
Clines Corners
40
3
To Tucumcari

■ HISTORY AND CULTURE

Pueblo culture along the northern Rio Grande began to flourish in the 1300s when an influx of Anasazi people from the north drifted into this area, intermarried, and began to farm along the river and its tributaries. The most notable pueblo is the extraordinary five-story village at Taos, first built in the mid-1200s and rebuilt around 1700 after a fire destroyed the original structure. In the 17th century, north-central New Mexico was a far-flung outpost of the Spanish colonial empire, the province of haciendas, Apache incursions, and a faltering pueblo culture. In the mid-1800s, the area opened to trade with the United States and its churches came under the administration of the American Catholic Church. Today, the past is evident everywhere—in adobe buildings, old churches, pueblos, and backcountry farms. Pueblo culture has rebounded, population size has increased, and an extraordinary tradition of pottery making continues.

❖

The pueblos stretching from Santa Fe to Taos are banded together in a council called Eight Northern Indian Pueblos. Many tourists visit them expecting to encounter exotic culture, architecture, and art, and those who do are often disappointed. However, each pueblo has a scattering of small shops, many of them in private homes, selling everything from bolo ties to excellent jewelry and pottery. Many pueblos have developed a distinctive pottery style: glossy black vases for Santa Clara, undecorated micaceous ceramics for Taos. But there has been so much innovation and cross-fertilization that today it is hard to identify some pieces with any certainty.

The area is changing. New people move in, young people go to the cities, and the desert in places takes on the look of an unzoned mobile home park. The most controversial thing to happen here has been the construction of enormous gambling casinos on Indian land, an enterprise that takes advantage of exceptions from U.S. laws granted to tribes.

■ SANTA FE TO TAOS ROAD TRIP

Route: *Follows US 285 to Española which continues as NM 68 along the Rio Grande north to Taos.*

Just north of Santa Fe, US 285 passes lovely open country before reaching the huge gambling casinos owned by Tesuque and Pojoaque pueblos. They advertise gambling on dazzling signs visible for miles, at the expense of great natural beauty.

❖

Nambé Pueblo. A tiny pueblo of around 600 members, Nambé lies at the foot of the Sangre de Cristos, and thus enjoys a spectacular attraction: Nambé Falls and Lake, which provide excellent opportunities for fishing, sightseeing, or hiking. (Because of its high elevation, the site is closed from November to March.) An especially colorful day to visit the park would be July 4th, when the Nambé Waterfall Ceremonial takes place at the foot of the falls. The pueblo, located east of the highway, NM 285, has perhaps the most beautiful setting of any along this route, occupying a green, level valley with panoramic vistas of the Sangre de Cristos.

San Ildefonso Pueblo. With its great tradition of pottery, San Ildefonso is an excellent place to explore the art—the population is only about 500, but most of the pueblo's families are involved in it. Black-on-black—a shiny background contrasted with a matte-black finish—remains the most popular style. Many people here are descendants of María Martínez, New Mexico's most famous potter, and her husband Julian. Both were producing pottery in the traditional polychrome style of San Ildefonso before Julian in 1919 developed matte black-on-black. Because María and Julian began signing their pieces early, and at a time when this was not common, their remarkable career can be traced by collectors.

María's sisters also worked in pottery: Maximiliana, Desideria, and Juanita. Clara, the youngest, did most of the polishing. Santana and Adam Martínez, Maria Poveka, and Juanita's daughter, Carmelita Dunlap, were also important in the history of San Ildefonso pottery.

There is a small museum here, the San Ildefonso Pueblo Museum, next to the mission church (rebuilt in 1968). Most buildings in this village are new or reconstructed. To the north of the village lies the natural tabletop fortress of Black Mesa, where in 1694 Pueblo Indians attempted to defend themselves against the Spanish reconquest. *15 miles north of Santa Fe on US 285, turn left at NM 502, then six miles to entrance on right.*

PUEBLO ETIQUETTE

Each pueblo in the Santa Fe–Taos region celebrates an annual feast day, a remarkable tradition that includes ceremonial dancing to the accompaniment of drums, rattles, and bells, and feasting. Although each of these celebrations honors the Catholic saint for whom the *conquistadores* named the village, ancient indigenous seasonal ceremonies and rites underlie these festivities. Tribe members will frequently invite non-Indian visitors into their homes to share the food, although this practice may be endangered because of its expense to the Pueblo families and the occasional boorishness of the guests. Some ceremonial events are closed to visitors. Call in advance; the best single source for information is the Eight Northern Indian Pueblos Council, (505) 852-4625. An annual visitors' guide to the Eight Northern Indian Pueblos is also available free at the Santa Fe Convention and Visitors' Bureau.

There are several rules of etiquette for visiting the pueblos, some of which may be culturally foreign to non-Indian visitors. These apply not only to feast days, but at all times.

- Rules on photographing pueblo buildings or ceremonies vary. Before you snap, ask at the pueblo governor's office or visitor center. Some, such as Taos Pueblo, levy a fee. Never photograph an individual or private property without asking permission.
- Don't talk or walk around during dances or other ceremonies, don't applaud, and don't ask for an explanation of the ceremony. Vernon Lujan of Taos Pueblo told the *Santa Fe New Mexican* that sometimes he responds to requests for explanations by saying, "If I tell you, I'll have to kill you." He's only kidding— but it gets their attention. Most Puebloans simply ignore the requests.
- On feast days, don't ask to come into a home for a meal, but graciously accept the invitation if one is offered. The Official Visitors' Guide to the Eight Northern Pueblos adds: "Thank your host, but a payment or tip is not appropriate."
- Never enter a pueblo *kiva* or graveyard.
- Never bring pets, firearms, alcohol, or illegal drugs into a pueblo.
- Finally, call before traveling to a pueblo to make certain it's open. Some ceremonial days are closed to outsiders.

Santa Clara Pueblo. Santa Clara is also known for its pottery, in particular the famous pottery families, Gutíerrez and Tafoya. The Tafoya family's black carved bowls, polished inside and out, have a decidedly contemporary appeal. *From Española 1.3 miles on NM 30; cross to west side of the Rio Grande, entrance on the left.*

Puyé Cliff Dwellings. Reached by a paved road about nine miles west of Española, these cliff dwellings were once one of the most extensive cliffside villages in northern New Mexico and are perhaps the most compelling attraction in the area. Some houses were mere caves, others had porches or open rooms attached. Wooden ladders and steps carved into the volcanic tuff were used to get from one dwelling to another and up to the pine-covered mesa above. Puyé's residents, who lived there from A.D. 1450 until the latter part of the 16th century, constructed *kivas* on the cliff's edge, along its base, and on a ledge halfway to the top of the mesa. Their glazed red pottery was painted with serpents who were said to guard the springs that provided their lifeblood. The dwellings, which are sometimes closed in the winter, were the prehistoric home of the Santa Clara Indians, who now live nearby on more than 40,000 acres of rich farmland, rangeland, and forests. *From Española drive south on NM 30 about three miles. At the sign for Santa*

Anita Suazo (above), a Santa Clara potter, displays one of her works.

The Puyé Cliff Dwellings. (Both photos by Eduardo Fuss)

Clara Pueblo, follow the road about six miles. The entrance to the Puyé Cliff Dwellings is on the left; call (505) 753-7326.

Those more engaged by nature than archaeology can continue on beyond the cliff dwellings into the Santa Clara Canyon, a lovely recreation area with four lakes, a stream, and canopies of pine, spruce, and aspen. The canyon offers 86 campsites and one cabin.

At Española, NM 68 continues a long open stretch of country to Taos, passing Velarde—with its apple orchards and roadside stands. Also at Española, US 84 heads north to Chama near the border. This trip is described on page 135.

■ TOWN OF TAOS

When the sun sets over low Carson Mesa, it leaves a thin crepuscular strip of pink and yellow light evaporating into the night sky above. Ahead, in the gathering gloom, Taos's lights blink on in the valley, below Taos Mountain. Above the great rock, when the moon is full and forces its way through silvered wisps of clouds, romantics call it "love at last light."

In daylight, predictably, Taos Mountain is different—no less of a magisterial presence, but there are now roadside distractions—a blend of low-grade commercial squalor leavened by classic Taos funk and high kitsch.

A settlement called **Ranchos de Taos**, four miles south of the center of town, provides the entrée to Taos's allure. There is a cordon of quaint galleries here, but the real attraction is the **mission church of San Francisco de Asís**, which sits flush with NM 68. This is actually fortuitous, because the hand-sculpted, adobe-buttressed back of this modest church is one of the purest architectural forms in North America. Its blank, brown adobe walls and uneven geometry drink in the sun as it glides across the sky, integrating the Spanish concept of *sol y sombra* (sunlight and shadow) into the architecture.

Painter Georgia O'Keeffe reduced the church to near abstraction by stripping away everything but light and form. "I had to paint it," she wrote. "The back of it several times, the front once. I finally painted a part of the back thinking that with that piece of the back I said all I needed to say about the church."

Taos is a corruption of the Tewa Indian words "Tua-tah," meaning "Red Willow Place." Its Spanish presence is even older than Santa Fe's, with the pioneer explorer Juan de Oñate having appointed a priest, Francisco Zamora, to the mission at Taos Pueblo in 1598. By 1615 a number of Spanish farmers were staking out the valley in the lee of the haunting mountain.

Taos began to assume an important economic role in New Mexico in the 1700s with its annual trade fair, a convergence of convenience in which Puebloans, Comanches, Utes, Apaches, and eventually Spaniards, Frenchmen, and Americans would all suspend their usual hostilities for a month and meet to trade furs, slaves, food, whiskey, and other goods. This was possible only because of Taos's isolation 70 miles north of the capital, where the Spanish governor would have enforced the Spanish crown's ban on commerce with "foreigners."

According to one account, relative values were as follows:

Soldier's monthly salary	15 pesos
Large antelope skin	2 pesos
Two small antelope skins	1 peso
One horse	3 pesos
Saddle, bridle, stirrups, spurs	12 pesos
Indian slave woman	30 pesos

By the early 1800s, Anglos were settling in Taos in significant numbers, the most famous of whom was Christopher "Kit" Carson. He was a fascinating contradiction of a man—a noted killer of Apache warriors who spoke several Indian languages and eventually adopted an Apache orphan, among numerous other foster children. An 1860 newspaper profile described him as a man with "an in-fy-nite small chance of legs [who] sits upon a horse like a king. I have never seen a man presenting a more regal aspect than this veteran mountaineer, when mounted upon his favorite steed, and dashing along like the wind." He married a Taoseña, Josefa Jaramillo, described by a contemporary as has having "beauty of the haughty, heart-breaking kind—such as would lead a man with a glance of the eye, to risk his life for one smile." Carson lived with her in a rambling house (now the Kit Carson Museum) just east of the Taos Plaza from 1843 to 1868.

The most famous (and notorious) event in 19th-century Taos was the Revolt of 1847, a bloody footnote to the quiet American seizure of New Mexico the year before. A few months after Gen. Stephen W. Kearny had claimed the territory for the United States, a core of Mexican loyalists in Taos, allied with some Pueblo Indians, revolted, storming the governor's house and killing him with arrows as his wife and children and Kit Carson's wife, Josefa, desperately tried to cut a hole through the back wall of the house and escape. The revolutionaries then scalped the governor and, after tacking his scalp to a board, paraded it around the Taos Plaza. The revolt lasted less than three weeks, and Indians suffered the severest losses—more than 150 dead in a final, decisive battle at Taos Pueblo. When the rebel leaders were tried at Taos before a judge whose own son been killed in the revolt, their accusers included the three Mexican women who'd been in the house with Governor Bent, the governor's wife, a Mrs. Boggs, and Mrs. Kit Carson.

Between 1898 and 1942, Taos became a mecca for disaffected artists, writers, and intellectuals seeking a new spiritual landing, and it continues to draw people of artistic and spiritual temperament to this day.

❖

The town of Taos, four miles north of Ranchos de Taos and two miles south of Taos Pueblo, is an enjoyable place to wander on foot, taking in galleries, small cafes, and the laid-back ambiance.

Even in the dark of winter Taos can be filled with light. Brilliantly sunlit white snow blankets the rugged peaks of the Sangre de Cristos, forming a spectacular stage set. Stark cottonwood trees guard icy rivulets running through the town. As in Santa Fe, thousands of *farolitos* illuminate the Plaza and nearly every building in town during the Christmas season.

Tiny Taos is actually congested, thanks to the fact that US 64 and NM 68 meet in the middle of town, a block from the Plaza. Everyone should stop where the two highways intersect and take a look at the wonderful mural of a *santero* (carver of saints) painted by local artist George Chacón on the side of a building in 1989. Bristling with symbolism, the anonymous *santero* is carving sculptures representing the Mexican-American family, the individual with a positive outlook, and the struggling single parent. But his *santos* look eerily like ghosts.

This heart of town looks as though it is trapped in a time warp between the 18th century and the impending 21st. As in Santa Fe, the old, brown adobe buildings are mostly protected and preserved (though nothing in Taos has the temerity to rise more than two stories); the enormous, stately cottonwoods lining the main roads seem to have been there at the dawn of time—and yet, the buzz of commerce permeates everything. Taos seems to have been invented for tourism.

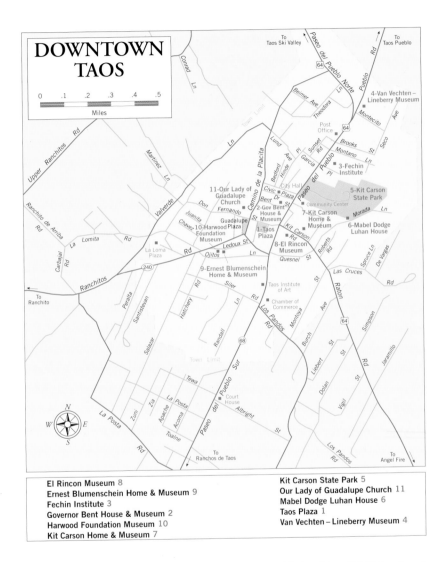

DOWNTOWN TAOS

0   .1   .2   .3   .4   .5

Miles

El Rincon Museum 8
Ernest Blumenschein Home & Museum 9
Fechin Institute 3
Governor Bent House & Museum 2
Harwood Foundation Museum 10
Kit Carson Home & Museum 7

Kit Carson State Park 5
Our Lady of Guadalupe Church 11
Mabel Dodge Luhan House 6
Taos Plaza 1
Van Vechten – Lineberry Museum 4

There are nine art and historical museums, the world-class Taos Ski Valley (maximum 4,800 skiers per day), and more boutiques (one specializes in wine and garlic) than seem possible in a town of 4,500. There are enough historic homes and museums in Taos to keep any visitor occupied for several days.

■ TAOS POINTS OF INTEREST

Taos Plaza. Located just west of the highway intersection and founded in 1790, this small plaza has a modest charm, even if it was remodeled mainly in brick in 1976. The shops clustered around the Plaza tilt more toward curio than art, especially T-shirt shops. One curio is the D. H. Lawrence art collection in the cluttered manager's office of La Fonda Hotel on the Plaza's south side. Lawrence lived in Taos in 1922–23 and 1925. He produced these ten paintings later. The cops seized them from a London exhibition in 1929. They're hardly lewd by modern-day standards—a few rather vague butts and breasts peek out—but they do demonstrate that Lawrence was a more gifted writer than painter. A small fee paid at the check-in desk gains admission to the exhibit.

Governor Bent House and Museum. Charles Bent, a prominent trader along the Old Santa Fe Trail and the first U.S. governor of the territory, lived here until he was scalped in January 1847. Exhibits include frontier memorabilia and period furnishings. *117-A Bent St., one block north of the Plaza; (505) 758-2376.*

Fechin Institute. Expatriate Russian artist Nicholai Fechin lived in and remodeled this two-story adobe house from 1927 to 1933, investing it with his own exquisitely hand-carved Russian-style furniture, doors, windows, corbels, and beams. The non-profit institute also offers more than a dozen five-day workshops in painting, drawing, and sculpture for students at all levels. *227 Paseo del Pueblo Norte, a few blocks north of the Plaza; (505) 758-1710.*

Kit Carson State Park. A lovely park in the middle of town. Kit Carson is buried in the small graveyard beside his wife and near several other Carson namesakes. Mabel Dodge Luhan is also buried in the same graveyard. *Paseo del Pueblo Norte, between Garcia Place and Civic Plaza Drive.*

Mabel Dodge Luhan House. Today a bed-and-breakfast, Mabel Dodge's three-story hacienda was once the gathering place for writers and artists including Georgia O'Keeffe, Willa Cather, and Aldous Huxley. Years later actor Dennis Hopper lived in the house while filming *Easy Rider. 240 Morada Lane; (505) 751-9686.*

Kit Carson Home and Museum. Carson bought this 1825 adobe house, now in downtown Taos, in 1843 as a wedding gift for his 14-year-old bride, Josefa

Jaramillo. The courtyard house holds hundreds of artifacts—guns, furniture, dresses, and contemporary newspaper profiles of Carson. *Half a block east of the Plaza on Kit Carson Road; (505) 758-0505.*

Ernest Blumenschein Home and Museum. In 1912, artist Ernest Blumenschein became one of the six co-founders of the Taos Society of Artists. This rambling house exhibits the Blumenscheins' collection of Japanese and American Indian art as well as their own work. *222 Ledoux Street; (505) 758-0505.*

Harwood Foundation Museum. Operated by the University of New Mexico, this art museum features a permanent exhibit of paintings, drawings, prints, photographs, and sculpture dating from the earliest (1910s) years of Taos as an art colony. The paintings and photographs testify eloquently to the reasons so many artists have congregated here: the power of the land and the irresistible images of its people. *238 Ledoux Street; (505) 758-9826.*

Chapel of Our Lady of Guadalupe. A lovely adobe chapel built in the 1970s. A large, brilliantly colored portrait of the patron saint adorns a wall inside the chapel. *404 San Felipe Street NW, Patio Escondido.*

Van Vechten–Lineberry Taos Art Museum. This large and ambitious private museum features the work of Taos artist Duane Van Vechten, who died in 1977. Virtually unknown because she chose not to sell her paintings, she was a gifted artist who mastered many different styles. Other Taos and New Mexico artists are on exhibit as well; the museum's taste is conservative. *501 N. Pueblo Rd; (505) 758-2690.*

Millicent Rogers Museum. This private museum, founded in 1956, maintains a stunning collection of Pueblo and Navajo jewelry, textiles, and pottery. Centerpiece: the Martínez Room, which showcases the development of the pottery of María Martínez and her family of San Ildefonso Pueblo. *Millicent Rogers Museum Road, four miles north of the Plaza off NM 64; (505) 758-2462.*

Martínez Hacienda. An exactingly restored Spanish hacienda dating from 1804 to 1827, originally belonging to Don Antonio Severino Martínez, the *alcalde* (mayor) of Taos. This fortress-like 21-room adobe house is built around two courtyards with few exterior openings, testifying to the danger of Apache attacks.

There are several interesting displays of Spanish colonial furniture and implements, such as an *artesa,* a wooden bowl resembling a shallow crib, used for making cheese. *Ranchitos Road (NM 240), two miles south of Taos Plaza; (505) 758-1000.*

■ TAOS PUEBLO

Taos Pueblo is famous in literature and art, and is the most architecturally ambitious of America's pueblos, an awesome achievement by any standard. The pueblo probably first arose in the 1200s, but what we see today—contrary to popular legend—mostly dates from a reconstruction following the Pueblo Rebellion of 1680. This hardly matters. The audacious idea of constructing a five-story apartment building out of mud and straw and maintaining it for several hundred years has to stand as a landmark in any architectural notebook.

A rug loom in the weaving room of Martínez Hacienda.

Taos Pueblo (opposite) was once the largest of New Mexico's pueblo communities.

The Taoseños don't live in their ancestral home anymore—no electricity, water, or phones—but are scattered around in modern houses on their reservation. The pueblo is divided into north and south villages. Walk around the edges of the plaza between them, rather than across it, which is not considered polite. Most of the ground-floor apartments have metamorphosed into shops, and a legion of *hornos*—outdoor adobe beehive fireplaces—have sprouted around them to produce hot bread for the tourists. Taos Pueblo is not an Indian Disneyland, but it does have that potential—and perhaps temptation. *Two miles north of the town of Taos. Self-guided and guided tours of the pueblo are offered daily. (505) 758-8626.*

■ THE HIGH ROAD

The High Road is the famous back-country route between Taos and Santa Fe. The best direction for appreciating the stunning vistas that unfold with every curve in the road is from north to south.

About 25 miles south of Taos on Highway 76 is the tiny pastoral village of **Las Trampas,** founded in 1751 by a colony of 12 families from Santa Fe. There's little commerce here; the prime attraction is the **church of San José de Gracia** (1760 –1776). The beautifully restored mission has broad adobe shoulders capped with delicate wooden pyramids with crosses. Interesting modern *santos,* carved in juniper and aspen wood by local artists, are for sale at La Tiendita, a store facing the church across the parking lot.

At first view—from an overlook along the highway—the town of **Truchas** appears to float across a grassy valley below the snow-capped Truchas Peaks, spectacular mountains soaring up to 13,100 feet. The village was founded with a land grant in 1749 and changed little until the late 20th century, many generations of residents making a living by small-scale farming. Even today the main street of Truchas looks very much like an isolated Mexican village snoring away the centuries.

Truchas's isolation actually ended in 1986 when Robert Redford brought a crew there to film *The Milagro Beanfield War.* Since then, about a dozen gift shops, galleries, and B&Bs have opened.

The Córdovas' Handweaving Workshop is one of two essential stops in Truchas. Harry and his father, Alfredo Córdova, produce beautiful custom-woven rugs. The other is Bill Franke's **Hand Artes Gallery,** one of the most interesting

PUEBLO FEAST DAYS AND DANCES

Call ahead to verify dates and for precise directions. Also consult maps, as the pueblos can be tricky to find.

Ácoma
Feast day: September 2. West of Albuquerque off I-40. (505) 470-4967

Nambé
Feast day: October 4; Nambé Falls Celebration, July 4. North and east of Santa Fe off NM 503; (505) 455-7708

Picurís (aka San Lorenzo)
Feast day: August 10; dances in February; sunset dance in August. North and east of Española on NM 75; (505) 587-2519

Pojoaque
Feast day: December 12. Fifteen miles north of Santa Fe off US 285; (505) 455-2278

San Ildefonso
Feast day: January 23. Corn dance in June. North and west of Santa Fe on NM 502; (505) 455-3549

San Juan
Feast day: June 24. Deer dance in February. Footraces and arts and crafts show in July. Just north of Española on NM 68; (505) 852-4400

Santa Clara
Feast day: August 12. Various dances in February and June. Just west of Española off NM 30; (505) 753-7326

Taos
Feast Day: September 30. Los Comanches dance in February; foot races in May; corn dance in June. Two miles north of town of Taos; (505) 758-9593

Tesuque
Feast Day: November 12. Corn dance in June and July. Ten miles north of Santa Fe on US 285; (505) 983-2667

and eclectic art galleries in northern New Mexico. There's furniture, folk art, fine art, religious art, Hispanic art, and provocative art.

From Truchas the High Road descends into the drier and warmer piñon-juniper scrub land of the Chimayó Valley. Córdova is a tiny village here, located in a narrow valley below the road, and has been home to generations of woodcarvers. Of all the villages strung along the High Road, Chimayó is the most interesting. It has a famous restaurant, Rancho de Chimayó Restaurante; a venerated family of weavers that has maintained their business for eight generations; and a historic and (according to believers) miraculous chapel.

Before the Spanish town was founded around 1700, there was a Tewa-speaking pueblo in this fertile valley. According to Indian legend, there was a pool—perhaps a hot spring—here whose water or mud held healing properties. The present Santuario de Chimayó may have inherited that very site. Around 300,000 people a year visit the Santuario—some out of curiosity, some to relish its architectural beauty, and many because they believe in the curative power of the soil here. Dirt is supplied from a hole in the floor in a room off the main chapel, and people rub it on their afflicted parts or scoop it up and take it with them. During Holy Week each year, more than 10,000 believers undertake a pilgrimage to Chimayó. Interstate 25 from Albuquerque and US 285 from Santa Fe will be lined for miles with pedestrians, some carrying crosses on their backs.

One of the alternative miracles of Chimayó is its chile, usually dried and ground into powder. Nowhere else in the country, or probably the world, does chile attain such a precise balance of fire and profound flavor. Several family markets in Chimayó sell bags of ground chile; one near the Santuario opportunistically markets it as "Holy chile." Holy or hellish, freeze it when you get home: this will help preserve the flavor.

■ BANDELIER NATIONAL MONUMENT

Extraordinary Anasazi pueblo ruins are protected here. They were discovered one October day in 1880, when a Swiss-born geologist named Adolph Bandelier peered over the rim of Frijoles Canyon 20 miles northwest of Santa Fe and saw something that would change the course of his life: the ruins of stone houses at least half a millennium old. Southwestern archaeology did not then exist, but over the next two decades Bandelier, along with a Swedish naturalist named Gustaf

Nordenskiold and a Colorado cowboy named Charles Wetherill, would invent it. Thirty-six years later the forested Pajarito Plateau and the dramatic canyon that so captivated Bandelier would become a national monument, named in his honor. This was evidently a good place to live in prehistoric times; there is evidence of human presence on the plateau and in the canyon since A.D. 950. The canyon's year-round creek was obviously its key attraction throughout the millennia. The pueblo ruins of Frijoles Canyon, however, date from about A.D. 1175 to 1550.

There is no way to guess whether the ancient Anasazi who lived here were also enchanted by the canyon's stunning natural beauty, but modern visitors certainly are. In fall the box elder and narrow-leaf cottonwood trees flanking the stream explode with color. In summer, the canyon is a moist, green, cool oasis. In winter, at an elevation of over 7,000 feet, the canyon is cold.

The canyon's largest ruin is Tyuonyi, an oval-shaped pueblo built of roughly molded volcanic tuff stones. Its construction took about a century, beginning around 1350. At its peak it had 400 rooms on several levels, and it would have had a defensive, forbidding attitude: the rooms completely encircle the large central plaza, and there was only one ground-floor entrance—which had large poles installed in it in a zigzag pattern, suggesting a maze. Today, however, the ruin is oddly beautiful, hugging the earth, its remaining walls a muted rainbow of salmon, auburn, gray, and black stones.

Several cliff dwellings line the south-facing canyon wall along a 1¹/₂-mile self-guided trail. Visitors in good physical condition also should not miss climbing the ladders 140 feet up to Ceremonial Cave, a reconstructed *kiva* in a large natural alcove in the canyon wall. There are 75 miles of maintained hiking trails. In summer, the Park Service conducts free night walks through the ruins under the stars with stops to read native poetry, fires lit in the cliff dwellings behind you. This is quite a marvelous thing to do, especially during the Perseid meteor showers in August. *(505) 672-3861.*

■ LOS ALAMOS

During the summer of 1922, a young physics professor from Berkeley, J. Robert Oppenheimer, accompanied a pack trip from Frijoles Canyon into the Valle Grande. During subsequent trips into the Jémez wilderness, Oppenheimer often passed by the site of Los Alamos, then only a ranch school.

Twenty years later, when Oppenheimer was asked to select an isolated site for a laboratory to develop the world's first atomic bomb, he thought of the ranch school. In 1941, it was forced to close to make room for the Manhattan Project. For the next three years, scientists secretly gathered in a makeshift government town, sharing ideas. Prefabricated apartment houses and wooden barracks were erected to house hundreds of scientists and technicians who arrived by train, many not even apprised of their destination. They were issued drivers' licenses with only numbers, no names, and all mail was sent to a Santa Fe post office box. People who applied to empty trash were hired only if they were illiterate. Even the scientists' families who accompanied them to the mountain outpost that came to be called "The Hill" didn't know exactly why they were there. Their wives taught in classrooms, shopped in Santa Fe, and attended ceremonies at nearby pueblos.

On July 16, 1945, the secret came out. The first atomic bomb was detonated in the desert at Trinity Site, 60 miles north of Alamogordo.

Although the laboratory maintains high security, the **Norris E. Bradbury Science Museum,** outlining the bomb's development and providing a basic course in nuclear energy, is open to the public. *Caravan tours of Trinity Site take place in April and October. Call (505) 667-4444 for more information.*

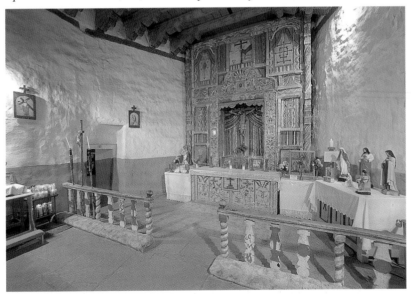

Must-see sights of the region surrounding Santa Fe include the Santuario de Chimayó (above) and the ruins of Bandelier National Monument near Los Alamos. The entrance to a kiva *is shown at left.*

8/06
only
beautiful

■ JÉMEZ CANYON

New Mexico 4 winds through the Jémez Mountains, past the Valle Grande, clear blue streams full of brown and rainbow trout, and pine-covered hillsides. One million years ago, a mighty explosion from a volcano that scientists estimate was between 14,000 and 27,000 feet high blew a hole in the ground 12 miles across and 3,500 feet deep. For thousands of years, eruptions poured forth, some ash settling up to a thousand miles away. This violent activity left behind an entire mountain range with its tallest point, Redondo Peak, at 11,254 feet.

Long extinct, the volcano also left behind an extensive network of geothermal pockets. Many remain locked in the earth, while others have burst forth in hot springs scattered throughout the Jémez Mountains. Ironically, the volcano's caldera, known as Valle Grande, has turned into a lush green meadow.

Volcanic tuff from the massive explosion blankets the landscape for miles, creating cone-shaped tent rocks and hoodoos (free-standing formations with a pancake-shaped rock on top). Black volcanic glass, obsidian, covers some of the tuff.

Jémez Springs is a shady hideaway, the town where burned-out Santa Feans come for R&R amid the pines and the natural mineral springs that gave the town its name. A handful of guest cottages and bed-and-breakfasts ranging from Spartan to cozy to New Age eclectic are available for overnighters.

Just north of town, the eight-foot-thick rock walls of the church of **San José de los Jémez** and the nearby prehistoric pueblo of Giusewa (a Tewa word that means "Place at the Boiling Waters") are preserved at **Jémez State Monument.** The massive church was founded in the early 1620s by Franciscan missionary Fray Alonso de Lugo. A self-guided tour takes you inside the fortress-like church, built with small windows for protection from invaders. *NM 4, 13 miles north of Jémez Pueblo; (505) 829-3530.*

Jémez Pueblo has one of the loveliest settings in the region. As you approach it, you may find yourself inhaling heavenly smells, for under shady *ramadas* that line NM 4 north of the pueblo, women sell bread they have baked inside adobe ovens. They also cook up fry bread on the spot, and the pleasing smell of baking dough mingles with the sweet piñon scent from the fire.

In the early 1630s, Jémez Pueblo became the center for religious activities for pueblo dwellers displaced from their settlements to the northeast by Spanish settlers. The pueblo's low adobe homes hug the brilliant brick-red earth. Coyote fences made with thin sticks form small corrals, and *hornos* the color of the rich earth appear beside nearly every home. Roadside galleries and shops sell local crafts, including the earth-toned pottery that is the pueblo's signature craft. Young Jémez men are famous as cross-country runners and firefighters; many spend their summers fighting forest fires throughout the United States.

At the village of San Isidro, take NM 44 east to reconnect with I-25 between Albuquerque and Santa Fe. It passes **Zía Pueblo,** a picturesque adobe village perched atop a mesa visible from the road. Zía is known for fine pottery. Its feast day and corn dance take place on August 15. *(505) 867-3304.*

■ ESPAÑOLA TO CHAMA ROAD TRIP

Route: *This trip picks up the road past Tesuque and Pojoaque (US 84/285) described in the beginning of this chapter on page 115. It follows US 84 which branches northwest at Española.*

❖

NM 84 passes the village of **Hernández,** which looks fairly ordinary at midday to the passing motorist, but has attained wide recognition from an Ansel Adams photograph. "Moon over Hernández" captures the light in the sky, the crosses in the graveyard, a magic of landscape, so perfectly that thousands of people have this photo in poster form hanging on their walls. Perhaps this says something about photography as an art that can capture the mood of a place.

Past Hernández is the 5,930-foot-high town of **Abiquiú,** most famous today for being the place where one of America's most revered artists, Georgia O'Keeffe, lived and painted much of her adult life.

In the mid-1700s, Abiquiú was a home to *genízaros,* people of mixed tribal blood released from slavery by Apaches or Spaniards. The serenity of this spectacular red-rock country seemed to tap their spirituality or otherworldliness. Indian "sorcerers" (a word used advisedly) were known to be powerful here, so powerful that a Spanish priest sent to Abiquiú from Santa Fe flushed out suspects in the tradition of the Spanish Inquisition and sentenced them to become servants of a prominent colonist. (One can't help wondering what spells the sorcerers put on the colonist.)

Raids by Ute warriors were endemic, and though they seldom killed people while raiding, their raiding was so prevalent that pueblos and small settlements often moved rather than endure another depletion of all they'd worked to harvest.

(following pages) Going to the Waterhole, Santa Clara, *ca. 1920 by Walter Ufer. He was one of the first artists from Taos to be internationally recognized. (Eiteljorg Museum of American Indian and Western Art, Indianapolis)*

By 1800, Penitentes became prominent here—a confraternity of Catholics who believed in experiencing the suffering of Christ by flagellation. Formed by Spanish men in isolated towns without resident priests, this order (also known at the "Brotherhood of Light") sought forgiveness for its members' sins, as well as for the sins of those who crucified Christ. Penitentes performed community service, helping the sick and poor, comforting the bereaved, and counseling those who were troubled. By voting as a block, they wielded much political power. In Abiquiú, the Brotherhood built two *moradas,* or meeting houses—rectangular adobe structures that had no windows, one door, and a wooden cross in front. As curiosity spread among outsiders, Penitente gatherings and rituals became secret. Penitente sects still exist, although little is publicly known about their numbers and activities.

Rumors say there are still practitioners of black magic in Abiquiú. One Penitente *morada* supposedly has been cursed. Local *santeros* who worked to restore it after it was vandalized have fallen mysteriously ill.

Established in 1766, **Ghost Ranch** is a collection of adobe buildings nestled among maroon shales and dusty orange and purple sandstone hillsides. It was named for the *brujas* (witches), who are said to inhabit its canyons. In 1934, Arthur Newton, a wealthy Easterner, turned the ranch into a fancy dude ranch. One of his early guests was painter Georgia O'Keeffe. Once she set foot on Ghost Ranch, O'Keeffe never left it for long. Eventually, she bought a portion of the ranch and lived in a small U-shaped adobe house with whitewashed walls.

Today, the Presbyterian Church operates a study center here with seminars offered year round. Topics range from archaeology, paleontology, and theology, to pottery and wood carving. Next to the ranch's main buildings are fine museums of anthropology and paleontology, as well as the **Ghost Ranch Living Museum,** which takes in injured wild animals and cares for them. *14 miles north west of Abiquiú at US 84; (505) 685-4312.*

A town of about 1,000 people, **Chama** lies at the northernmost edge of New Mexico at an altitude of 7,800 feet. Here from late May to mid-October you can board the **Cumbres and Toltec Scenic Railroad,** a coal-fueled, narrow-gauge train that pulls seven passenger cars through groves of aspens and up the steep 10,000-foot Cumbres Pass. Golden eagles soar overhead, and orange lichens cover craggy volcanic outcroppings. The day-long journey ends in Antonito, Colorado, where passengers can spend the night, or return to Chama via train or van. *Call (505) 756-2151 or (719) 376-5483.*

Photographer Charles F. Lummis took this portrait of an elderly Penitente with an image of the Virgin during Easter week celebrations in 1888. (The Southwest Museum, Los Angeles)

North-Central New Mexico Food & Lodging

■ FOOD & LODGING

> *Restaurant prices:*
> Per person, not including drinks, tax, and tips:
> $ = under $10; $$ = $10–20; $$$ = over $20
> *Room rates:*
> Per night, per room, double occupancy:
> $ = under $50; $$ = $50–100; $$$ = over $100

Abiquiu

population 809   elevation 6,060

✕ **Cafe Abiquiú at the Abiquiú Inn.**
US 84; (505) 685-4378 $$
Choose between Middle Eastern salads
and Indian curries, or stick with New
Mexican enchiladas and fajitas. The
dining room is comfortably casual.

⌂ **The Abiquiú Inn.** US 84; (505) 685-
4378 $$
Multi-hued pastel cliffs and sky form
the backdrop for this comfortable roadside lodging. The Chama River, which
flows nearby, adds to the natural beauty.

Chama River Area

✕ **Chama Cattle Company Blue Duck
Brewery.** 1128 Main St.; (505) 756-
2808 $$
Handcut steaks are the specialty at this
microbrewery.

✕ **Viva Vera's.** Chama; (505) 756-2557 $
Vera has been feeding the folks here
since 1963 and she's still their favorite
cook. You'll long remember her hearty
New Mexican dishes and sopaipillas.

⌂ **Casa del Rio Bed & Breakfast.** Ten
miles north of Española off US 84;
(505) 753-2035 $$
Elegant guesthouse with kiva fireplace
situated on the Chama River.

⌂ **Casa de Martínez Bed & Breakfast.** US
84, Los Ojos; (505) 588-7858 $$
Restored 1869 Spanish adobe two-story
farmhouse. Non-smoking. Across high-
way from Rio Chama.

⌂ **Corkins Lodge.** Brazos River, Chama;
(505) 588-7261 $$$
Log-cabin luxury at this full-service
wilderness lodge at the foot of the
Brazos Cliffs.

⌂ **The Lodge at Chama.** US 84; (505)
756-2133 $$$
Luxury at its finest in this elegantly
rustic hunting lodge that overlooks the
Chama Valley.

Chimayó

population 2,789   elevation 1,993

✕ **Rancho de Chimayó Restaurante.** NM
520 one mile S. of Chimayó; (505)
351-4444 $$
The Jaramillo family settled around

present-day Chimayó in 1695; nine generations later their descendants run this prodigiously popular restaurant in a rambling 19th-century hacienda. How popular? Try 300,000 meals a year. Try also not to arrive at lunchtime in summer when tour buses are disgorging diners by the hundreds; strike at an odd hour. Excellent traditional New Mexican food.

☒ **Hacienda Rancho de Chimayó.** Santa Fe County Rd., off NM 503; (505) 351-2222 $$
A lovely B&B across the road from the famous Restaurante Rancho de Chimayó. Seven rooms in an old adobe hacienda surround a courtyard. Much peace and quiet. About 40 miles north of Santa Fe.

Española

population 8,389   elevation 5,585

✗ **Angelina's.** Paseo de Oñate; (505) 753-8543 $
Highly seasoned New Mexican cooking is served at this wood-floored adobe. For extra "atmosphere," eat inside the teepee-shaped booth.

✗ **Anthony's at the Delta.** 228 Paseo de Oñate NW; (505) 753-4511 $$-$$$
Once a home, this sprawling, high-ceilinged mansion now houses a restaurant known for its steaks and fresh seafood.

✗ **El Paragua.** 603 Santa Cruz Rd; (505) 753-3211 $-$$
Mexican food, mesquite-grilled steaks and seafood in an elegant setting.

✗ **Embudo Station Restaurant and Brewery.** Fifteen miles north of Española on NM 68; (505) 852-4707 $-$$
A beautiful place nestled under ancient cottonwoods on the west bank, literally, of the Rio Grande. Succulent smoked meats and vividly flavored green chile beer from Embudo Station's own smokehouse and brewery. Open April through October only.

✗ **Gabriel's.** Thirteen miles north of Santa Fe off US 285; (505) 455-7000 $-$$
Expertly prepared Mexican and Southwest cuisine—the guacamole, made fresh at your table, is sheer genius. If you arrive around sunset, try for a table on the outdoor patio, order a fabulous margarita, and take in the spectacular views of the Sangre de Cristo Mountains.

☒ **Inn at the Delta.** 304 Paseo de Oñate; (505) 753-9466 $$$
Original artwork and southwestern furnishings adorn each over-sized room in this bed-and-breakfast.

☒ **Rancho de San Juan.** US 285; (505) 753-6818 $$$
Explore the Ojo Caliente River Valley while staying at this elegant country inn.

Los Alamos

population 18,100   elevation 7,410

✗ **De Colores.** 820 Trinity Dr.; (505) 662-6285 $-$$
Enjoy fare ranging from New Mexican classics to mesquite-grilled steak at this popular local gathering place.

North-Central New Mexico Food & Lodging

North-Central New Mexico Food & Lodging

✕ **Hill Diner.** 1315 Trinity Dr.; (505) 662-9745 $-$$
Down-home food in down-home atmosphere. Great chicken-fried steak and homemade desserts.

▦ **Hilltop House Hotel and Los Alamos Suites.** 400 Trinity Dr.;(505) 662-2441 $$
A pleasant, centrally located hotel with stunning views of the Jémez Mountains. Indoor pool.

▦ **Orange Street Inn.** 3496 Orange St; (505) 662-2651 $$
Views are lovely from this lodging, situated in a canyon forest.

Taos

population 23,118   elevation 6,950

✕ **AppleTree.** Taos Plaza; (505) 758-1900 $$
A popular restaurant with fireside tables in the winter months and a breezy patio in the warmer seasons. The menu offers a range of dishes from curried chicken to shrimp quesadillas.

✕ **Casa Fresen Bakery.** Arroyo Seco; (505) 776-2969 $
The smell of fresh-baked goods mixes with steaming espressos in this European-style gourmet cafe on the road to Taos Ski Valley. Lunch only.

✕ **The Chow Cart.** 402 Paseo del Pueblo Sur; (505) 758-3632 $
A renovated '50s-style drive-thru well-known for its sensational chiles rellenos fried and wrapped in tortillas. Devour this brilliant creation inside or sit out-

side under the shady trees.

✕ **El Taoseño.** 819 Paseo del Pueblo Sur; (505) 758-4142 $
Tourists don't come here, but they should. The breakfast crowd arrives in pickups and cop cars and engorges big, cheap plates of chorizo and eggs, potatoes with green chile sauce, and huevos rancheros. There are "American" breakfasts here too, but Taoseños stare quizzically at people who order them.

✕ **Eske's, A Brew Pub.** 106 Des Georges Ln.; (505) 758-1517 $
Bratwurst and tabouleh are on the menu, but it's the daily changing beer selection that's worth an afternoon stop at Taos' first brew pub.

✕ **Fred's Place.** 332 Paseo del Pueblo Sur; (505) 758-0514 $-$$
In a town known for its quirkiness, this restaurant stands out. The ceilings are painted with murals of heaven and hell, the walls are adorned with locally made crucifixes and santos. Exceptionally well-prepared northern New Mexican specialties are served by a congenial young waitstaff sporting tattoos and pierced body parts. No reservations, so go early or be prepared to wait in line with the rest of the mostly local patrons.

✕ **Jacquelina's Southwestern Cuisine.** 1541 S. Paseo del Pueblo Sur; (505) 751-0399 $-$$
Taos's hottest feed bag. The menu weaves through traditional and nuevo New Mexican, both delectably executed.

✕ **Lambert's of Taos.** 309 Paseo del Pueblo Sur; (505) 758-1009 $$–$$$

This pretty, cottage-like restaurant serves new American cuisine such as grilled lamb chops with mushrooms, and slips in an occasional New Mexican accent with smoky chipotle sauces.

✕ **Marciano's Ristorante.**112 Placita; (505) 751-0805 $$
This quiet, intimate, and unpretentious Italian cafe serves mostly pasta dishes, some spiked with chile. Emphasis is on organic vegetables and meats, home-made sauces, and a long wine and beer list. Very good; rather expensive for pasta.

✕ **The Outback.** 712 Paseo del Pueblo Norte; (505) 758-3112 $
Gourmet pizzas made with organically grown flour. During winter don't miss the homemade soups.

✕ **Villa Fontana.** Five miles north of Taos on NM 522; (505) 758-5800 $$$
Owner-chef Carlo Gislimberti here serves up stunning northern Italian dishes such as piccata of venison with wild mushrooms bathed in vodka demi-glace. Service seems excessively formal for Taos, but diners in tattered jeans still are perfectly welcome.

⊟ **Casa Benavides.** 137 Kit Carson Rd.; (505) 758-1772 $$-$$$
A modern and colorful B&B. Navajo rugs, Native American pottery, flagstone floors, and other Southwestern trappings adorn the spacious rooms.

⊟ **Casa de las Chimenas.** Los Pandos and Cordoba roads; (505) 758-4777 $$$
Four charming rooms look out upon an English garden.

⊟ **El Monte Lodge.** 317 Kit Carson Rd.; (505) 758-3171 or (800) 828-8267 $$
An old but very nicely maintained mom 'n' pop motel near downtown. Quiet, spacious rooms, some with beehive fireplaces or kitchens.

⊟ **Fechin Inn.** 227 Paseo del Pueblo Norte; (505) 751-1000 $$$
This elegant hotel embraces the Russian artist Nikolai Fechin's home physically as well as spiritually; the lobby furniture is hand-carved in Fechin's distinctively rustic style.

⊟ **Historic Taos Inn.** 125 Paseo del Pueblo Norte; (505) 758-2233 or (800) 826-7466 $$$
Taos's famous old downtown hotel opened in 1936, but parts of the building date from the 1600s. Most rooms have fireplaces. Local art on display.

⊟ **Mabel Dodge Luhan House.** 240 Morada Ln.; (505) 758-9456 $$-$$$
Early in the century, Mrs. Luhan coaxed many literati, including D. H. Lawrence and Willa Cather, to come West and stay in her rambling, old house. Even in it's present incarnate as an 11-room B&B, the artistic tradition continues with frequently held workshops and writers' conferences. There's a casual, rather rustic flavor to the place.

Tesuque

population 1,500   elevation 6,000

✕ **Tesuque Village Market.** Junction of NM 591 and Bishop's Lodge Rd.; (505)

North-Central New Mexico Food & Lodging

North-Central New Mexico Food & Lodging

988-8848 $

Locals usually drop by this cafe/grocery store for a cup of coffee, a stack of blue corn pancakes, and a copy of the *New York Times*.

Rancho Encantado. Rte. 4, off NM 592; (505) 982-3537 or (800) 722-9339 $$$

Few accommodations offer more spectacular views. Sprawled across 168 acres above the stunning Rio Grande Valley, the resort attracts celebrity guests from Robert Redford to the Dalai Lama.

Santa Clara Canyon Campground. Fourteen miles south and west of Española off NM 30; cross to west side of the Rio Grande, entrance on the left; (505) 753-7326.

A lovely recreation area with four lakes, a stream, and canopies of pine, spruce, and aspen. The canyon offers a 83 campsites and 32 sheltered sites.

Tesuque Pueblo RV Campground. Off I-25 take St. Francis exit ; (505) 455-2661.

A tribal-owned campground with hot showers, restrooms, and hookups. Fine views extend from this campground.

The high mountain meadows of northern New Mexico make for some of the best hiking and camping in the United States. Pictured above is the east fork of the Jémez River in the Jémez Mountains.

Chiles in Chimayó. When braided together like this they are called ristras.

FOUR CORNERS

■ HIGHLIGHTS
Mesa Verde
Navajo Reservation
Shiprock
Chaco Canyon
Canyon de Chelly
Hopi Villages
Betatakin and Keet Seel
Monument Valley
Hovenweep
Four Corners Monument

■ LANDSCAPE

This is high desert and canyon country, a landscape of wide vistas and unearthly land formations made oddly familiar by car commercials. Everybody who has the bright idea to name a truck after an Indian culture ("Navajo," "Dakota") seems compelled to film it in this setting of improbable sandstone monoliths, impossible roads, and indescribable sunsets. Admittedly, it sometimes takes a truck, a horse, or a hike to visit some of the most dramatic history in what is now the Navajo Nation.

An arbitrary political division appears to center this space on the adjacent corners of Utah, Colorado, New Mexico and Arizona. But its geographic heart is the San Juan River Basin, a vast expanse of peaks and mesas draining into the San Juan River, which itself empties into the Colorado. If the Four Corners landscape is unique, so are its sky, clear light, shifting shadows, and profound sense of isolation.

■ TRAVELERS ORIENTATION

The Four Corners region is dry, isolated country, but there are towns with adequate facilities near most of the sites listed here. Mesa Verde is only eight miles from Cortez, Colorado, but the more inviting town is Durango, Colorado, about 35 miles east of the park. Chaco Canyon is 175 miles from Albuquerque, New Mexico, and only 75 miles from Farmington, New Mexico. Canyon de Chelly is just outside the town of Chinle and 164 miles from Flagstaff, Arizona. Quick forays into the area are worthwhile, but it's also a place where a person of contemplative temperament or an interest in ancient and modern Indian cultures, who appreciates beautiful landscapes and quiet, could drift about happily for a month. Many sites were inhabited by Anasazi Indians, who disappeared before the modern tribes who live here came into this region. The Ute, Navajo, and Hopi reservations cover a wide reach of the Four Corners region. Always travel with extra water, and check weather conditions before venturing too far on unpaved roads, as they are impassable in wet weather. AAA's Indian Country map is the best available for this area.

Food & Lodging appears on page 183.

This high, arid plateau receives little rain, most falling during thunderstorms in July and August. The best time to visit is from late spring to early fall when the altitude prevents the summer heat from becoming excessive. Winters are dry and occasionally bitterly cold with temperatures often falling far below 0° F (-16° C) at night, although the intense sunshine warms the days to well above freezing. Three weather stations which best represent the climate of the area are at Chaco Canyon (elev. 6,175) in northwest New Mexico, Mesa Verde (elev. 7,070) in southwest Colorado, and the town of Kayenta (elev. 6,600) in Arizona's Monument Valley on the Navajo Reservation.

| TEMPS (F°) | AVG. JAN. | | AVG. APRIL | | AVG. JULY | | AVG. OCT. | | RECORD | RECORD |
	HIGH	LOW	HIGH	LOW	HIGH	LOW	HIGH	LOW	HIGH	LOW
Chaco	43	12	72	38	91	55	70	38	102	-38
Kayenta	39	15	70	39	93	58	72	40	104	-17
Mesa Verde	41	19	69	40	88	58	68	43	100	-20

PRECIPITATION (INCHES)	AVG. JAN.	AVG. APRIL	AVG. JULY	AVG. OCT.	ANNUAL	SNOW
Chaco	0.3	0.2	1.2	0.6	8.5	17
Kayenta	0.5	0.4	1.3	0.8	8.6	20
Mesa Verde	1.2	0.4	1.3	0.8	8.6	20

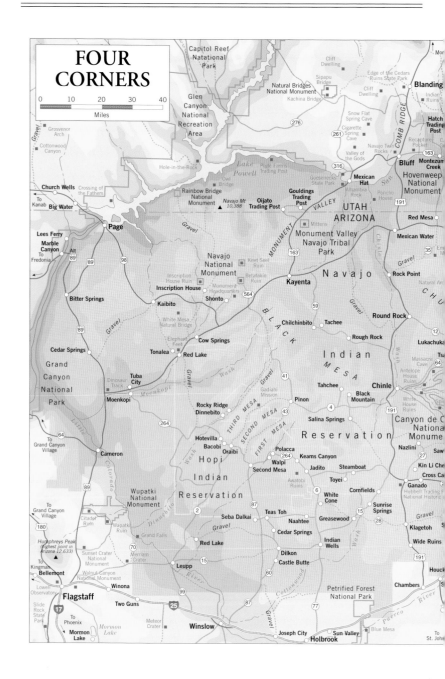

FOUR CORNERS

0   10   20   30   40
Miles

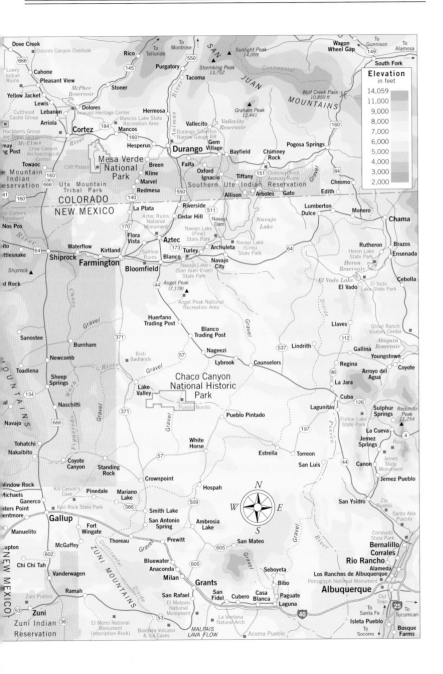

Elevation
in feet

14,059	
11,000	
9,000	
8,000	
7,000	
6,000	
5,000	
4,000	
3,000	
2,000	

■ HISTORY

The Four Corners region used to be Anasazi land, and the remnants of that culture are littered throughout the canyons of the reservation. Traditional Navajos still shun the ruins, believing them haunted by ghosts. "Anasazi," a Navajo word, means "enemy ancestors."

Archaeologists call the early Anasazi "Basketmakers." Beginning around 100 B.C., they began to settle into a sedentary life of farming, and wove yucca-fiber baskets so finely that they could hold water. They lived in dismal pithouses, half below ground and roofed with sticks and mud mortar. Around A.D. 200, pottery made its first appearance; between A.D 500 and 700, the bow and arrow began to replace the spear and *atlatl* (a wooden extension of the spear-thrower's arm); and beginning about 750, the concept of the pueblo revolutionized both Anasazi architecture and culture.

Spectacular reminders of Anasazi culture today are the cliff dwellings, large masonry pueblos preserved in natural canyon alcoves in places such as Mesa Verde, Canyon de Chelly, and Betatakin and Keet Seel in Navajo National Monument. Equally astounding are the ruins at Chaco Canyon, where the Anasazi built a massive city on the floor of a shallow canyon.

Along with the architecture came beautifully decorated pottery, ornamental jewelry, and clothing—a sash woven of dog hair on display at Mesa Verde National Park features a repeating diamond pattern as elegant as anything in a Santa Fe boutique today. To judge by the number of wooden flutes found in Anasazi burial sites and represented in rock paintings, it seems likely that the people of the canyons appreciated music.

Given all this, it is easy to romanticize the Anasazi culture, but the hard evidence is that lives were hard and short. The physical environment, for all its beauty, was blisteringly hot in the summer, dismally cold in winter, with unpredictable rainfall and unreliable running water. Anthropologists analyzing Anasazi remains have found pitting of bones, which suggests poor nutrition and anemia. The men were no taller than about five feet three inches, and they lived about 35 years. The cliffside pueblos, hauntingly beautiful in ruin, would have been decidedly less engaging as actual dwelling places—cold, dark, cramped, and smoky.

The disappearance of the Anasazi around A.D. 1300, probably was caused by a long, persistent drought in the Four Corners region from 1276 to 1299, which must have devastated agricultural production. At the same time the Anasazi population had grown to the point that this dry, cold land—marginal even in good times—could no longer support the people. Disease may have played a pernicious role. The role of nomadic tribes such as the Utes and Navajo in bringing about the demise of the Anasazi is a subject of much controversy. If they arrived in the 14th century, as some anthropologists maintain, their raids may have been the coup de grâce that finally destroyed this civilization. Most anthropologists are equally adamant that these nomadic people did not arrive until the 16th century, after the Anasazi had deserted their villages and migrated elsewhere.

By 1300, the great Anasazi centers at Chaco Canyon, Mesa Verde, and in Canyon de Chelly were deserted. Whether these people were all of one tribe, or belonged to several different tribes who evolved similar and interconnecting cultures, is unknown. One modern Arizona tribe, the Hopi, speak a Uto-Aztecan language and trace their ancestry to the Sinagua of Walnut Canyon and the Anasazi of Canyon de Chelly. The Ácoma people, just east of Albuquerque, speak a Keresan language and trace their ancestry to Anasazi of Mesa Verde in Colorado.

■ MESA VERDE

The entrance to Mesa Verde lies 10 miles east of Cortez, Colorado, and includes some of the most enthralling ruins of an ancient civilization to be seen anywhere in the world. Beyond the visitors center at the entrance, it's an uninterrupted drive through piñon-covered hills and mesas where long ago (and almost unbelievably) corn, beans, and squash were grown. No streams are now visible, nor are there any remnants of irrigation works. In the mesa area, you will see numerous half-ruined pit houses and other structures that belonged to ancestors of the later cliff-dwelling Anasazi, whose dwellings lie deeper into the park.

Given the length and desolation of the ensuing miles, it seems likely that the Anasazi chose this spot to live in for purposes of defense or because it was easy to hide in. Potential enemies certainly would have found it difficult to wage war on such a remote people. Yet these Anasazi were a part of a vast network of similar sites and traded all over the Four Corners area.

After the site was abandoned about 1300, these buildings sat unnoted and unused for centuries. The wandering Utes—who may have raided these areas before the demise of the Anasazi—later decided these rock cities were best avoided. After

AN ANCIENT TRADITION IN POTTERY

Pottery makers of the Southwest have been experimenting with clays, slips, and forms, both useful and decorative, for about 1500 years. Designs common in the pots shown below are still part of the pottery tradition today.

HOHOKAM POT

This sacaton red-on-buff style pot was found at Casa Grande National Monument in Arizona. Its sloping shoulders make it typical of this period of pottery-making among the Hohokam people. A.D. 1100.

ANASAZI POT AND BOWL

Found at Canyon de Chelly in Arizona, the cooking pot to the right was made for everyday use by the Kayenta Anasazi. The corrugations are made by pinching coils of clay. The black-on-white bowl below was found at Mesa Verde in southwestern Colorado. It measures more than 13 inches in diameter. The Mesa Verde region was a major center of pottery manufacture. A.D. 500–1300.

SINAGUA BOWL

The redware bowl to the right was made by the paddle and anvil technique and was found near Flagstaff, Arizona. The Sinagua culture, whose name means "without water," flourished between A.D. 500–1450.

SALADO JAR WITH HANDLE

An unusual pottery type, found in the vicinity of Roosevelt Dam in central Arizona. Its linear design was applied after the piece was polished. A.D. 1150–1450.

EASTERN PUEBLO POT

This glazed pot was made in an Anasazi pueblo in the Rio Grande Valley in New Mexico between A.D. 1425 and 1475. It was probably used for storing food or water.

(all photographs by George H. H. Huey)

that no one thought much about the ruins at Mesa Verde for a long, long time. Then, in the winter of 1888, two cowboys out looking for stray cows suddenly stopped in their tracks in a state of shock. What Richard Wetherill and Charlie Mason had caught sight of was an intact, abandoned stone city fit for hundreds of inhabitants. It's not recorded whether they found the cows, but there is a record of what they did find: the **Cliff Palace,** a complex of about 200 individual homes, 23 underground ceremonial *kivas,* and towers rising as high as four stories.

The world came to see what the cowboys had found, with every new visitor seeming to come away with something, be it a stone or pottery shard, from the surrounding area's estimated 800 cliff dwellings. Congress finally took action in 1906 to stop the random looting and created Mesa Verde National Park, the first national park designed to preserve archaeological treasures.

Built from A.D. 1100 to 1278 and then abandoned almost as soon as they were completed, the cliff dwellings still stun and mystify. Tucked underneath huge overhangs, some of the stone-crafted dwellings, such as Cliff Palace, could

The first photograph ever taken of Mesa Verde by William H. Jackson in 1874 shows famed frontiersman John Moss standing at left. Had they ventured to the side canyons they would have been the first white men to stumble upon Cliff Palace.

accommodate up to 400 people. The masonry walls were not just rocks and mortar slapped together, but were crafted with care, plastered, and in some cases decorated. The fact that many of these buildings are still standing 700 years later is testimony to the masons' skill.

The entrance, where you can pick up information on the park's ruins and accommodations, is located 10 miles east of Cortez on US 160; (970) 529-4465. From here the ruins are 21 miles south; some ruins are open only in summer. Two main areas are Wetherill Mesa and Chapin Mesa. The latter includes Cliff Palace and a museum describing Anasazi life. The Far View Visitor Center, a 15-mile drive from the entrance, provides background information and directions, and is the only place nearby to buy food; (970) 529-4543.

Hovenweep. This extraordinary Anasazi site lies due west of Cortez—much of it just over the Utah border. It is described in this chapter on page 181.

❖

Nearby Towns. The closest towns to Mesa Verde are Cortez, Dolores, and Durango. **Cortez** has become a repository of current Southwest Indian art and culture, thanks to its several arts and crafts galleries featuring work from Ute, Navajo, Apache, and other Native American artisans. The **Crow Canyon Archaeological Center** just outside Cortez, specializes in lectures and tours of current archeological digs. *Four and a half miles northwest of Cortez; (970) 565-8975.*

Nearby, in the small town of **Dolores**, the **Anasazi Heritage Center** houses educational and participatory exhibits. It is also the storehouse for two million artifacts that would have, without some arm-twisting, been drowned by the McPhee Reservoir, farther north. *(970) 882-4811.*

Less than an hour's drive east of Mesa Verde off US 160 is the quaint Western town of **Durango.** Born into existence with arrival of the Denver and Rio Grande Western Railroad, Durango was a booming rail hub for 70 years and was dubbed the "Queen City of the West." Today the town is an inviting combination of turn-of-the-century architecture and a broad selection of modern and restored Victorian hotels and restaurants.

The restored **Durango & Silverton Narrrow Gauge Railroad,** an authentic steam-powered locomotive, makes daily runs along the Animas River between April and October. *479 Main Street; (970) 247-2733 or (888) 872-4607.*

■ UTE MOUNTAIN INDIAN RESERVATION

South of Cortez off US 160/666 lies the Ute Mountain Indian Reservation where the land is barren and dry, with just a sprinkling of native shrubs and bushes. A Shoshonean people, the Utes were first described by Europeans in the diary of Father Silvestre Vélez de Escalante, when he crossed into Utah on an exploratory expedition in 1776. By the early 19th century, the Utes had acquired horses and became known as expert horsemen, hunters, and raiders of livestock.

Physically, the Utes are a stocky, powerfully built people with dark, bronze-colored skin. Historically, they moved their camps into the high country for summer hunting, but retreated to lower elevations to wait out winters.

The Utes "knew" the bear and how to coax him from hibernation with the Bear Dance that signalled the beginning of spring. The Sun Dance, initiated in the middle of summer, was to ensure good hunting.

The Utes were known as a playful people, and many of their dances—the Circle Dance, Coyote Dance, Tea Dance—were strictly social in nature. Social, but more serious, were the melodies from handmade flutes that a man used to court his true love. All sorts of games occupied idle time, including stick dice, archery, ring spearing, juggling, wrestling, and foot races. Horse racing was without question their most popular sport. The Utes were (and are) also known for their beadwork, valued for its intricacy, exceptional use of color, and refinement.

Today, the most substantial town on the reservation is **Towaoc**, nestled against the hills off the highway. Towaoc's **Ute Mountain Tribal Park** has a pottery showroom, and guides offer tours to a number of extraordinary Anasazi dwellings. *Located on US 160/666, 15 miles south of Cortez; (970) 565-3751.*

Despite the establishment of Ute cultural centers, the national park and historic sites, and the preservation actions taking place from Cortez to Ignacio, the federal government maintains what can diplomatically be described as an uneasy relationship with the Indians here. Water rights have long been an acrimonious issue.

■ NAVAJO RESERVATION

Of all the Indian tribes in the United States, the Navajo are the most populous. The Spanish estimated their population at about 9,000 in the 1700s, and today it is close to 350,000. Their reservation (they prefer the term "Navajo Nation") sprawls over 18 million acres—vast acres of New Mexico, Arizona, and Utah. Like

Flute playing was an important Ute courting ritual. (Center of Southwest Studies, Fort Lewis College, Durango, Colorado)

their neighbors, the Hopis, the Navajo have been able to retain much of their ancestral land and therefore maintain some of their old ways of life. Their traditional octagonal mud-and-log hogans are scattered throughout the reservation, although today most Navajo live in modern, government-issue housing.

The Navajo crossed into North America with the last great migration across the ice bridge roughly 2,000 years ago. Speakers of an Athapaskan language, they brought with them the sinew-backed Mongolian bow and the moccasin. Between the 14th and 16th centuries, the Navajo reached what they call Dinétah, their legendary homeland near the headwaters of the San Juan River in New Mexico.

The Navajo were an aggressive nomadic people, hunters who traded with and harassed village-dwelling Puebloan people, including the Hopi, whose own reservation is contained uneasily within the Navajo. With the arrival of the Utes, the Navajo were pushed out of Dinétah.

From the Spanish the Navajo acquired sheep and goats, and they took naturally to a pastoral life as herdsmen. They are famous for their craftsmanship, in particular their rugs and their silver and turquoise jewelry. Today the tribe operates logging operations and a huge power plant, whose chimneys can be seen belching smoke into the desert horizon north of Flagstaff.

The Navajo language is a tonal language, and pitch helps distinguish words. Animate nouns are either "speakers" (humans) or "callers" (plants and animals); and inanimate nouns may be corporeal or spiritual. Because Navajo names have power and it is not always correct to use them, the language utilizes a grammatical fourth person that allows a speaker to speak politely with someone nearby without naming that person.

The dusty town of **Shiprock**—on the San Juan River in north-central New Mexico—sits squarely within the Navajo Reservation and is focused more on serving residents than attracting tourists. Navajo tribal lands are patrolled by the Navajo Tribal Police (the same force that employs the fictitious protagonists of Tony Hillerman's detective series: Officer Jim Chee and Lieutenant Joe Leaphorn).

To the southwest of the town of Shiprock, its namesake—a 7,178-foot jagged rock monolith—dominates the semi-desert landscape. Shiprock itself begins as an apparition, fuzzily coming into view. But once you've spotted it, this core of an extinct volcano commands your attention. Navajos call the mystical rock **Tse Bida'hi**

(Rock with Wings) and many tribal legends surround it. As the land around it is owned by the tribe, it is not usually possible to walk up to it.

The wide, placid San Juan River flows east between Shiprock and Farmington, which sits at the edge of the Navajo Reservation. The fertile fields fed by the river suggest the origins of Farmington's name. Small farms and orchards of apple, pear, and peach trees flourish, but it's the vast deposits of coal, oil, and natural gas that have come to dominate the area's economy.

To the Navajo, the area of present-day **Farmington** was known as "To-tah," which means "Among the Waters." Three of the region's major waterways meet three miles apart: the gently flowing Animas River skirts Farmington's eastern edge, then empties into the wide San Juan River south of town. The smaller La Plata enters the San Juan west of town after irrigating fields of hay and corn.

When local residents talk about the pleasures of the Farmington area, they describe an outdoorsman's paradise: great fishing and hiking. The main thoroughfares of Farmington are crowded with small businesses, restaurants, and shops.

■ AZTEC AND SALMON RUINS

Aztec and Salmon ruins lie just outside of the towns of Aztec and Bloomfield, respectively. When they were built, they were outliers of the great Chaco Canyon area to the south and served by the Chaco road network.

The communal dwellings of Aztec Ruins were built on a rise overlooking the blue-green Animas River, and they reveal construction methods similar to those used at Chaco Canyon. (The crumbling walls and rectangular rooms were named by 19th-century settlers who mistakenly assumed the pueblo was built by the Aztec Indians of Mexico.) A walk through the largest pueblo, a U-shaped village that covered two acres and contained 500 rooms in three stories, allows you to look across the decaying walls into a maze of square and rectangular adjoining rooms and to crawl through tiny doorways. You can peer into subterranean *kivas*, built with thousands of soft taupe sandstone slabs. Anchoring the pueblo is the Great *Kiva*, constructed in the 12th century and reconstructed in 1934. The grand underground space was broken only by massive columns that supported a roof estimated at 90 tons. This is the only reconstructed great *kiva* in the Southwest.

Navajo girl Linda Rodriquez atop Hunts Mesa in Monument Valley.

NAVAJO GIRL

Some of the men of Jemez rode out to meet the Navajos. John Cajero was one of them. He was then a man in his prime, a Tanoan man, agile and strong in his mind and body, and he was a first-rate horseman. He was mounted on a good-looking gray quarter horse, which he handled closely and well, and he cut a fine figure upon it in his blue shirt and red headband, his manner easy and confident. He singled out old friends among the Navajos, and soon there was a cluster of riders holding up on the side of the road, convened in a high mood of fellowship and good humor—and a certain rivalry.

❖   ❖   ❖

I was watching him so intently that I did not at first see the girl. She came from nowhere, a lithe, lovely Navajo girl on a black horse. She was coming up fast in John Cajero's dust, faster than he had come, and her horse was holding steady in a long, loping stride, level and low. When I saw her she was already hanging down nearly the whole length of her arm from the saddle horn, her knee cocked and her long back curved like a bow, her shoulders close against the deep chest of the horse; she swung her left arm down like a scythe, and up, holding the dollar bill with the tips of her fingers until it was high over her head, and she was standing straight in the stirrups, and her horse did not break stride. And in that way she rode on, past John Cajero, along the wagon train and into the village, having stolen the show and the money, too, going in beauty, trailing laughter. Later I looked for her among the camps, but I did not find her. I imagined that her name was Desbah Yazzie and that she looked out for me from the shadows.

—N. Scott Momaday, *The Names, a Memoir,* 1976

(following pages) Shiprock looms above the northern New Mexican desert plateau.

Much of this site remains unexcavated under sandy mounds scattered in the shade of cottonwood trees, and no one knows if the mounds cover dwellings or trash heaps.

Salmon Ruins sit atop a bluff overlooking the farmland of the San Juan River valley two miles west of Bloomfield. A well-traveled Chacoan road leads directly north from Chaco Canyon for 50 miles through dusty arroyos and across desert mesas to the C-shaped, 250-room pueblo. Most building materials here were imported: sandstone was quarried at sites 30 miles distant, and timbers used for the *vigas* (roof beams) were hauled from southern Colorado. Nearby petroglyphs depict ears of corn on a stalk, and some archaeologists speculate that the small community was developed as an agricultural center to serve the main Chaco Canyon villages.

Salmon Ruins were named for George Salmon, an 1880s homesteader who protected the site from vandals and thieves. His home still stands nearby.

The pueblos of Aztec and Salmon were abandoned by the mid-12th century, only to be reoccupied in the early 13th century by Indians from the nearby Mesa Verde culture of southwestern Colorado. But they, too, left after the great drought, never to return.

The town of **Aztec** is as misnamed as the ruins; nothing about its tree-shaded streets filled with Victorian brick buildings recalls the ancient Aztec Indians of Mexico. Shops and businesses along Main Street have retained an early 20th-century Midwestern appearance, and the only modern touches are a few pastel-painted storefronts.

Sidetrip: Fourteen miles east on NM 173 is **Navajo Dam,** and nearby, fine fishing in the clear, cold, blue-green waters of the San Juan River. A nearly four-mile stretch, called the Quality Waters, harbors trophy-sized trout.

■ BISTI BADLANDS

South of Farmington off NM 371 lie the Bisti Badlands, 3,968 acres of giant mushroom-shaped spires surrounded by red, green, and bone-white cliffs in the San Juan Basin. The eerie desolation of this wild moonscape is all that remains of what once was a shallow sea bordered by swamps and forests and inhabited by dinosaurs. Eons of wind and water have carved the sandstone and shale formations. The Bisti, along with the nearby De-na-zin area, are rich in fossils, left behind from the days 75 million years ago when duckbill and horned dinosaurs sloshed along the seashore. Huge conifers towered above a jungle of ferns and palms. Salamanders, snails, worms, sharks, and crocodiles choked the waterways.

Today, snakes and lizards scurry across rocks devoid of vegetation. Unfortunately, billions of tons of coal lie near the surface underneath the Bisti, posing the constant threat that this magical, unspoiled land could be destroyed by open-pit mining.

■ CHACO CANYON

Between A.D. 700 and 1100, a vital culture thrived in Chaco Canyon along the flowing Chaco River and atop high desert mesas. Something of a population explosion occurred during the 11th century, when 13 Great Pueblos were built, some four stories high, with more than 600 rooms. Their masonry walls were of rubble, faced on both sides with a course of small flat stones, and larger stones. Their fortress-like structure suggests they were to keep out prying eyes, or possibly invaders.

Chaco is the most mysterious place in all Anasazi country. The Great Pueblos could have housed as many as 4,000 people, but this cold, arid canyon couldn't have provided enough resources to sustain more than a fraction of that population. Either it was a great ritual center, drawing pilgrimages from a wide region for periodic ceremonies, or it was a kind of city-state, like ancient Sparta or Soviet Moscow, supporting itself by extracting tribute and forced labor from satellite pueblos.

Chaco's astonishing road systems might support either theory. They were almost uniformly 30 feet wide and absolutely straight, powering their way over mesas or through arroyos, even where common sense dictated an easier way around. They connected with outlying pueblos as much as 75 miles away. Why would a people who had no horses or wheels need freeways 30 feet wide? Possibly they served as symbols to remind the outliers of the nucleus of power, or perhaps they had a ceremonial purpose. They might have had a secondary use as trade routes. Seashells, copper bells, and the remains of parrots and macaws prove the Chacoans also had contact with people as far south as Mexico.

The large number of *kivas* found in Chaco's pueblos suggests that Chaco served as a religious center for the numerous outlying villages. Astronomy also played a major role, as evidenced by the placement of small corner windows built into the thick walls at Pueblo Bonito, the largest excavated ruin. A sun priest in charge of planting and harvesting rituals perhaps scheduled those events based on the play of light along an interior wall at the pueblo.

High on Fajada Butte is a Chaco solstice marker which signaled when planting should commence. Two stone slabs were set in such a way that on a solstice or equinox they were penetrated by a shaft of sunlight at an angle that hit two spiral petroglyphs.

By A.D. 1000, Chaco had established itself firmly as the political, economic, and possibly the ceremonial center of the northwestern plateau. Improved farming methods provided abundant food, and these productive people had the leisure to develop their artistic abilities. They etched petroglyphs of snakes and spirals into the soft sandstone, wove baskets and sandals from desert grasses, and fashioned

Pueblo Bonito in Chaco Canyon is the most extensive archaeological monument in the nation.

clay bowls, pitchers, jars, and mugs with detailed black-on-white geometric designs.

The hundreds of ponderosa pine used as roof beams in the construction of Great Pueblos—5,000 at just one—were most likely cut from forests east at least 25 miles away. Inside the canyon, the riparian environment may well have been destroyed by all the cutting, causing the Chaco River to cut a deeper channel. Water was thus more difficult to divert, lowering agricultural productivity at the same time the population was expanding. By 1100, refugees from Chaco were heading north to live at Aztec, the largest pueblo being built there in 1100. Other Chaco refugees went on to Mesa Verde on Wupatki.

Within a hundred years the once-flowing river was dry and ran only after summer rainstorms. The fields of corn and beans had been overtaken by desert grasses and sagebrush, and the voices of a vibrant culture were silent.

Today, the ruins are preserved in Chaco Canyon National Historical Park. Extensive rock ruins blend with towering sandstone cliff faces that provided the

The interior of a kiva. This one is the Great Kiva of the Aztec ruins, located north and west of Farmington.

ancient masons with their building materials. Along the banks of the bone-dry riverbed, partial walls appear rust red against an azure sky, steel gray under a blanket of clouds, or dull umber when covered with snow.

At **Pueblo Bonito**, Anasazi masons shaped thousands of rocks of all sizes with crude stone hammers and axes in the construction of more than 600 rooms and 40 *kivas*. The varying construction techniques reflect the order in which these carefully crafted walls were built. For example, the oldest walls were one stone thick with generous applications of mud mortar. Later walls had thick inner cores of rubble topped off by a veneer of stonework so precisely fitted that little mortar was needed. Stone bases remain that once steadied masonry pillars supporting heavily beamed roofs at the fourth story.

Across the dry wash from Pueblo Bonito is the **giant *kiva* of Casa Rinconada**, which was built apart from other communities, indicating that it was possibly used as some sort of ceremonial center. A smooth stone bench that traces the inner wall is a perfect place to rest and listen to the silence, broken only by occasional gusts of wind. The musty smell of sandstone mingles with imagined memories of the many ceremonies that must have taken place here at one of the largest "great *kivas*" in the Southwest.

Behind Pueblo Bonito, **Pueblo Alto** sits atop a mesa. Its location at the junction of several prehistoric roads suggests it served as a trade and distribution center.

The drive to Chaco can be quite a challenge. Two gravel roads lead to the park —one from I-40 to the south and another from NM 44 to the northwest, either way means a 45-minute drive on fairly rough terrain. The only accommodation is a campground. Tours are offered daily, and pamphlets for the self-initiating also are available at each of eight restored ruins that stretch for a few miles alongside Chaco Wash. Well-marked hiking trails lead to additional ruins such as Pueblo Alto, Peñasco Blanco, and the symmetrical village of Wijiji. Check with the visitors center before setting out; bad weather or a sudden storm can render roads impassable without a four-wheel-drive vehicle, and there are no supplies or food available within the park. (505) 786-7014.

■ SOUTH AND WEST OF CHACO

South of Chaco Canyon—by a backcountry route that necessitates an excellent map—lie Window Rock, Ganado, Chinle, and Canyon de Chelly. Directly west of Gallup, on I-40, lie the Petrified Forest and the Painted Desert and beyond that, Flagstaff, Arizona (187 miles west of Gallup). These latter two are described in "CENTRAL ARIZONA" on pages 259 and 264.

■ WINDOW ROCK TO CHINLE

Window Rock, just northwest of Gallup, is the capital of the Navajo Nation. Named for the rock formation that dominates the landscape, Window Rock is home to tribal government offices as well as the Tribal Arts and Crafts Center and the Navajo Tribal Museum. Both offer examples of fine Navajo rugs and demonstrations of how they're made.

A better stop is 20 miles west at Ganado, where the historic **Hubbell Trading Post National Historic Site** has dealt in first-rate Navajo weavings since 1878. In fact, it was trader John Lorenzo Hubbell who helped the Navajo turn weaving into their signature art form and most lucrative industry by advertising their rugs in catalogs in the eastern states. Rugs from Hubbell were known as Ganado-style rugs, typically black, white, and grey designs on a red background. Warning: Good Navajo rugs are expensive. Hispanic weavers in northern New Mexico towns such as Chimayó produce woolen rugs that are just as beautiful at a fraction of the cost. *Located on AZ 264, one mile west of Ganado.*

❖

A few miles west of Ganado you can pick up US 191 and head north for 33 miles to Chinle, gateway to Canyon de Chelly.

Chinle, a town of 3,400 people in the high desert Navajo badlands, is a modest, even bleak town. A scruffy huddle of government-issue houses and utilitarian stores line the highway. The natural spectacle yawning at the back door of Chinle is Canyon de Chelly, a three-pronged gash in the earth whose sculptured sandstone walls and soft, ruddy coloring rival the Grand Canyon in mesmerizing beauty.

■ CANYON DE CHELLY

Canyon de Chelly (pronounced "d' Shay") earned its pseudo-Spanish name from the inability of early 19th-century Spaniards to pronounce the Navajo word *tsegi,* which means "rock canyon."

There actually are several adjoining canyons here, with the largest tributary, Canyon del Muerto, stretching nearly as long as Canyon de Chelly's 27 miles. While the greatest depth is only about 1,000 feet, the walls themselves form an astonishing spectacle. Generally even steeper and more sheer than the Grand Canyon's walls, some appear to have eroded in layers, like a flaking biscuit, while others look as though they were sliced by a 600-foot knife. One remarkable

NAVAJO RUGS

The designs used in Navajo rugs were largely developed towards the end of the 19th century when traders encouraged the Indians to produce blankets to sell to tourists arriving on the railroad. Consequently, certain designs have come to be associated with the trading posts that supplied them. Following is a brief outline of some of the more distinct examples of these traditional designs.

CHINLE

Named after the town of Chinle in Arizona. These patterns feature designs such as squash blossoms (pictured) within bands of plain color. (Woven by Evelyn Curley)

TWO GREY HILLS

Named after a village in New Mexico. Usually woven from very fine, natural, handspun wool in white, black, and brown colors with a dark border. (Woven by Maraline John)

GANADO

Named for the town where the Hubbell Trading Post is located. Almost always has a red background and dark border. Considered by many as the classic Navajo rug design because of its long history. (Woven by Evelyn Curley)

BURNTWATER

Named after an area south of Ganado. Features earth tones, a large variety of pastel colors, and complex border designs.
(Woven by Brenda Spencer)

CRYSTAL

Named after a trading post in New Mexico. Noted for the wavy lines within the bands produced by alternating colors of weft strands. This example features patterned squash blossoms similar to the Chinle. (Woven by Fannie Begay)

(all photographs by George H. H. Huey)

A Navajo wanders through Canyon de Chelly in this photo from the 1890s.
(Underwood Archives, San Francisco)

feature is Spider Rock, a needle-like sandstone monolith shooting 800 feet out of the canyon floor. In autumn, particularly, Canyon de Chelly is a festival of color, with the auburn walls playing off the lime-green and golden cottonwoods along the river at the bottom.

Humans have occupied Canyon de Chelly for almost 2,000 years. The Anasazi left some 400 ruins, beginning with primitive pit houses and ending with the construction of a three-story masonry highrise around A.D. 1284. Between the time the Anasazi left Canyon de Chelly and the Navajo claimed it, about 400 years elapsed. Small groups of Hopis lived here during that time. One planted the first peach orchards in the canyon, trees that still bear fruit.

The Anasazi and later the Hopi left thousands of paintings on the canyon walls, and when their Navajo successors began to move into the canyon in the mid-1700s, they added their pictorial stories. One Navajo canyon painting depicts the Spanish military expedition of Antonio Narbona in 1804-05, and behind it lies a tragic story.

On a chilly January morning in 1805, Narbona and his men discovered more than a hundred Navajos hiding in a remote cave 600 feet above the canyon floor. Narbona later claimed that after a battle "with the greatest ardor and effort," his valiant troops killed "90 warriors" along with a few women and children holed up in the cave, but Navajo oral history holds that the victims were all women, children, and old men. The Navajo version has more of the resonance of truth: the first Spaniard to climb to the cave that day was attacked by a woman defender armed with a knife. The massacre gave Canyon del Muerto its haunting Spanish name: it means "Canyon of the Dead."

Canyon de Chelly became a national monument in 1931, although the Navajo, who still farm the canyon floors, restrict access to much of it.

Near the entrance to the canyon (follow signs) is the venerable **Thunderbird Lodge**, a Southwest-style hostelry with charm and character from which jeep tours, led by knowledgeable Navajo guides, leave daily and are worth the expense. Both half- and full-day tours lead you into Canyon de Chelly and Canyon del Muerto. In the cooler months remember to take a jacket, as the canyon can be freezing cold on a very sunny day. *Call Thunderbird Lodge at (520) 674-5841.*

You may also pick up maps and directions, and sign up for ranger-led tours (summers only) or guided hikes at the visitors center on the mesa rim near the entrance. *Call Canyon de Chelly Visitor Center at (520) 674-5500.*

You may drive around the north and south rim to overlooks that gaze down thousand-foot red cliffs, to cottonwood trees, a stream winding in a swath of sand, a few farms, and Navajo hogans. Today about 30 Navajo families still live in the canyon in summer.

South Rim Drive begins at the visitors center, passes White House Overlook and ends at Spider Rock Overlook. **North Rim Drive** also begins at the visitors' center, then follows Canyon del Muerto, and ends at Massacre Cave Overlook where 115 Navajo were killed by Narbona's party. One trail winds down to the White House Ruin.

■ BETATAKIN AND KEET SEEL

Northwest of Chinle toward the Utah border lies spectacular countryside that encompasses eerie rock formations, mesas, and distant mountain ranges. The separate units of **Navajo National Monument** lie near the small town of Kayenta.

Betatakin and Keet Seel were both built by Anasazi in deep sheltering alcoves in

The Hubbell Trading Post, located just west of Ganado, has been selling fine Navajo weavings since it opened in 1878.

the walls of Tsegi Canyon. Betatakin is a three-hour hike in and out, led by a park ranger, and limited to 60 people a day (first come, first served). Keet Seel is a 16-mile round trip best taken on horseback; the hike is a grueling march through soft, wet sand.

Betatakin is open from the beginning of May to the end of September; Keet Seel from Memorial Day through Labor Day. Reservations for Keet Seel are essential and must be made one to two months in advance. Navajo National Monument, (520) 672-2366. If you take only the half-day Betatakin tour, return to Kayenta in the afternoon, then take US 163 19 miles north to Monument Valley. See page 180.

■ HOPI RESERVATION

The Hopi Reservation is completely surrounded by the Navajo Nation, an uneasy living arrangement born of ancient rivalries and U.S. government interference. The 10,000 people who make up the Hopi nation are culturally related to the Pueblo people of New Mexico, and their rituals and art reflect those ties. Contemporary Hopi pottery and kachina dolls are refined works of art.

Hopi life, religion, and society are organized around an all-encompassing

The much photographed Teardrop Arch at the northern end of Monument Valley is not easily accessible. The only way to reach it is with a Navajo guide and a four-wheel-drive vehicle.

belief system called *Hopivotskwani,* the Hopi Path of Life. According to legend, it began when the first ancestors of the Hopi emerged from the spirit underworld to wander until they arrived at the arid mesas that would become their home. The Bear Clan, so called because they found a dead bear during their pilgrimage, settled at Shungopovi, in northeastern Arizona. As other groups arrived, they were given land to farm and accepted into Hopi society once they could demonstrate their acceptance of Hopivotskwani.

The concept of the Hopi Path is extremely difficult for an outsider to grasp, but it has to do with the presence of the spirit world in virtually everything. Every plant and animal has a spirit; every summer thunderstorm is generated in the spirit universe—those storms being critical to Hopi farming. Every winter solstice marks the beginning of ceremonial kachina dancing, which continues until mid-July. The kachinas, which appear to outsiders to be men dressed in elaborate and astounding costumes, are in Hopi belief the spirits of departed ancestors. They sing songs of admonition and perfected life, and they take the Hopis' prayers for rain, health, and fertility back to the spirit world.

Not surprisingly, many ceremonies center on the need for rain. Most astonishing is the snake dance, in which Hopi priests carry live snakes—including rattlesnakes—in their mouths.

For hundreds of years the Hopis have lived on three mesas that rise above a wide valley. A road runs through the valley, where a scattering of schools, churches, and government issue housing stand. Above them on the three mesas are the ancient Hopi villages. Hopis are at best ambivalent about tourism; some of their villages do not welcome visitors, and those that do generally ask outsiders to register at the local community office.

First Mesa. A narrow, gravel road leads up to First Mesa from the more modern town of Polacca. On top, the view is sweeping. Some sections of the stone and adobe houses may predate the arrival of Columbus by 300 years. Of the three small, interconnected villages on top, the first is **Hano,** a Tewa settlement, formed in 1696 by Tewa Indians from the Rio Grande region who had fled from the Spanish. The Hopi let them live here on the condition they guard access to the mesa top. Amazingly, the Tewa have maintained their own customs and language despite centuries of Hopi influence. The most famous Hopi reservation pottery family, the Nampeyo, is from the Hano settlement. The first of these potters, known simply as Nampeyo, was born here about 1860. Her designs were influenced by prehistoric pottery found by her husband, Lesou, at a nearby archeological dig in 1895. Their descendants carry on the tradition they began, using clay taken from an ancient and proprietary Hopi source, and painting designs with a yucca spine brush.

Adjacent to Hano is the village of **Sichomovi**, where visitors will find **First Mesa Visitor Center at Ponsi Hall**. It is necessary to park here and register for a guided walking tour. At tiny **Walpi**, ancient houses and old defenses jut out from the rocky cliffs, forming a dramatic contrast of stone against the surrouding expanse of sky. *Take AZ 264 west of US 191 through the Navajo Reservation and past Keams Canyon. Visitor Center telephone is (520) 737-2262.*

Second Mesa. Of the three mesas, Second Mesa is the most amenable to visitors. Below the mesa on the western edge, a complex of buildings, including a restaurant and motel, connect with the **Hopi Cultural Center**. The center's museum has fascinating exhibits of Hopi history culture. A second cafe, Nova-ki, is also located here. The mesa's three villages are **Shipaulovi, Mishongnovi, and Shunopavi.** *AZ 264 and AZ 87 join below Second Mesa. Cultural Center, (520) 734-2401.*

Third Mesa. One mile south of AZ 264, at the eastern base of Third Mesa, stands the village **Kykotsmovi**, which means "Mound of Ruined Houses." **The Office of Public Relations** is here, along with the **Kykotsmovi Village Store**—stocked with groceries—and a few arts and crafts stores.

Two miles west of Kykotsmovi, **Old Oraibi** is perched on the edge of Third Mesa. Inhabited since A.D. 1150, Old Oraibi is considered by many to be the oldest continually inhabited community in the United States. (Ácoma also vies for the title). In 1900, the population neared 800, but six years later a widely publicized dissension caused many to leave. To settle a dispute between two chiefs, Youke-oma and Tawa-quap-tewa, the two village leaders staged a "push-of-war" contest where the two groups stood on either side of a line cut into a mesa. They pushed each other until one group lost. You-ke-oma and his faction left to establish **Hotevilla**, about four miles away. Both villages welcome visitors and are known for their basketry and other crafts. The residents of **Bacavi**, situated across the highway, are also descendents of Oraibi's former inhabitants.

■ MONUMENT VALLEY

Monument Valley, a Navajo tribal park, straddles the Arizona-Utah border a few miles north of the town of Kayenta. Described by some as the "Eighth Wonder of the Natural World," it is one of the most beautiful and awe-inspiring desert landscapes on earth. Visitors generally drive the 17-mile unpaved loop drive through Monument Valley, but some of the valley's most fascinating and eerie sandstone totems lie well away from the road. The Navajo strictly forbid hiking, rock climbing, and off-road driving. Guided tours with more intimate photo opportunities may be booked at the visitors center.

In the south end of the park, **Mystery Valley** has several hundred Anasazi dwellings, most of them small and unnamed. Visitors must hire guides to explore this section. *Monument Valley Visitor Center is 3¹/₂ miles south and east of US 163 and about 24 miles north of Kayenta; (435) 727-3353.*

A trading post, motel, and gift shop are located at **Goulding's Lodge and Trading Post** two miles west of the US 163 turnoff for the park.

Only 30 miles to the north of Monument Valley, **Valley of the Gods** is a similar cluster of enormous spires and buttes and can be visited without restrictions.

On the way north stop at the Muley Point overlook to see the **Goosenecks of the San Juan,** one of the grand scenes of the West. The river curves back and forth so tightly that six miles of tortuous bending back and forth advances only one and a half miles as the crow flies. *To reach the overlook at Goosenecks turn west from US 163 onto UT 261, four miles north of the small community of Mexican Hat, then turn left onto UT 316 and proceed four miles to the vista point.*

Sidetrip: Fine examples of Indian jewelry and blankets can be seen and purchased from stores like **Hatch Trading Post** (also handy for groceries) on the way from Monument Valley to Hovenweep National Monument (via AZ 163 and UT 262), and **Montezuma Creek Trading Post,** just east of Bluff, Utah. **Ismay Trading Post** is 14 miles southeast of Hovenweep in Colorado. Some people set up roadside stands in this area to sell their wares. If prices are high, don't be surprised. It takes a very long time to produce what is often truly a work of art.

(previous pages) Monument Valley is one of the world's most scenic and spectacular wonders.

■ HOVENWEEP NATIONAL MONUMENT

Hovenweep is a Ute word meaning Deserted Valley, an apt name for this remote and hauntingly beautiful spot. It is a curiosity in the Anasazi world because of its distinctive towers perched on the edges of canyons. Six separate, ruined settlements are found here.

The Hovenweep area was inhabited for 350 years before it was abandoned, about the time that Mesa Verde, 100 miles to the west, fell silent as well. The culture had much in common with Mesa Verde; perhaps they were migrants, maybe even outcasts. They lived in scattered villages, where they cultivated corn, beans, squash, and melons. From studying tree rings, it has been determined that by A.D. 1200, annual rainfall had decreased substantially. The outlying farm villages were abandoned and new ones rebuilt near canyons with permanent springs. The style of the towers and the location of the dwellings in the cliffs suggest the inhabitants of Hovenweep may also have been preparing for attack by other Anasazi clans or Shoshone raiders looking for food and water. Each tower contained only one small doorway protected by a parapet, and most towers also have peepholes pointing outward, away from the canyon.

Archaeologists have offered another theory concerning the use of the towers. At least three sites at the monument, including the major ruin, Square Tower, may have been used as observatory sites. Certain windows in the towers are situated in such a way that sunlight enters only during the summer and winter solstices and the autumn and vernal equinoxes, striking particular points marked on the interior walls. *Hovenweep is located in Utah near the Colorado border. It is south of Blanding and northeast of Bluff off US 191 on UT 262. The ruins are always open. Access to the monument is on unpaved roads generally passable by passenger cars, but tricky to navigate when it rains. Hovenweep is administered by Mesa Verde National Park in Colorado; (970) 529-4465.*

■ FOUR CORNERS MONUMENT

Directly south of Hovenweep is the Four Corners Monument. If ever there was a big nothing, this is it: a parking lot surrounding the spot where Utah, Colorado, New Mexico, and Arizona meet. But big nothing or not, lots of people come here, and stand on all fours, spread eagled, in order to claim the dubious but amusing distinction of being in four states simultaneously. *Follow sign off US 160 where the four states meet.*

■ FOOD & LODGING

> *Restaurant prices:*
> Per person, not including drinks, tax, and tips:
> $ = under $10; $$ = $10–20; $$$ = over $20
>
> *Room rates:*
> Per night, per room, double occupancy:
> $ = under $50; $$ = $50–100; $$$ = over $100

Aztec, NM

population 5,479   elevation 5,686

- **Miss Gail's Inn.** 300 S. Main; (505) 334-3452 $$
  Eight rooms in a 90-year-old B&B, each decorated in unique style.
- **Step Back Inn.** 103 W. Aztec; (505) 334-1200 $$
  In tribute to the families who settled the town in the late 19th century, this 40-room inn is filled with pioneer photographs and histories. Modern amenities (television, hairdryers) are here too.

Blanding, UT

population 3,160   elevation 6,105

- **Elk Ridge Restaurant.** 123 E. Center; (435) 678-3390 $
  Open daily for breakfast, lunch, and dinner. The menu offers a variety of American and Mexican dishes.
- **Best Western Gateway Motel.** 88 E. Center; (435) 678-2278 $$
  Clean and comfortable motel with pool. Indian jewelry sold here.

- **Grayson County Inn.** 118 E. 300 South; (435) 678-2388 $$
  Private baths and lovely antiques in each of seven guest rooms, some with kitchenettes. Full country breakfast includes pancakes, granola, fresh eggs.
- **Hovenweep Campground.** Approached via UT 262, one mile from US 160 West to C. Road then 40 miles to campground. (970) 749-0510
  Located one mile from Hovenweep National Monument Visitor Center, these campsites have water and restrooms.

Chinle, AZ (Canyon de Chelly)

population 5,060   elevation 5,058

- **Junction Restaurant.** Next to Best Western. A block east of US 191 on Navajo Rte 7; (520) 674-8443 $$
  Hot sandwiches and Navajo entrees.
- **Thunderbird Restaurant.** Inside the Thunderbird Lodge, just southeast of Canyon de Chelly National Monument Visitors Center; (520) 674-5841 $-$$
  Cafeteria-style with a predictable menu—salads, sandwiches, steaks.

Four Corners Food & Lodging

⌑ **Best Western Canyon de Chelly Inn**
One block east of US 191 on Route 7;
(520) 674-5875 $$
There are 102 rooms, with standard
motel furnishings, and the only swim-
ming pool in Chinle.

⌑ **Thunderbird Lodge.** 1/4 mile southeast
of Canyon de Chelly National Monu-
ment Visitor Center; (520) 674-5841
$$-$$$
Adobe-style rooms decorated with
Native American and Southwest fea-
tures. Gift shop.

Durango, CO

population 12,400   elevation 6,523

✗ **Ariano's Italian Restaurant.** 150 E.
College Dr.; (970) 247-8146 $$-$$$
Northern Italian cuisine. Homemade
pastas and the chef's special veal. For a
less formal affair try the sister restaurant
next door, **Pronto Pizza & Pasta.**

✗ **Carver's Bakery/Brewery.** 1022 Main
Ave.; (970) 259-2545 $
This meeting place for locals is particu-
larly busy at breakfast and lunch. It's
also open for dinner when a nightly
special (e.g. fajitas) is added to the usual
options: burritos, enchiladas, soups,
and stews.

✗ **Durango Diner.** 957 Main Ave.;
(970) 247-9889 $
This hole-in-the-wall diner is best
known for its spicy green chile.

✗ **Edgewater Grill.** Located in the Dou-
bletree Hotel, 501 Camino del Rio;
(970) 259-6580 $-$$
On the banks of the Animas River, of-

fering simple breakfast and lunch fare
on the patio; more elaborate dinners
and a Sunday brunch.

✗ **Gazpacho.** 431 E. Second Ave.; (970)
259-9494 $
A lively crowd gathers here for traditional New Mexican cooking (heavy on
the green chiles), sensational sopaipillas, and the best margaritas in town.

✗ **Griego's.** 2603 N. Main Ave.; (970)
259-3558 $
A drive-in Mexican restaurant in an old
A&W with good food and sweat-
producing green chile.

✗ **Henry's at the Strater Hotel.** 699 Main
Ave.; (970) 247-4431 $-$$
Breakfast and dinner in a Victorian-
style historic hotel *(see below).* Summertime specials include all-you-can-eat
prime rib buffet.

✗ **Mama's Boy.** 36th and Main St.;
(970) 247-0060 $
Italian fare: New York pizza, calzones,
heros, pasta, and hard-to-find Italian
beers.

⌑ **Jarvis Suite Hotel.** 125 W. 10th St.;
(970) 259-6190 or (800) 824-1024 $$
A 19th-century theater converted into a
set of suites and rooms complete with
kitchens and baths and combo rates
that include either train tickets or lift
tickets. Recently refurbished.

⌑ **Strater Hotel.** 699 Main Ave.; (970)
259-5373 $$-$$$
Will Rogers, JFK, and Louis L'Amour
have all stayed at this Victorian, origi-
nally built in 1887. The lobby, guest
rooms, and saloon exude old-fashioned
elegance: crystal chandeliers, brass
lamps, and walnut antiques.

Farmington, NM

population 34,000 elevation 5,395

X **K. B. Dillon's.** 101 W. Broadway; (505) 325-0222 $$-$$$
Steaks and seafood in dimly lit setting.

🛏 **Best Western Farmington Inn.** 700 Scott Ave.; (505) 327-5221 or (800) 528-1234 $$
Centrally located, near restaurants and downtown shopping district.

🛏 **Holiday Inn.** 600 E. Broadway; (505) 327-9811 or (800) HOLIDAY $$
Fitness center, outdoor heated pool, and sports lounge are amenities at this comfortable motel.

🛏 **Anasazi Inn.** 903 W. Main; (505) 325-4564 $$
Pastels of the desert adorn this quiet roadside motel on the western edge of town.

Flagstaff, AZ

See Central Arizona Food & Lodging *on page 273*

Hopi Reservation (Second Mesa)

X **K.D.s Diner.** On AZ 264, Second Mesa; (520) 737-2525 $
A simple eatery specializing in burgers, Mexican entrees, and hot entrees.

X **Tunosvongya Restaurant.** On AZ 264, Second Mesa; (520) 734-2401 $
This Hopi Cultural Center restaurant serves traditional Native American dishes such as Hopi blue-corn pancakes, fry bread, Indian tacos, and *nok qui vi* (lamb stew).

🛏 **Hopi Cultural Center Motel.** On AZ 264, Second Mesa; (520) 734-2401 $$
A pleasant pueblo-style motel set high atop a Hopi mesa. The immaculate rooms are decorated in soothing shades and Native American touches.

Kayenta, AZ

population 4,400   elevation 5,641

X **Amigo Cafe.** US 160 at US 163; (520) 697-8448 $
For all its other attractions, it's almost impossible to find a good meal on the Navajo Reservation. Richard and Esther Martínez's unassuming little cafe is, well, the place. All the Mexican food is good, particularly the steak picado (chopped beef sauteed with green chile), and the salsa was, at last taste, the hottest in Arizona.

🛏 ⚘ **Goulding's Lodge and Trading Post.** Two miles west of US 163 turnoff for Monument Valley; (435) 727-3231 $$-$$$
Just north of the Utah-Arizona border, this trading post consists of a motel, campground, restuarant, museum, grocery store, and gift shop. Stunning views of Monument Valley.

🛏 **Wetherill Inn.** P.O. Box 175, US 163; (520) 697-3231 $$
Pleasant 54-room motel in town. Native American gift shop.

Four Corners Food & Lodging

UTAH CANYONLANDS

■ HIGHLIGHTS

Zion National Park
Cedar Breaks
Bryce Canyon
Paria Wilderness
Escalante
Capitol Reef
Arches
Bridges
Canyonlands
Glen Canyon
Lake Powell

■ LANDSCAPE

The Colorado Plateau dominates southern Utah and affords some of the most spectacular scenery anywhere in the world. This is a sparsely vegetated landscape of plateaux, terra-cotta mesas, deep canyons, gleaming sandstone cliffs, and barren badlands. Most of the impressive sandstone cliffs seen by visitors to Arches, Zion, Capitol Reef, and Canyonlands national parks are solidified sand dunes.

Roaring through this dry magnificence is the Colorado River, which cuts down from the Rocky Mountains, joins with the Green River, and subsides into Lake Powell. At the far end of Lake Powell, beyond Glen Canyon Dam, the river flows placidly to Lee's Ferry, after which the gradient steepens, cliffs soar above the river once more, and the Colorado, resuming its wild nature, begins its plunge through the Grand Canyon. The San Juan River also twists and curves through the far southeastern corner of Utah, before emptying into Lake Powell.

■ TRAVELERS ORIENTATION

This is isolated country, high and wild. There are three small cities in the area, to the west Cedar City and sunny St. George; to the east outdoorsy Moab.

If you wish to visit the backcountry, take the obvious precautions: carry water (twice what you estimate you need), bring along an extra tire, and fill up your gas tank before you take off. The state and national parks and the Bureau of Land Management provide many places to camp and cook out.

Crossing Lake Powell is possible by car ferry between Halls Crossing and Bullfrog marinas. The very southeastern corner of Utah is also described in "Four Corners," page 181.

Food & Lodging appears on page 220.

Virtually all types of climate zones co-exist within the amazingly diverse topography of southern Utah. In general, the bottoms of the valleys and areas of relatively low elevation (under 4,500 feet) such as Canyonlands, Zion National Park, or the town of St. George are hot, sometimes exceedingly hot, and dry most of the year, but they may be comfortably visited anytime between early March and late November. The higher plateaus and canyon rims above 7,000 feet such as those at Bryce Canyon have deep winter snows and bitterly cold temperatures. There summers are short but sweet, and these areas can be visited without winter gear only between mid-May and early October. These two extremes are represented in the climate charts below for Bryce Canyon Airport (elev. 7,600) and Zion (elev. 4,050). Flash floods plague the entire area, caused by sudden thunderstorms dropping enough rain to fill narrow slot canyons to the brim with rushing water. Before venturing into narrow canyons, consult rangers and weather forecasts.

TEMPS (F°)	AVG. JAN. HIGH	LOW	AVG. APRIL HIGH	LOW	AVG. JULY HIGH	LOW	AVG. OCT. HIGH	LOW	RECORD HIGH	RECORD LOW
Bryce Canyon	36	4	54	23	80	44	61	26	92	-30
Canyonlands	42	17	70	39	97	62	72	40	113	-24
Zion	52	29	72	43	99	69	78	49	115	-15

PRECIPITATION (INCHES)	AVG. JAN.	AVG. APRIL	AVG. JULY	AVG. OCT.	ANNUAL	SNOW
Bryce Canyon	0.7	0.6	1.1	1.0	9.5	61
Canyonlands	0.4	0.7	1.2	0.7	9.0	12
Zion	1.6	1.1	1.3	0.9	15.4	15

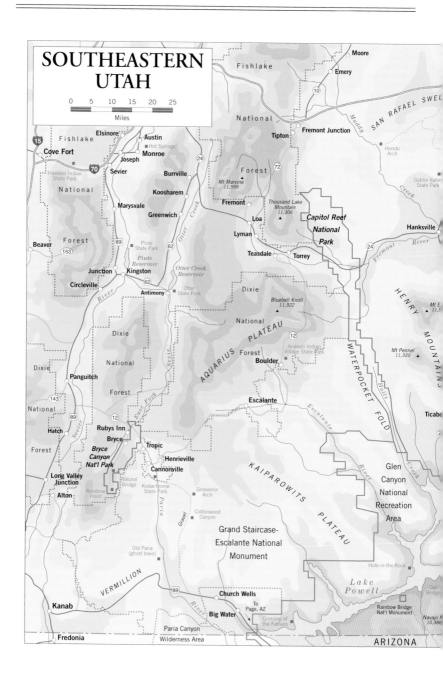

SOUTHEASTERN UTAH

0   5   10   15   20   25
Miles

Moore

Fishlake

Emery

10

Fishlake

San Rafael Swell

Muddy

15 Fishlake

Elsinore   Austin

Cove Fort

National

Tipton   Fremont Junction

Hondu Arch

Hot Springs

Joseph   Monroe

70   Sevier

Fremont Indian State Park

24

Forest

72

Goblin Valley State Park

National   Burrville

Mt Marvine 11,599

Creek

Koosharem

Fremont

Thousand Lake Mountain 11,306

Capitol Reef

Marysvale

Greenwich

Loa

National

Hanksville

Forest

89

Piute State Park

Lyman

Park

24

River

Beaver

153

62

Teasdale   Torrey

Fremont

Piute Reservoir

Otter Creek

Junction   Kingston

Circleville

62

Otter Creek Reservoir

Dixie

Bluebell Knoll 11,322

Henry

Mt E. 11,5

Antimony

Otter State Park

National

12

Mountains

Waterpocket

River

Dixie

Plateau

Anasazi Indian Village State Park

Mt Pennel 11,320

Dixie

National

Aquarius   Forest

Boulder

National   Panguitch

Fold

Ticaba

Forest

143

Escalante

National

Escalante

Hatch   89

12

Rubys Inn

Glen

Forest   Bryce

Tropic

Kaiparowits

Canyon

Long Valley Junction

Bryce Canyon Nat'l Park

Henrieville

Cannonville

Natural Bridge

Kodachrome State Park

Grosvenor Arch

National

Recreation

Alton

Rainbow Point

Paria

Gravel

Cottonwood Canyon

Plateau

Area

Hole-in-the-Rock

Grand Staircase-

Old Paria (ghost town)

Escalante National

Monument

Lake Powell

Owl Bridge

Vermillion

89

Rainbow Bridge Nat'l Monument

Navajo M 10,388

Kanab

Church Wells

To Page, AZ

Big Water

River

Crossing of the Fathers

Fredonia

Paria Canyon

Wilderness Area

ARIZONA

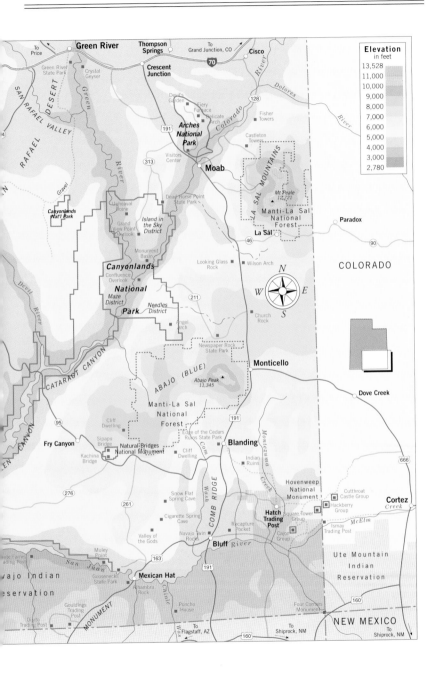

Elevation
in feet

13,528
11,000
10,000
9,000
8,000
7,000
6,000
5,000
4,000
3,000
2,780

■ HISTORY AND CULTURE

"Hell of a place to lose a cow." There are several variants of what pioneer home-steader Ebenezer Bryce supposedly said about the grand garden of hoodoos now called Bryce Canyon, but they all have to do with cows disappearing in it. No wonder; the staggering beauty of southern Utah's canyonlands belies the incredible hardships faced by the early pioneers: bitter winters, spring floods, and hostile Indians. And then there was the American public, raising eyebrows at Mormon polygamy.

The first white pioneers to risk losing their animals in Utah's labyrinthine land-scapes were not Mormons, of course, but Spaniards. In 1776, two Franciscan friars, Francisco Atanasio Domínguez and Francisco Silvestre Escalante, explored a large measure of this *terra incognita* in a fruitless search for a new overland route to the new missions of California. Some members of their party, however, were help-ful in mapping it.

When in 1847 Brigham Young led an advance party of 148 followers into Utah, he was searching not for a wagon route but for a respite from persecution—"a place on earth that nobody else wants," as he described his dream. He found that place, as well as 27 women willing to be his wife. The Mormons first settled the Salt Lake Valley, but eventually fanned south to populate the canyonlands. Mean-while, a famous non-Mormon adventurer, John Wesley Powell, braved the canyons and rapids of most of Southern Utah's wild rivers, smoothing the way —figuratively if not literally—for the thousands who would follow.

Utah joined the union in 1896, six years after the Mormon Church's president, Wilford Woodruff, announced that God had kindly suggested his followers quit polygamy. The practice still persists in some isolated Utah and Arizona communi-ties and is generally overlooked by outside law enforcement.

Between 1909 and 1964 Congress created five national parks in southern Utah. Each is worth a long, contemplative visit. It would take weeks to see even the most important ones.

❖

Outside of the few substantial towns in this region, most people here work on ranches or in isolated settlements. Families tend to be traditional; many of them are Mormon. Small-town friendliness can be tempered with suspicion of outsiders. The ethic of most people here is hard work, cordiality, and honesty. One recent

Jex and Sons Broom Factory was typical of the many small town Mormon businesses that prospered in the late 19th century. (Courtesy of Rell G. Francis)

traveler records the following incident in the town of Henrieville near Bryce Canyon. He bought two bags of groceries and inadvertently left one behind. After a week of traveling, he drove back through Henrieville and stopped at the same store to buy a coke. The clerk recognized him and said, "You left a bag of groceries here last week. It's in the food locker. Just a minute."

■ ZION NATIONAL PARK

Zion: the promised land of the Bible. The deeply religious Mormon pioneers who came upon the canyon were inspired by its sweep and grandeur, its unearthly beauty, thousand-foot walls, grand vistas, and waterfalls. They named its remarkable formations after icons in the Book of Mormon: Great White Throne, Angels Landing, Temple of Sinawava, Guardian Angels, Pulpit, Mount Moroni, and Tabernacle.

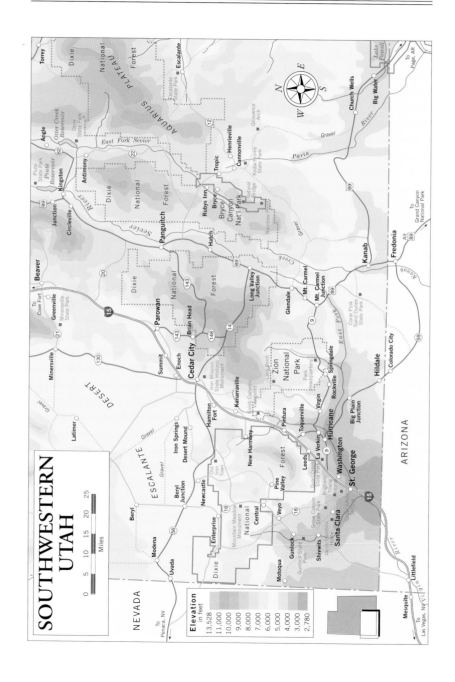

SOUTHWESTERN UTAH

Zion National Park is beautiful and accessible in all seasons. In the fall, cottonwoods and oaks, ablaze with yellow and rust-colored leaves, shimmer at the bottom of gigantic red-brown cliffs. Winter brings snow to the sandstone peaks, ice formations, and a chilly solitude. In spring, the Virgin River, which cuts through Zion, swells with runoff and roars through the canyon. Summer brings blazing heat, but the canyon and the people in it are somewhat cooled by the river, the waterfalls, and the deep shade of the canyon walls.

Zion is a "civilized" national park, with visitors centers at both Zion Canyon and Kolob Canyon, several paved hiking trails, and large developed campgrounds. Yet, for all its civilized (and, in the summer, crowded) atmosphere, Zion is essentially a wild place full of unexpected adventures for those willing to explore.

❖

The park is bisected by UT 9, connecting US 89 on the east, and Interstate 15 on the west. Within the boundaries of the park, the 13 miles of this two-lane highway are known as the **Zion–Mt. Carmel Highway.** This road makes its most remarkable entrance into Zion Canyon (and indeed, one of the most spectacular roads anywhere) from the eastern entrance.

Louis Prang painted Valley of the Babbling Waters *from a sketch made by Thomas Moran during one of his early explorations of what is now Zion National Park. (Library of Congress)*

About a mile past the east entrance rises the **Checkerboard Mesa,** a great petrified sand dune carved into a checkerboard pattern, where large trees grow sideways out of bare rock. Soon after, the road disappears into the **Mt. Carmel Tunnel,** which is regulated to allow alternate directions of one-way traffic. As you descend in near darkness, great windows suddenly open up in the rock wall, framing astounding portraits of breathtaking cliffs and canyon walls. Emerging at the lower end, the road descends in a series of dizzying switchbacks to the chasm floor.

Whether approaching from east or west, a logical and convenient first stop for any visitor is the **Zion Canyon Visitor Center,** near the mouth of the great canyon itself. Here you can learn about how the Virgin River, a surprisingly small stream on most days, carved this mighty gorge. Displays and programs highlight the park's rich natural and human history, and rangers can supply you with maps, books, and information on hiking and other interpretive programs.

From the Visitor Center, the seven-mile **Zion Canyon Scenic Drive** winds up the Virgin River into the canyon proper, beneath brilliantly hued, reddish rock walls and sublime rock formations that tower 2,000–3,000 feet above the river, none more majestic than the **Great White Throne.**

East of the road at the **Grotto Picnic Area** are two popular trailheads. (Parking is available here, but lots fill up early, particularly on summer days.) An easy, two-and-half-mile walk leads across the Virgin River to the **Emerald Pools**—three idyllic pools dwarfed by red sandstone cliffs. A longer and more strenuous hike, but one of the most spectacular in Zion, is to **Angels Landing.** This 9.6-mile roundtrip climbs to the summit of a thin, vertical slab of rock with a vertigo-inducing, 1,500-foot sheer drop down both sides at the summit. The Park Service has installed steel cables as handholds, but the last 400 feet of the ascent is still scary indeed; you appear to be climbing directly into the sky. Don't attempt this hike in wet, snowy, or threatening weather.

The Zion Canyon Scenic Drive ends at the **Temple of Sinawava,** a giant natural amphitheater. From here you can take the **Riverside Walk** beside the Virgin River. Along the trail the canyon narrows and deepens, shaded from above by cottonwood trees. In the summer, the air may be in the 90s, but the river runs quite cold, and all along the route are lovely grottos. This is a hike where you may get wet, so wear shoes that are appropriate (sport sandals work quite well). The first few miles are not particularly strenuous and are often traversed by families and school groups. *Zion Canyon Visitors Center is about a mile inside the south entrance; (435) 772-3256.*

❖

Kolob Canyon. In the remote **Kolob region** of the park, some 45 miles east and north by road from Zion Canyon, backpackers can hike to Kolob Arch; with a span of 310 feet, it is the world's longest. Cougar, ringtail cat, bobcat, coyote, mule deer, and fox all live in the backcountry. Rarely visible, they leave their footprints in the dry sandy washes or on the banks of the tiny creeks. *Kolob Canyon Visitor Center is at exit 40, off I-15; (435) 772-3256.*

■ ST. GEORGE AREA

St. George is an ideal base for exploring Zion National Park, located 40 miles to the east. The town *bustles,* and its skyline is dominated by a brilliant, white Mormon Temple. Locals like to compare the weather to that of Phoenix or Palm Springs, although at an elevation of 2,880 feet, St. George is more temperate than either city in the summer. The city has some good restaurants, modern hotels, pools and spas, and more than half a dozen golf courses.

Near the town of Rockville, a few miles from the south entrance to Zion National Park, is the **ghost town of Grafton**. Movie-goers may recognize it as the setting of the bicycle scene in *Butch Cassidy and the Sundance Kid.*

Kanab is a pretty town located 41 miles southeast of Zion on the Utah-Arizona border, close to both Lake Powell and Arizona's Grand Canyon. The town has been a center of the Western movie industry for many years. The Frontier Movie Town was built to show tourists a bit of the Hollywood West. Admission is free. *297 W. Center Street; (435) 644-5337.*

Coral Pink Sand Dunes State Park is known for its stark, ruddy-colored hills of sand. These dunes, made of billions of tiny particles of quartz, reach heights of several hundred feet. *12 miles west of Kanab off US 89; (435) 648-2800.*

Pipe Spring National Monument recreates pioneer life in its living history program. In the summer, docents dressed in period garb act the parts of pioneers and profess to know nothing about the 20th century. In September, local citizens try to put together a covered wagon ride from Pipe Springs to St. George along the **Honeymoon Trail**. It takes about four days by wagon to cover what is a 90-minute automobile drive. The trail received its name because Mormon couples from all over the Arizona Strip (the part of Arizona north of the Grand Canyon) used it to reach the temple in St. George, where they were married. Thus, they spent their honeymoons riding back on the trail—men bringing home a new wife to meet the others; women no doubt hoping they'd all get along. *On UT 389, southwest of Kanab.*

■ CEDAR BREAKS AND CEDAR CITY

Shaped like a gigantic coliseum, **Cedar Breaks National Monument** has a drop of 2,500 feet and a diameter of more than three miles. Stone spires, columns, arches, and canyons in hues of tan, red, and orange change color and, seemingly, texture as the sun moves across the sky.

Cedar Breaks was named, erroneously, by Mormon pioneers who settled Cedar City in 1851. The "cedars" growing near the base of the cliffs were actually juniper trees. The pioneers referred to the steep badlands topography as "breaks."

A particularly enchanting way to explore Cedar Breaks is to walk along the **Alpine Pond Trail** in early summer, when meadows are ablaze with wildflowers.

Mormon leader Brigham Young's winter home in St. George was built of adobe bricks.

A summer storm clears over Point Supreme in Cedar Breaks National Monument.

In the summer months, hikers can take a rugged 10-mile backpacking trip into **Rattlesnake Creek** and the nearby **U.S. Forest Service Ashdown Gorge Wilderness Area,** located on the western boundary of the national monument. The trail descends 3,400 feet into the gorge. Backpackers can arrange to be picked up at the bottom of the hike rather than hiking back out.

Summer visitors to Cedar Breaks often take side trips to **Panguitch and Navajo lakes.** Both have rustic lodges and U.S. Forest Service campgrounds. Mountain bikers are discovering the scenic dirt roads and trails in this area. *Cedar Breaks is located east of I-15 and Cedar City, off UT 14, or south from Parowan on UT 143. Check maps for other routes via US 89.*

Brian Head. Even though Cedar Breaks sometimes does not open until mid-June, when the snow clears, winter is the prime season at the nearby Brian Head Ski Resort. Use of the nordic ski trails is free, although there is a small charge for the trail maps. Brian Head Nordic Center also offers tours and a variety of special programs. Take the full moon ski tour. *(435) 677-2035.*

Cedar City. With 11,000 residents, Cedar City is the second largest settlement in southern Utah. North/south-running I-15 roars into town against a backdrop of a dark mountain crest. Along the highways blink the signs of chain hotels and motels, giving the area an unplanned, raw look. The smaller, older part of town has quite a few restaurants and motels as well as Southern Utah University. The main event of summer is the Shakespeare Festival, which runs from early July through the first week of September. Southern Utah's love of Shakespeare dates to pioneer times, when Mormons who settled nearby Parowan staged a Shakespearean play three weeks after moving down from the north.

■ BRYCE CANYON

Bryce is not really a canyon at all. It's a series of 14 huge amphitheaters which descend a thousand feet down through the pink and white limestone of the Paunsaugunt Plateau. The Pink Cliffs on the east side contain thousands of fantastically eroded hoodoos—pinnacles, windows, and walls of stone carved out of the soft limestone. Depending on the time of season, the hour of the day, and the weather, the fantastic formations of limestone visible from Inspiration and Rainbow points turn vivid shades of white, orange, yellow, red, and purple.

Indian legend claimed that Bryce was built as a city for the people of Coyote. Because they worked too long beautifying their city, Coyote became angry. He turned the people all to stone and overturned the paints they were using. They are still standing there, rows and rows of them, with the paint dried on their faces.

Early settlers came up with poetic names: Queen's Garden, Navajo Loop, Peeka-boo Loop, Under-the-Rim, and Fairyland. Trails give hikers intimate views of formations like the Chinese Wall, Mormon Temple, Fairy Castle, the Cathedral, the Alligator, the Sinking Ship, Wall of Windows, and Boat Mesa.

The road into the park traverses spectacular scenery, and passes some motels and shops. Maps are available at the visitors center entrance at 8,000 feet; after that the road follows a gradually rising scenic drive. Plan to get out and walk along the rim or down onto the trails. If possible, arrive at the rim at dawn or sunset, and sit for awhile on one of the benches overlooking the amphitheaters, when the colors glow as if freshly applied on a canvas. Sunrise and Sunset points are about one mile past the visitors center and from each you can see a broad panorama.

The walks down into the Bryce amphitheater are deceivingly easy. Climbing back out with elevation gains of anywhere from 300 to more than 800 feet can be grueling, especially during the hot summer months. The easiest hike is the 1^{1}/2-mile Queen's Garden Trail, which begins at Sunrise Point and takes about two hours to complete.

Less crowded trails meander through the meadows and forests of the Paunsaugunt Plateau on the west side of the park. In the spring, sego lilies, penstemons, asters, clematis, evening primrose, scarlet gilias, Indian paintbrush, and wild iris turn this part of Bryce into a garden full of wonderful color. Ancient bristlecone pines, 2,000 years old, still inhabit Bryce Canyon.

Seasonal extremes are great at Bryce Canyon, mainly because of its elevation, which reaches 9,105 feet at Rainbow Point. This means temperatures in winter dip well below freezing. The Park Service closes trails into the canyon in heavy snow. *East of Cedar City off UT 12. Visitors Center, (435) 834-5322.*

■ BACKCOUNTRY EAST OF BRYCE

Kodachrome Basin State Reserve, east of Bryce off UT 12, occupies a scenic little valley full of towering monolithic chimneys unlike anything else in the world. Yet, because Kodachrome Basin—which was named by the National Geographic Society—is located on the northern edge of Grand Staircase–Escalante National Monument (UT 12). Kodachrome Basin campground has fresh water and a modern restroom, complete with showers. A concessionaire provides guided horseback, wagon, and stagecoach rides.

The trail to **Shakespeare Arch** passes a wealth of desert flora: juniper, sagebrush, buffalo berry, Indian rice grass, false buckwheat, saltbrush, snakeweed, yucca, Mormon tea, and rabbitbrush.

The rugged dirt road which leads south from Cannonville to Kodachrome Basin gets considerably rougher beyond the park (check with Kodachrome rangers before attempting to drive it). It goes to **Grosvenor Arch**, an unusual, yellowish-tan span named in honor of the founder of the National Geographic Society. Farther south lie the unusual rock formations of Cottonwood Canyon—named the Cockscomb because they resemble the top of a rooster's head.

The flower of the prickly pear cactus blooms once a year during the spring.

■ PARIA WILDERNESS

Paria Canyon, a water-tortured gash in the Paria Plateau just north and west of Marble Canyon, offers a spectacular canyon trek into the Paria Canyon–Vermilion Cliffs Wilderness Area on the Utah-Arizona border, but it's not for the timid,

Flash floods pose a real danger to hikers in narrow slot canyons, which may unexpectedly fill with raging torrents of water, the result of thunderstorms miles away.

inexperienced, or claustrophobic. Backpackers, who sometimes must wade through waist-deep water, tell many "thrilling" stories of their experiences in the narrow, twisting canyons of the Paria River. In places, Paria is 1,100 feet deep and 10 feet wide. Flash floods roar through on occasion, drowning some and stranding others for days. Water that formed a broad, shallow flash flood on a normally dry arroyo a few miles away, will within Paria's narrow walls, rise well over hikers' heads in seconds. This is also quicksand country.

This narrow canyon is as wildly beautiful and isolated as any spot in the Southwest. If it's blistering hot up on the desert floor, in the shade of the vermilion cliffs it's cooler. The narrow sky overhead is a brilliant cerulean blue, and the smallest hint of greenery seems like a miracle. High overhead, the jumbled sticks that look like bird nests are really flash flood flotsam.

If you come prepared with water and bedding for a three- to four-day trek, you can hike to the banks of the Colorado River at Lee's Ferry. Late summer hiking (July–September) is discouraged because a thunderstorm could quickly flood the canyon. But before setting out, at any time of year, hikers should call the BLM weather service in Kanab, Utah, *(435) 644-2672*.

The trailhead is reached from US 89 between Kanab and Big Water in southern Utah. Turn in at the ranger station for maps, then follow the dirt access road south to the campground. The trail follows the canyon for 35 miles until it ends at the Colorado River adjacent to Lee's Ferry.

■ LEE'S FERRY

Lee's Ferry is a rocky spot on the river below a break in the cliffs above Marble Canyon. Missionary-explorers Domínguez and Escalante tried ferrying the river here but were unable to negotiate a crossing. There is little shade, a parking lot, and a small house on the National Register of Historic Places. John Doyle Lee lived here for three years with one of his 18 wives, operating a small farm and regular ferry service, beginning in 1872. Fifteen years before he began running the ferry, Lee had led the Mountain Meadows Massacre, in which he and other Mormons, along with Paiutes, murdered a wagon train of 140 non-Mormon immigrants. Lee was finally tried for these crimes in 1875, found guilty, and executed.

Lee's Ferry is where motorized rafts, carrying passengers on half-day float trips from Glen Canyon Dam, pull up to let people walk around before they are motored back. River rafters are picked up here for magnificent journeys by raft into the Grand Canyon. The trip from Lee's Ferry to Phantom Ranch in the

Grand Canyon requires three days and traverses a completely isolated world. (For more information see pages 241.) *To reach Lee's Ferry follow the paved road which turns north from US 89A just west of Navajo Bridge.*

■ GRAND STAIRCASE–ESCALANTE NATIONAL MONUMENT

When President Bill Clinton designated the 1.7-million acre Grand Staircase-Escalante National Monument on September 18, 1996, millions discovered what a few southern Utah red-rock fanatics knew all along.

East of Cannonville on UT 12 lies a wild land of arches, "goblins," hoodoos, and assorted canyons. This red-rock country of the Escalante River is believed by most historians to be the last major river "discovered" by government surveyors in the continental United States.

Before doing much exploring in this area, it's a good idea to stop at the interagency travel office in Escalante to obtain literature, safety information, maps, historical data, and reports on weather and road conditions. Information, a good interpretive museum and ruin site are also available at Anasazi State Park in Boulder. There are few developed facilities in the monument.

Hole-in-the-Rock, a narrow slit in the 2,000-foot cliff overlooking the Colorado River, was discovered by pioneers seeking a shortcut into southeastern Utah. More than 200 people, 82 wagons with two or more teams of horses, about 200 additional horses, and more than 1,000 head of cattle made the 290-mile journey in 1879, traveling 1.7 miles per day.

Today, some of the Hole-in-the-Rock Road has been drowned by Lake Powell, but enough signs of the original trek remain that boaters on Lake Powell, or drivers willing to brave the rigors of a sometimes rugged 61-mile county-maintained gravel road, can still view the places where pioneers struggled to cross. The road passes **Dance Hall Rock,** a huge sandstone amphitheater where dances kept pioneer morale high, en route to the crevice above the Colorado, where the party used blasting powder and picks to open a passage to the river. If you thread your way down the steep, narrow sandstone slit, you will find yourself appreciating the immense hardships the pioneers endured.

Another interesting site is **Devil's Garden Natural Area,** a fantastic collection of red and white hoodoos reminiscent of Arches National Park and Goblin Valley.

Perhaps the best-known Escalante destination is **Calf Creek Falls,** 15 miles east of the town of Escalante. The trail passes small natural arches, thousand-year-old Indian rock art, an Anasazi ruin and, after a somewhat difficult terrain, the falls

Big Drop 2 rapid in Utah's Cataract Canyon of the Colorado River consists of a standing 15-foot wave, the volume of which peaks at 50,000 cubic feet per second during spring snowmelt.

itself. In the summer visitors can fish in the deep pools of Calf Creek. There are also a few picnic sites here and 13 camp sites. *Information, (435) 826-5499.*

■ ESCALANTE CANYON COUNTRY

Nearby **Escalante Petrified Forest State Park** has some shade, a grassy area, camping facilities, and access to **Wide Hollow Reservoir,** a good place to swim and fish. Hiking trails lead to the small petrified forest.

Anasazi Village State Park conserves the remains of an ancient village constructed on top of a mesa. With a year-round water supply, fertile fields, a broad view of the surrounding countryside, and abundant wild game, wood, and stone, the village was able to support 200 people for 75 years. By A.D. 1300, suffering from drought, the Anasazi abandoned all of their outposts in Utah.

At a reconstructed pueblo visitors can sit down and grind corn the Indian way, with a *mano* and *metate.* The University of Utah Natural History Museum sponsors annual digs here for amateur archaeologists who want to help excavate. *Located on UT 12, 28 miles northeast of Escalante and 38 miles south of Torrey. Call*

(435) 335-7308 for more information.

After passing through the lovely small town of **Boulder** with its green trees, and pastures, UT 12 climbs north to the 9,200-foot summit of the Boulder Mountains, offering glimpses of Capitol Reef and the Waterpocket Fold to the east, the Aquarius Plateau to the west, and the Escalante canyons, Straight Cliffs, and Kaiparowits Plateau to the south. There are three developed Dixie National Forest campgrounds along the road, from which you can hike into one of the many lakes on Boulder Mountain itself—lakes teeming with brook trout.

■ CAPITOL REEF

Capitol Reef gets its name from two geological curiosities of the Waterpocket Fold, a 100-mile bulge in the earth's crust containing eroded pockets that catch water after each rainfall. Early settlers who looked at this landscape of bulges and pockets decided it looked like a coral reef. Then they encountered a round

The aptly named Temple of the Sun in Capitol Reef National Park's Cathedral Valley.

sandstone formation, and decided it looked like a capitol dome. The Fremont River runs through the middle of Capitol Reef, along UT 24, and archaeologists believe Indians inhabited this area from about A.D. 700 to 1275. Fremont Indians have left petroglyphs and storage bins, or *moki* huts, along the walls of the canyons.

There's a fine paved road through Capitol Reef, and many wonderful hikes along the way. Walks to **Hickman Bridge**, through **Capitol Gorge**, or along **Grand Wash** reveal fascinating geology. Children enjoy scrambling up the sandstone and through the little stone alcoves. Longer, more difficult treks go to Cassidy Arch, Frying Pan Canyon (where a shout turns into an echo heard several times over), Spring Canyon, and the Golden Throne. An excellent hiking guide detailing the most popular trails is available at the visitors center.

The **Burr Trail** is a solitary, mostly paved track cutting down the eastern boundary of the park, with one spur south to Lake Powell and another west to the town of Boulder. There are washes to explore and arches to discover in this land. With four-wheel drive you can explore the rugged dirt road on the north end of the park leading to **Cathedral Valley.** Here, huge monolithic sandstone remnants form jutting buttes that resemble cathedrals in the desert. *(435) 425-3791.*

■ SAN RAFAEL SWELL

The scenic stretch of Interstate 70 between Salina and Green River cuts through Fishlake National Forest—the heart of the red-rock San Rafael Swell and Sinbad Valley—without passing a town for over 100 miles. The Swell has been described as the jagged remains of a dinosaur backbone, an exposed sandstone coral reef, a saw blade, and a scene from the Arabian Nights.

North of Interstate 70 at **Buckhorn Draw** are pictographs and petroglyphs left by the Indians who roamed this area thousands of years ago. Backpackers and horseback riders can discover places like the Black Box, the Little Grand Canyon, Wedge Overlook, Black Dragon Canyon, the Muddy River, Crack Canyon, Iron Wash, Little Wildhorse Canyon, and the Copper Globe. Outlaws and cattle rustlers once hid in the narrow, winding canyons of the San Rafael Swell.

On the southern edge of San Rafael Swell, roughly midway between I-70 and Hanksville, **Goblin Valley State Park** is a delightful playground overrun by stone goblins. Wind through a maze of stone babies, red goblins, ghosts, and toadstools, ranging 10 to 200 feet tall. *South of US 70, the turnoff to the park is on UT 24.*

Maps and information for exploring the San Rafael Reef are available from the Price Chamber of Commerce and BLM offices in Salt Lake City, Price, and Hanksville. Michael Kelsey's guidebook, *Hiking Utah's San Rafael Swell,* provides detailed information.

■ MOAB

Most visitors go to Moab by way of Interstate 70, turning south at US Route 191. A more scenic route is by way of Cisco, where UT 128 hooks south from the interstate. After crossing the Colorado River, it leads past Fisher Towers and through Castle Valley to Moab. **Fisher Towers** are isolated remnants of a 225-million-year-old floodplain. They gained some fame in 1964 and 1974 when helicopters placed cars atop the pinnacles to make some automobile commercials. A 2.2-mile hiking trail around the base of the towers takes about three hours to complete.

The town of Moab (population 4,000) is a good base of operations for exploring southeastern Utah, and in particular, Arches and Canyonlands national parks and the La Sal Mountains. It is also the center of operations for river trips, bicycle excursions, hikes, and four-wheel-drive expeditions. Thousands of visitors from all over the United States come for the special yearly events, like the Moab Half-Marathon in March, the Easter Jeep Safari, the Friendship Cruise powerboat voyage on the Green and Colorado rivers, the Labor Day Jeep Jamboree, and the October Fat Tire Festival for mountain bikers.

Though it does occasionally snow in the winter and temperatures can dip down below freezing, this part of Utah generally enjoys mild weather. The ideal months to visit the Moab area are April and October.

Founded in the 1870s by Mormon farmers and ranchers after an 1855 mission attempt failed, Moab was named for the biblical kingdom at the edge of Zion, the promised land. The town itself is located in a green valley on the edge of the Colorado River and is surrounded by high sandstone cliffs. The scenic countryside has been a backdrop for Western movies such as John Wayne's *Rio Grande* and *The Comancheros,* the biblical movie *The Greatest Story Ever Told,* and *Indiana Jones and The Last Crusade.*

The Moab Slickrock Bicycle Trail, originally constructed for use by trail machines and motorcycles, has been taken over by mountain bikers, who ride over the pale orange Navajo sandstone "petrified" dunes. Overlooks at Updraft Arch, Negro Bill Canyon, Shrimp Rock, Abyss Viewpoint, and Echo Point provide glimpses of the Colorado River, the La Sal Mountains, and Arches National Park. Those with plenty of mountain-biking experience may want to take a day to explore the 10.3-mile main loop ride.

Day and night jet-boat trips and one-day rafting trips into the canyons are offered by a number of outfitters, and most Colorado River trips into Cataract and Westwater canyons begin here.

Hikers should investigate the uncrowded trails that cross the country around Moab outside the boundaries of Arches and Canyonlands national parks. Portal Overlook, Corona, and Bowtie arches, Mill Creek Canyon, Negro Bill Canyon, Hidden Valley, and Hunters Canyon often reward explorers with solitude.

■ ARCHES NATIONAL PARK

Containing no fewer than 2,000 arches, Arches National Park is divided into six sections: Courthouse Towers, The Windows, Delicate Arch, Fiery Furnace,

Riding the Slickrock Trail (above) near Moab provides glimpses of Arches National Park nearby. Delicate Arch (right) is just one of the spectacular formations to be found within the park.

Klondike Bluffs, and Devil's Garden. Hiking guides are available and the trails are, for the most part, well marked.

In the Windows section, short trails leads to Double Arch (which appeared in *Indiana Jones and the Last Crusade*), Turret Arch, and North and South Windows. From claustrophobic Fiery Furnace, a spur off the trial to Broken Arch leads to little Sand Dune Arch.

The longest series of maintained trails in Arches are found in the Devil's Garden area at the end of the paved road, just north of the campground. The five-mile loop trail, with only a gentle 200-foot gain in elevation, leads past narrow fins to Double O Arch and **Landscape Arch.** At 291 feet long and 188 feet high, Landscape is the longest span in the park and second longest in the world.

The most famous sight in the park is **Delicate Arch** (which is anything but delicate and might well have been named Schwarzenegger's Biceps), an improbable natural wonder of salmon-colored sandstone, about 65 feet high, and with an opening nearly 35 feet wide. There are few more spectacular hikes in this world than the trek to Delicate Arch. The arch was once dubbed "The Schoolmarm's Bloomers" by local cowboys. Later it was named "Landscape Arch," but a cartographer switched this name with an arch named Delicate Arch and now each has become the other. The 1.5-mile trail begins at the historic Wolfe Ranch, built by Civil War veteran John Wesley Wolfe, who tried to make a living out of this desolate country in the late 1800s. The beauty of the hike is that the arch itself isn't visible until the last possible second. The view here is extraordinary at sunset, when the light and shadows play tricks with the arch and the natural amphitheater around it. *Arches National Park Visitors Center; (435) 259-8161.*

■ CANYONLANDS NATIONAL PARK

The late Edward Abbey, iconoclast, cynic, and author of some of the best essays and fiction written about the deserts of southern Utah, described the Canyonlands country of southeastern Utah best when he called the place "the least inhabited, least developed, least improved, least civilized, most arid, most hostile, most lonesome, most grim bleak barren desolate and savage quarter of the state of Utah —the best part by far."

In acreage, Canyonlands is the largest of Utah's five national parks. It is also the least developed and most difficult to tour. The park is divided into four principal

STONE BRIDGE IN A STORM

*T*he dark spruces were tipped with glimmering lights; the aspens bent low in the winds, as waves in a tempest at sea; the forest of oaks tossed wildly and shone with gleams of fire. Across the valley the huge cavern of the cliff-dwellers yawned in the glare, every little black window as clear as at noonday; but the night and the storm added to their tragedy. Flung arching to the black clouds, the great stone bridge seemed to bear the brunt of the storm. It caught the full fury of the rushing wind. It lifted its noble crown to meet the lightning. Venters thought of the eagles and their lofty nest in a niche near the arch. A driving pall of rain, black as the clouds, came sweeping on to obscure the bridge and the gleaming walls and the shining valley. The lightning played incessantly, streaking down through opaque darkness of rain. The roar of the wind, with its strange knell and the recrashing echoes, mingled with the roar of the flooding rain, and all seemingly were deadened and drowned in a world of sound.

—Zane Grey, *Riders of the Purple Sage,* 1912

districts. Island in the Sky is a broad, level mesa wedged between the Green and Colorado rivers. It serves as a kind of observation platform for the other three wards of this rugged park: the Needles District, the Maze, and the River District. A separate chunk of parkland, the Horseshoe Canyon Unit, lies northwest of the main body of the park.

The River District takes in Cataract Canyon and the confluence of the Green and Colorado rivers, and can be visited only by river runners and experienced hikers. The other districts can be approached by road, though in some cases that means only by four-wheel-drive vehicle, or on foot.

Island in the Sky District is reached by UT 313, which runs west from its junction with US Route 191, six miles north of the turnoff to Arches National Park. The highway is a dead end. One spur leads to Dead Horse Point State Park, and another into Canyonlands. Much of the park can be surveyed from **Grandview Point.** On a quiet, cold winter morning, the distant peaks of the La Sal, Henry, and Blue mountains stand like snow-covered sentinels in the midst of twisting, convoluted canyons. To the south, the Needles jut like monoliths erected by some ancient culture. Rock formations with descriptive names like Lizard Rock, the

(following pages) Canyonlands National Park is home to magnificent arches, such as Mesa Arch pictured here at sunrise.

Doll House, Chocolate Drops, the Maze, and the Golden Stairs rise up in the southern background near the canyon of the Colorado River. Take some time to be alone in this outpost to contemplate the vast tract of wilderness below you.

Long hiking trails and rugged dirt roads lead down to the White Rim Trail, remote arches, and interesting side canyons. Only the hardiest backpackers and people experienced in maneuvering four-wheel-drive vehicles in the backcountry should attempt these routes. Shorter, easier trails lead to Mesa Arch, Upheaval Dome, and Whale Rock. Standing on the brink of the cliff at Mesa Arch is like walking on the edge of infinity.

The view from the lip of a 2,000-foot drop-off overlooking the Colorado River at **Dead Horse Point State Park**, 34 miles west of Moab, gives a sense of the depth, size, and majesty of the canyon country. Cowboys used to trap wild mustangs on the promontory by closing off the narrow neck of land. According to one legend, the gate was once left open so a band of corralled mustangs could return to the range. Instead, the mustangs remained on the point, dying of thirst within sight of the Colorado River, 2,000 feet below; hence the morbid name.

South from Moab is another staggeringly beautiful view, that at **Needles Overlook**, reached by detouring to the **Canyon Rims Area** at the marked junction, 32 miles south of Moab. Run by the BLM, this reserve has campsites and trails, one leading to Jail Rock. Legend has it that a sheriff's posse held a captured outlaw in the large pothole at the center of the rock. Another story says a rancher used to keep his wife there when he visited a local saloon.

Seven miles south of the Needles Overlook road, UT 211 heads west from US Route 191 toward Newspaper Rock and the Needles District of Canyonlands National Park. **Newspaper Rock State Park** preserves a wall of sandstone covered with Indian petroglyphs that date back 1,500 years. Several theories have been proposed to explain the meaning of the rock graphics. Contemporary Indians recognize some symbols; the Hopi, for instance, still use some in their religious ceremonies. Some graphics have been found to have direct connections to astrological occurrences. Archaeologists have used some as maps to lead them to water. Others see the strange manlike figures as records of extraterrestrial visits.

The Needles District is an amazing landscape of wind-carved sandstone fins. Plan on spending a day or two here camping in their midst and hiking to the Roadside Ruin, Cave Spring, or Pothole Point. Lovers of cowboy lore should visit the reconstructed line camp next to Cave Spring.

Few jeepers will ever forget an expedition over Elephant Hill, one of the wildest, roughest, most challenging stretches of "road" in the entire West. Narrow slots barely wide enough for a vehicle to get through, silver stairs of sheer rock, and steep inclines force off-roaders to put their machines in the lowest possible gear. At one point in the 10-mile loop, four-wheel-drives are forced to back to the edge of a steep cliff in order to make the turn! (We know of one woman who left the vehicle in tears at this point, and walked until she perceived the trail to be safe again. It was a long walk.) A few backcountry campsites can be found in Chesler Park along this road.

The Maze District, located on the remote west side of the Colorado River, the Maze District can be reached only by jouncing over some 60 miles of dirt road from UT 24 near the Goblin Valley turnoff. Only hikers and four-wheel-drive vehicles should attempt the last few miles. The road to the Maze passes through a section of Canyonlands National Park detached from the main body of the park: the Horseshoe Canyon Unit. Some of North America's most outstanding ancient Indian rock art can be found there in the Great Gallery. The gallery's huge, ghost-like pictographs probably were painted by Fremont artists.

Large graceful cottonwoods grow along the trail. In places the water surfaces to nourish cattails, horsetails, reeds, and willows. Seeping water in occasional alcoves nurses delicate flower gardens and lacy ferns.

Canyonlands National Park is located south of Moab off US 163; or drive south from I-70 at Crescent Junction. National Park Service; (435) 587-2737.

■ NATURAL BRIDGES NATIONAL MONUMENT

The view from the road into the visitors center or the campground is typical of this country in that you can see for miles across reddish-brown, brush-and-piñon-covered range land without seeing directly the site you've come to see. Typically, that's because it lies below the surface of the landscape you're looking across, down in a canyon cut by a small river. Walking down to see the natural bridges, you come upon a palette of cream-white, ochre, soft salmon pinks, and deep red, marking rocks of sculptural beauty on a God-sized scale.

A stream runs through the bottom of the canyon at Bridges, and along it, in the mud, can be seen tracks of coyote, ringtail cat, and deer. About 200 Anasazi dwelling sites have been found here, under cliff overhangs, and near the

cottonwood trees along the creek. Horse Collar Ruin is accessible from the trail between Sipapu and Kachina bridges.

These natural bridges were given Hopi names: Kachina (a representation of a spiritual messenger); Owachomo, (a flat-rock mound); and Sipapu (gateway to this world from the other world below). Hopi clan symbols can be seen near several ruins, and it's possible that White Canyon Anasazi may have migrated south from here to join the ancestors of present-day Hopi. *From UT 95, turn northwest on UT 275 and drive about five miles to the visitors center; (435) 692-1234.*

❖

Grand Gulch Primitive Area, south of the monument, preserves a winding, many-fingered canyon where numerous graphic panels can be found along the rock walls. The area was occupied as early as A.D. 200 by Basketmaker Anasazi but

The petroglyphs (above) in Newspaper Rock State Park are about 60 miles north of Grand Gulch Primitive Area.

Lake Powell (opposite) is a water sports paradise. Swimming, waterskiing, and fishing may be enjoyed, and houseboats rented for comfortable exploration of 1,960 miles of shoreline.

was abandoned and reoccupied two centuries later. *Those who wish to explore Grand Gulch should call the* BLM *Office in Monticello at (435) 587-2141 for more information. Grand Gulch is 40 miles west of Blanding on UT 95; it's approached via a long road through piñon pine. There is a campground, but no other lodging nearby.*

■ GLEN CANYON AND LAKE POWELL

Lake Powell, the second largest man-made reservoir in the world, is likewise Utah's second most popular tourist destination. Lake Powell receives some 2.8 million visitors a year—more than either the Grand Canyon or Yellowstone National Park. Glen Canyon Dam, located near Page, Arizona, has created a 186-mile reservoir with a meandering, 1,960-mile shoreline. The recreation area itself consists of 1,869 square miles. Most of that is accessible only by boat; some of it can be reached by automobile, and other parts can be explored by hikers or rafters.

Wrote Arizona author Bob Hirsch in his book *Houseboating on Lake Powell*:

> There are few places on earth that cannot be adequately described. Lake Powell is one of them. You'll know the first time you nudge the bow of your houseboat onto some sandy shore in a lonesome canyon far up the lake. It is quiet and peaceful and your eye delights in the patch of blue sky above, framed by soaring walls of buff and pink and light chocolate. The day is yours . . . from the time dawn tints a far-off butte from black to gray to the blush of rose, to the final hour storing up memories beside a driftwood fire, watching shadows dance on the ancient walls.

Such pleasant thoughts may not be uppermost in your mind when you first arrive at Lake Powell, perhaps to take the car ferry from Bullfrog Marina to Halls Crossing. The water is blue, certainly, bright blue, and it laps a treeless, red-rock shore under a ferocious sun. On both sides of the ferry crossing there are campgrounds and swimming beaches, as well as grocery stores. Desperate-looking trees grow on out-of-place bright green lawns, and the moored houseboats look as if they are as hot as ovens.

Rent a houseboat anyway. Once you putt away, you'll feel as if you've left the interstate for a backcountry road. It's in quiet stretches of water, and in remote canyons, that the beauty of this place reveals itself. In faraway parts of the canyon there are arches to discover, Indian ruins to find, hiking areas to explore, and warm enough water around your boat to allow for languorous swims.

Fishermen can avoid the crowds of summer by renting a powerboat in either April or May or from mid-September to late October. Fishing for large- and small-mouth bass, striped bass, crappie, northern pike, walleye, and channel catfish is best during those times of year.

Lake Powell boaters would do well to purchase one of Stan Jones's maps. Updated annually, these maps use a system of numbered buoys to mark major landmarks, canyons, fishing areas, and other points of interest. Always take precautions: because this reservoir is so large, it is possible to get lost or to run out of gas and find yourself floating around out there.

■ RAINBOW BRIDGE

Probably the most famous sight along Lake Powell is Rainbow Bridge. With a height of 290 feet and a span of 270 feet, it is the world's largest natural bridge. This spot, sacred to the Navajo Indians, has been named one of the seven natural wonders of the world. When author Zane Grey came here around the turn of the century he carved his initials underneath a stone crevice behind the bridge. In Grey's day, only a few hearty souls made the long and difficult hike. Now, thousands of boaters visit the monument annually.

The easiest way to Rainbow Bridge National Monument is by boat tour on Lake Powell from Wahweap, Bullfrog, or Halls Crossing. Experienced hikers venture along rugged trails to get to the bridge. Pick up the trail at either the Navajo Mountain Trading Post just north across the Utah-Arizona border on the east side of Navajo Mountain or the Rainbow Lodge ruins just south of the Utah-Arizona border. For more information inquire with the National Park Service at Glen Canyon; (520) 645-2511/2471.

Utah Canyonlands Food & Lodging

■ FOOD & LODGING

> *Restaurant prices:*
> Per person, not including drinks, tax, and tips:
> $ = under $10; $$ = $10–20; $$$ = over $20
>
> *Room rates:*
> Per night, per room, double occupancy:
> $ = under $50; $$ = $50–100; $$$ = over $100

Beaver

population 2,000   elevation 5,898

Arshel's Cafe. Off of I-15 on 711 N. Main St.; (435) 438-2977
Inviting roadside cafe with great hamburgers, hand-cut French fries, and famous pies.

Bryce Canyon National Park

Best Western Ruby's Inn. One mile north of the park entrance on US 63; (435) 834-5341 $$
Operated by the Syrett family for several generations, this sprawling facility is one of the largest full-service hotels in the region. It features ski touring and snowmobiling in the winter, helicopter rides, and rodeos in the summer; hot tubs, a swimming pool, general store, gift shop, and restaurant. Nothing fancy, but the hospitality and variety of things to do make it the area's best.

Bryce Canyon National Park Campgrounds. Bryce Canyon on US 63; (435) 834-5322
North Campground, located just east of park headquarters, has 110 units.

Sunset Campground is located two miles south of park headquarters and has 115 units.

Bryce Point Bed and Breakfast. 61 N. 400 West, Box 96; Tropic, UT; (435) 679-8629 $$
Five rooms, all with baths. Redwood deck. Each guest room features a 7 x 5-foot picture window facing Bryce Canyon and cottage.

Bryce Canyon Lodge. Inside the park; (435) 834-5361 $$-$$$
Built for the Union Pacific Railroad in the 1920s and since refurbished, this lodge nonetheless retains its old charm. Open mid-April through October.

Bryce Canyon Pines. UT 12, 6 miles west of the park turnoff; (435) 834-5441 $$
Modern rooms with beautiful views in a relatively secluded setting. The restaurant and swimming pool are open spring through fall.

Dixie National Forest Campgrounds. Powell Ranger District; (435) 676-8815
A few miles west of the park, Kings Creek and Red Canyon campgrounds often have room when the sites inside the park are full. To reach **Kings Creek**

Campground drive west 2.8 miles on UT 12 from the park turnoff, then south seven miles on East Fork Sevier River Road. To reach Red Canyon Campground drive west 10 miles on UT 12 from the park turnoff.

Capitol Reef National Park

✕ **Cafe Diablo.** 599 W. Main St., Torrey; (435) 425-3070
Chef Gary Pankow has created his distinctive brand of Southwestern cooking. Fresh salsas and french fried sweet potatoes are just part of an eclectic menu.

✕ **Capitol Reef Inn Cafe.** 360 West Main St., Torrey; (435) 425-3271 $$
Sophisticated, healthy food features fresh salads, veggie dishes (stir-fried vegetables, for one), and beef, chicken, trout, and shish kebab, as well as fresh juice and espresso.

✕ **Sunglow Cafe.** Bicknell, about 10 miles west of the park on UT 24; (435) 425-3701 $
This tiny roadside cafe is known for its unusual pie selection. How does pickle, pinto bean, or oatmeal sound?

☴ **Best Western Capitol Reef Resort.** UT 24, one mile outside entrance to the park; (435) 425-3761 $$
One of the area's newer facilities. A pool is open in the summer.

⚑ **Fruita Campground.** Located one mile from Capitol Reef Visitors Center on the scenic drive; (435) 425-3791
Surrounded by orchards and lush greenery. First come, first served.

Cedar City and Vicinity

population 13,443   elevation 2,761

✕ **Cowboy's Smokehouse.** 95 N. Main St., Panguitch; (435) 676-8030 $–$$
Succelent meats—pork ribs, beef brisket, chicken, and turkey—are the specialties at this colorful eatery. Delicious fruit cobbler.

✕ **The Edge.** Brian Head. 406 S. Rte. 143; (435) 677-3343 $$
A popular spot for lunch and dinner. Hamburgers and sandwiches are large, to say the least, and the steaks, seafood, soup, and salad are all equally delicious.

✕ **Milt's Stage Stop.** 5 miles east of Cedar City in Cedar Canyon; (435) 586-9344 $$–$$$$
Rustic steak and seafood house in a quiet canyon setting. Steaks and prime rib are among Utah's best. Dinner only.

✕ **Pizza Factory.** 124 S. Main, Cedar City; (435) 586-3900 $
Good pizza, salads, and pasta. An excellent place to take the family.

✕ **Sullivan's Cafe.** 103 S. Main, Cedar City; (435) 586-6761 $–$$
Typical small-town southern Utah restaurant. Try the prime rib sandwich, potato bar, and the huge salad bar.

☴ **Abbey Inn.** 940 W. 200 North, Cedar City; (435) 586-9966 $$
One of southern Utah's modern hotels. The indoor swimming pool and hot tub make it a year-round favorite.

☴ **The Bard's B&B.** 150 S. 100 West, ; (435) 586-6612 $$
Taking its cue from the annual Shakespeare festival, this intimate B&B is

Utah Canyonlands Food & Lodging

filled with precious details including Elizabethan dolls, stained glass panels, and antique oak furnishings.

⊟ **Best Western Town & Country Inn.** 200 N. Main; (435) 586-9900 **$$** One of the larger and more centrally located motels in Cedar City, this inn features a popular gift shop inside an old train station.

⊟ **Cedar Breaks Lodge.** 223 Hunter Ridge Rd., Brian Head (Rte. 143); (435) 677-3000 or (800) 27-BRIAN **$$-$$$** The rooms here are spacious and pleasantly decorated. Friendly and helpful staff.

⊟ **Cedar City Holiday Inn.** 1575 W. 200 North; (435) 586-8888 **$$-$$$** A fairly typical Holiday Inn, but this one contains an exercise room, outdoor pool, and indoor hot tub. Close to I-15.

⊟ **Paxman Summer House Bed & Breakfast.** 170 N. 400 West; (435) 586-3755 **$$** This turn-of-the-century Victorian farmhouse with lace-curtained windows and antique beds stands within walking distance of the Utah Shakespearean Festival venues.

⊟ **Rustic Lodge.** 186 W. Westshore Rd, Panguitch Lake off UT 143; (435) 676-2627 **$$** On the west shore, offers cabins, RV park with showers and laundry, restaurant, small store, boat rentals, mountain bicycle rentals, and horseback riding.

Kanab

population 3,289   elevation 4,079

✕ **Chef's Palace.** 176 W. Center St.; (435) 644-5052 **$$** A local favorite for rib-eye steaks, prime rib, and seafood.

⊟ **Nine Gables Inn.** 106 W. 100 North; (435) 644-5079 **$$** A sunny, inviting ranch house with flower and vegetable gardens enclosed by a white picket fence. The four guest rooms each include baths and are furnished with family treasures.

Glen Canyon Lake Powell

✕ **Canyon King Paddlewheeler.** Board at Wahweap Lodge. (520) 645-2433 or (800) 528-6154 **$$$** Sunset dinner cruise on an 1800s-style riverboat. Prime rib dinner is presented buffet style on the glassed lower deck.

✕ **Rainbow Room in Wahweap Lodge.** On US 89, 7 mi northwest of Page, AZ; (520) 645-2433 or (800) 528-6154 **$$** A semicircular restaurant with panoramic views of the lake. Southwestern and standard American fare with creative specialties.

⚠ **Glen Canyon Campgrounds.** **Bullfrog Campground** 70 mi. south of Hanksville on UT 276 and has 86 units; **Halls Crossing,** just across Lake Powell from **Bullfrog Campgrounds,** is 72 mi. west of Blanding on UT 276

and has 65 units; **Hite Campground** (6 units) is 45 mi. south of Hanksville on UT 95, 6 units and **Wahweap Campground** near Page, AZ has 100 units.
☵ **Defiance Lodge.** 1.4 mile from Bullfrog Marina, at top of the hill. (435) 684-2233 $$-$$$
Overlooking Lake Powell and Bullfrog Marina, this two-story lodge offers fine views and luxury accommodations.
☵ **Best Western Arizona Inn.** 716 Rim View Dr., Page, AZ; (520) 645-2466 or (800) 525-1234 $$-$$$
Perched on a high bluff, this pleasant, full-service motel provides fine views of Lake Powell and Glen Canyon Dam.
☵ **Wahweap Lodge.** On US 89, 7 miles northwest of Page, AZ; (520) 645-2433 $$$
A well-appointed lodge with two swimming pools, a cocktail lounge, and a lovely restaurant (see above). The newest rooms are decorated in an attractive southwestern style with bright colors and oak furnishings; many have views of Lake Powell.

Moab and Vicinity

population 3,971   elevation 4,025

✗ **Buck's Grill Steakhouse.** 1391 N. US 191; (435) 259-5201 $$
Good choice of vegetarian gourmet dishes, as well as steak, chicken, and wild game entrees served by chef Tim Buckingham. Original western oils on the walls.
✗ **Center Cafe.** 92 E. Center St., Moab; (435) 259-4295 $$-$$$

Fresh fish, fine vegetarian dishes, gourmet pizzas, and espresso are served in a simple but elegant atmosphere. This standout restaurant is one of Utah's finest.
✗ **Eddie McStiff's.** 57 S. Main St., Moab; (435) 259-BEER $-$$
In addition to serving tasty lagers, this brew pub offers great pizza, pasta, steaks, and burgers. Late in the day it becomes crowded and fun—a great place to go after mountain biking.
✗ **Fat City Smoke House.** 36 S. 100 West, Moab; (435) 259-4302 $-$$
Texas-style barbecue and vegetarian dishes that are both delicious and inexpensive.
✗ **Sunset Grill.** 900 N. US 191; (435) 259-7146 $$$
Built by a colorful old uranium miner, this converted mansion affords great views of the red rock country and Colorado Plateau. Menu of fish, pasta, and mesquite-broiled steak.
☵ **Best Western Canyonlands Inn.** 16 S. Main St., Moab; (435) 259-2300 $$
Certainly among the nicest of the many typical franchise-type motels found in southeastern Utah.
⬙ **Canyonlands National Park campgrounds.** (435) 259-7164
Reservations not accepted. **Squaw Flat** is 35 miles west off US 191 on UT 211 and has 26 units. **Willow Flat** is 41 miles west off US 191 on UT 313 and has 12 units.
☵ **Castle Valley Inn.** 424 Amber Ln., Castle Valley, about 2.3 miles of UT 128; (435) 259-6012 $$-$$$

Utah Canyonlands Food & Lodging

Utah Canyonlands Food & Lodging

One of the state's quietest bed-and-breakfasts. An orchard, small cottages with kitchenettes, and a hot tub with views of Castle Valley's sandstone spires, add up to a serene experience.

☎ **Lazy Lizard Hostel.** 1213 S. US 191; (435) 259-6057 $
Dorm rooms run $7 to $10 a person. Individual cabins are $24. Hot tub.

☎ **Moab Valley Inn.** 711 S. Main St.; (435) 259-4419 $$-$$$
This spot offers a few more amenities than most motels with its hot tub, swimming pool, and nice private park with picnic tables and barbecue grills.

☎ **Sunflower Hill Bed & Breakfast.** 185 N. 300 East; (435) 259-2974 $$
Each room in this old house affords visitors a private bath, TV, and distinctive, elegant decor—try the Sun Porch Room with a sunflower bedspread or the Rose Room with stenciled roses twining the walls.

Richfield and Vicinity

✗ **Mom's Cafe.** 10 E. Main St., Salina; (435) 529-3921 $-$$
A homey diner with aqua-colored booths, a pink counter, and the simple pleasures of ranch-style fare: fried sweet bread scones, biscuits covered in thick gravy, tender chicken-fried steaks. Open from 7:00 AM to 10:00 PM.

✗ **Topsfield Lodge.** 1200 S. Main, Richfield; (435) 896-5437 $$
One of the area's finest steakhouses with prime rib a specialty.

St. George and Vicinity

population 28,502   elevation 2,761

✗ **Andelin's Gable House.** 290 E. Saint George Blvd., St. George; (435) 673-6796 $$-$$$
A St. George tradition, serving a limited but fine menu in elegant style. Wonderful homemade cornbread and rolls.

⛺ **Coral Pink Sand Dunes State Park.** 12 miles west of Kanab off US 89; (435) 648-2800
The small campground here provides an out-of-the-way experience.

☎ **Howard Johnson's Four Seasons Inn and Convention Center.** 747 E. St. George Blvd, St. George;(435) 673-6111 $-$$$
Palm trees, putting green, in-room steambaths, tennis courts, and pool.

☎ **Greene Gate Village Historic Bed & Breakfast.** 76 W. Tabernacle St., St. George; (435) 628-6999 or (800) 350-6999 $$-$$$
A larger-than-average bed-and-breakfast spread over several buildings; swimming pool and hot tub, too.

☎ **Green Valley Resort.** 1841 W. Canyon View Dr., St. George; (435) 628-8060/ (800) 237-1068 $$$
Off the main drag, and offering tennis, golf, racquetball, and exercise facilities.

☎ **Penny Farthing Inn.** 278 N. 100 West, St. George; (435) 673-7755 $$-$$$
Built in the 1860s and fully restored. Rooms have an English decor; there's a Jacuzzi in the Bridal Suite.

☎ **St. George Hilton Inn.** 1450 S.Hilton Dr., St. George; (435) 628-0463 or

(800) 628-0463 $$-$$$
Close to golf course.

⚎ **St. George Holiday Inn.** 850 South
Bluff St., St. George; (435) 628-4235
or (800) 457-9800 $$
Nice indoor sports complex and pool.

⚉ **Snow Canyon Campground.** Five
miles north of St. George off UT 18;
(435) 628-2255.
This scenic campground is among the
best in this part of the state.

Zion National Park Vicinity

✕ **Bit and Spur Saloon and Mexican
Restaurant.** 1212 Zion Park Blvd.,
Springdale; (435) 772-3498 $-$$
Interesting Mexican dishes make this
restaurant rank among the best south-
of-the-border-style spots in the state.
Music on weekends.

✕ **Flanigan's Inn.** 428 Zion Park Blvd.,
Springdale; (435) 772-3244 $-$$
Southwestern-style cuisine, especially
variations on salmon and pasta.

✕ **Pizza and Noodle Company.** 868 Zion
Park Blvd, Springdale; (435) 772-3815 $
In an old church. It's strictly serve-your-
self, but the pizza and pasta are the best
in the area.

✕ **Switchback Cafe.** 1149 S. Zion Park
Blvd., Springdale; (435) 772-3777 $$-
$$$
Large picture windows overlook Zion at
this pleasant cafe. The kitchen uses
fresh ingredients and specializes in
wood-fired pizzas, vegetarian dishes,
and fruit drinks.

✕ **Zion Lodge.** Zion National Park; (435)
772-3213 $$-$$$

Historic lodge offering traditional fare
such as trout and ribeye, as well as good
pastas. Great views of the park. Picnics
can be ordered in advance.

⚎ **Blue House Bed & Breakfast.**
Rockville; (435) 772-3912 $$
A modern home built to look old. The
three upstairs rooms are delightful.

⚎ **Flanigan's Inn.** 428 Zion Park Blvd.,
Springdale; (435) 772-3244 $$–$$$
A step above the franchise motels and
restaurants in the area. Both modern
and older units, a nice pool area, and a
very good restaurant (see opposite).

⚎ **Harvest House Bed & Breakfast.** 29
Canyon View Dr., Springdale; (435)
772-3880 $$
A classic, two-story Western ranch
house. Request the rooms with private
decks that sit beneath Zion's Watchman
Formation.

⚎ **O'Tooele's Under the Eaves Guest
House.** 980 Zion Park Blvd., Spring-
dale; (435) 772-3457 $$
Beautiful views of Zion National Park
with a garden Jacuzzi.

⚎ **Zion Park Inn.** 1215 Zion Park Blvd.
(435) 772-3200 $$
A new inn decorated with Southwest-
ern accents Hasa common sitting area
overlooking Zion Canyon.

⚎ **Zion Lodge.** Zion National Park; (435)
772-3213 $$–$$$
The only lodging in the park, this historic lodge is open year-round. The old
cabins, each with a fireplace, are popular, as are the more modern motel
suites, so reserve well in advance.

Utah Canyonlands Food & Lodging

GRAND CANYON ❖ LAS VEGAS

■ HIGHLIGHTS

Grand Canyon
Lake Mead
Hoover Dam
Las Vegas
Red Rock Canyon
Mojave Desert

■ BASICS

The 1,400-mile Colorado River drains the Rocky Mountains, crashing in a great flood through Utah, then backing up behind dams in the red-rock country on Arizona's borders with Utah and Nevada. West of Glen Canyon Dam the river cuts a mile deep into the Kaibab Plateau, forming the Grand Canyon: 277 miles long, four to 18 miles wide, varicolored, mysterious, and almost impossible to grasp.

From the Grand Canyon, the Colorado River backs up behind Hoover Dam to form Lake Mead, a blue, flat expanse of water among red-rock cliffs. The river turns south past Hoover Dam, through dry desert toward the Gulf of California. Just west of its curve to the south, lies the ultimate desert mirage, Las Vegas, gambling capital of the United States, and beyond it Red Rock Canyon and the Mojave Desert. The Colorado River flows out of Mojave Desert country, south into the Sonoran Desert. The southern wedge of Nevada that splits the Arizona-California border is the lowest point in Nevada, 450 feet above sea level, and the hottest. The country's highest temperatures are recorded here more than 20 days a year.

■ TRAVELERS ORIENTATION

Visitors to the Grand Canyon must decide first which rim to visit, as few people manage both on one visit. Reservations to stay in this area, or to raft the river or ride a burro into the canyon must be made long in advance. Spontaneous visits will probably mean staying 84 miles away in Flagstaff (for the South Rim), and driving in, walking about on overlooks, getting a snack, and driving back.

Lake Mead—like Lake Powell a vast expanse of water in the desert—is easily accessible. Hoover Dam makes a fascinating day trip. Las Vegas is easy to reach by freeway, usually has plenty of affordable lodging, and will bewilder or excite you depending on your predilections.

Food & Lodging appears on page 250.

The Grand Canyon is a microcosm of climate zones from Phantom Ranch (elev. 2,570) on the canyon floor, all the way up to South Rim (elev. 6,950), and North Rim (elev. 8,400.) On average, the temperature drops five degrees for every thousand feet of elevation, so summer temperatures are some 30° warmer at the bottom of the canyon than at the top. It's also drier, as rainfall tends to evaporate before reaching the canyon floor.

Las Vegas, set in a broad Mojave Desert valley, has the lowest humidity and driest climate of any metropolitan area in the country. Six months of the year it is pervaded by daunting heat. Thunderstorms are common in the summer, and winds can be fierce at any time of the year. Winter temperatures are mild.

TEMPS (F°)	AVG. JAN. HIGH	LOW	AVG. APRIL HIGH	LOW	AVG. JULY HIGH	LOW	AVG. OCT. HIGH	LOW	RECORD HIGH	RECORD LOW
North Rim	37	16	53	29	77	46	59	31	91	-25
South Rim	41	18	60	32	84	54	65	36	98	-22
Phantom Ranch	56	36	82	56	106	78	84	58	120	-9
Las Vegas	58	33	79	50	104	77	80	54	118	8

PRECIPITATION (INCHES)	AVG. JAN.	AVG. APRIL	AVG. JULY	AVG. OCT.	ANNUAL	SNOW
North Rim	3.2	1.7	1.9	1.4	22.8	129
South Rim	1.5	0.9	1.9	1.2	14.5	65
Phantom Ranch	0.7	0.5	0.8	0.6	8.4	0
Las Vegas	0.5	0.2	0.4	0.2	4.0	1

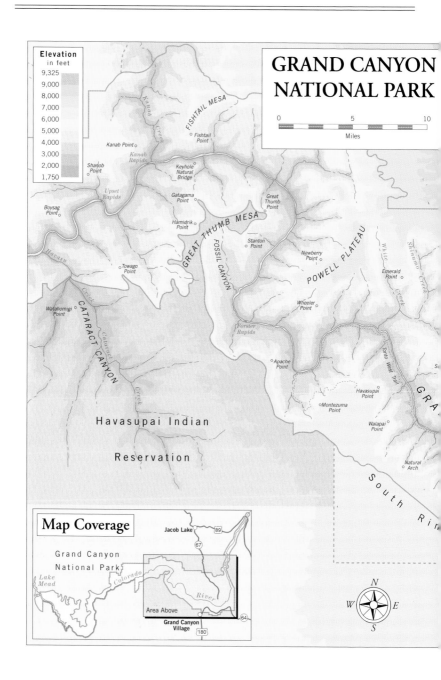

Elevation
in feet
9,325
9,000
8,000
7,000
6,000
5,000
4,000
3,000
2,000
1,750

GRAND CANYON
NATIONAL PARK

0   5   10
Miles

FISHTAIL MESA

Fishtail Point

Kanab Point

Kanab Rapids

Sharlob Point

Keyhole Natural Bridge

Upset Rapids

Gatagama Point

Great Thumb Point

Boysag Point

Hamidrik Point

GREAT THUMB MESA

FOSSIL CANYON

Stanton Point

Newberry Point

POWELL PLATEAU

White

Shinumo Creek

Emerald Point

Towago Point

Watahomigi Point

CATARACT CANYON

Cataract

Creek

Wheeler Point

Forster Rapids

Apache Point

Havasupai Point

Tonto West Trail

GRA

Se

Havasupai Indian

Montezuma Point

Walapai Point

Reservation

Natural Arch

South Ri

Map Coverage

Jacob Lake   89

67

Grand Canyon
National Park

Lake
Mead

Colorado

River

64

Area Above

Grand Canyon
Village   180

N
W   E
S

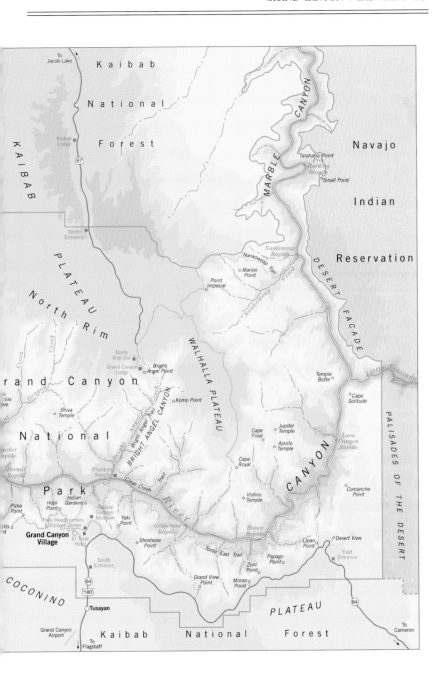

■ GRAND CANYON HISTORY

One-point-seven million years. Six million years. Twenty-five million. Sixty-five million. Consult three recent books on the Grand Canyon, and you'll get these four estimates of its age (One book couldn't make up its mind). Despite a century of intense study, one of the most fundamental questions about the canyon's geology, its birthday, remains mired in confusion and debate. What is known is that the once-mighty Colorado River carved a fantastic gash about a mile deep and four to 18 miles wide through the Kaibab Plateau, exposing 1.2 billion years of the earth's formation to glorious view. Or is it two billion?

Modern humankind has radically altered the process, however. Engineers at Glen Canyon Dam, completed in 1963, artificially vary the flow of water through the Colorado from a trickle to a torrent depending on how hard the air conditioners in cities such as Phoenix and Los Angeles are having to work. Ardent environmentalists, who despise the dam more than any other piece of civil engineering in North America, keep praying for an even greater flood than the one in 1983, which threatened to destroy the damn thing. Mother Nature being who she is, the Colorado undoubtedly will someday be a wild and free river once again.

Human beings have lived in and around the Grand Canyon for about 4,000 years. Anasazi left more than 2,000 ruins in the canyon, mostly at its eastern half, dating between A.D. 500 and 1225. In more recent times nomadic Paiute lived in the canyon, and the tiny Havasupai tribe still does.

Spanish explorer García López de Cárdenas, part of Francisco de Coronado's expedition, laid eyes on the Canyon in 1540 but found no way down inside it. The canyon's modern exploration was left to John Wesley Powell. A courageous and fascinating man who had lost his right arm in the Civil War, Powell led the first thorough expedition through the canyon in 1869. He set out from the Colorado tributary of Green River in Wyoming on May 24 with 10 men and a flotilla of four 16- and 21-foot rowboats. The tattered remains of the expedition—two boats, seven men—arrived more than three months later at the mouth of the Virgin River, now somewhere under Lake Mead in Nevada's southeastern corner. Powell's dramatic and meticulous chronicle, published by the U.S. Government Printing Office in 1875, ranks among the most compelling and literate explorers' journals ever written.

Three of Powell's companions died on the expedition—the ones, ironically, who had balked at running the stupefying Separation Rapid (also now inundated

RIDING THE RAPIDS WITH JOHN WESLEY POWELL

*A*nd now we go on through this solemn, mysterious way. The river is very deep, the canyon very narrow, and still obstructed, so that there is no steady flow of the stream; but the waters wheel, and roll, and boil, and we are scarcely able to determine where we can go. Now, the boat is carried to the right, perhaps close to the wall; again, she is shot into the stream, and perhaps is dragged over to the other side, where, caught in a whirlpool, she spins about. We can neither land nor run as we please. The boats are entirely unmanageable; no order in their running can be preserved; now one, now another, is ahead, each crew laboring for its own preservation. In such a place we come to another rapid. Two of the boats run it perforce. One succeeds in landing, but there is no foothold by which to make a portage, and she is pushed out again into the stream. The next minute a great reflex wave fills the open compartment; she is water-logged, and drifts unmanageable. Breaker after breaker rolls over her, and one capsizes her. The men are thrown out; but they cling to the boat, and she drifts down some distance, alongside of us, and we are able to catch her. She is soon bailed out, and the men are aboard once more; but the oars are lost, so a pair from the *Emma Dean* is spared. Then for two miles we find smooth water.

—John Wesley Powell, *Diary of Colorado River Explorations,* 1869

by Lake Mead) and tried to walk out of the canyon. Three days later, Shivwits Paiute Indians encountered them on the North Rim and killed them.

Powell's reports from this and a subsequent expedition in 1871 introduced the Grand Canyon to an astonished country, but tourism took hold slowly. Even to settlers in Utah and Arizona Territory, the canyon seemed remote and inaccessible. However, John Hance, an itinerant miner and raconteur, built a log cabin on the South Rim about 1883, and soon began leading paying guests into the canyon on trails.

It wasn't until 1901, when the 64-mile railroad punched through from Williams to the South Rim, that tourists began flocking to the canyon in serious numbers. By 1905, the luxurious El Tovar Hotel was complete, and in 1922, Phantom Ranch—then as now the only accommodation on the canyon floor —opened for guests. Today's routine amusement of river running, however,

Artist William Holmes, who accompanied John Wesley Powell in his exploration of the Grand Canyon, produced this spectacular chromolithograph in 1882. (Library of Congress)

remained an exotic and frequently deadly venture for a long time. After Powell's first successful river trip through the canyon in 1869, 80 years passed before 100 people, including the Powell parties, had done the same.

❖

The first major project to harness the Colorado to human benefit (other than aesthetic) was Hoover Dam, completed in 1935. It was (and still is) a stupefying piece of civil engineering and public sculpture, a curving buttress of concrete 726 feet high, at its completion the biggest dam in the world (it is now the 19th highest). It provided irrigation water, domestic water, and hydroelectric power for three states—as well as recreation in Lake Mead, backed up behind it.

However, what turned the Colorado into the relatively benign stream it is today was the completion of Glen Canyon Dam more than 200 miles upstream from Hoover. Ironically, the recreational lake created thereby is named Lake Powell, in honor of the pioneer explorer who undoubtedly would have been saddened to see this magnificent torrent and canyon obliterated.

■ SEEING THE GRAND CANYON

The Grand Canyon is a vast 277-mile furrow cut by the Colorado River into the Kaibab Plateau of northwestern Arizona. While you can see across the canyon, the drive from the South Rim Village to the North Rim Overlook is long, the shortest route being 235 miles via the Navajo Bridge. Most visitors choose one rim from which to see the canyon, and then figure out how to get down into it.

The South Rim of the canyon can be reached by driving north from Flagstaff, Arizona, on scenic US 180 to Grand Canyon Village or north off I-40 from Williams on AZ 64. Here are lodgings, restaurants, thousands of visitors, and few places to park. Yet with a little effort and ingenuity you can get away from the crowds and enjoy the canyon. **The North Rim**, located south and east of St. George, Utah, off US 89 and AZ 67, is more remote, has fewer amenities, and draws fewer visitors. Because its elevation is 1,500 feet higher, it's also cooler and gets more precipitation than the South Rim. Thanks to the abundant snow, it is open to visitors only mid-May through mid-October.

No single mode of exploring the Grand Canyon is enough to fully appreciate and comprehend it, and standing on the rim and staring in is the most inadequate of all. One needs to engage the canyon with all the senses. Hike its trails, feel its walls, challenge its river. Fly over it—at twilight, if possible, when its vivid afternoon colors of auburns, greens, purples, and browns slowly converge into a deep, mistlike, saturating blue, and its sharp edges melt away in the faint light, the sensation of mystery growing as bottomless as the chasm itself.

■ DRIVING

Roads follow both the North and South rims of the canyon for short distances. Overlooks are marked, and it's quite possible to simply drive along, park your car, get out, and look. Refer to the map on pages 228–229. At the South Rim orient yourself at the **Park Headquarters and Visitors Center,** four miles into the park from the South Entrance Station. Less than a mile farther is the **Yavapai Geologic Museum,** which explains the geologic history of the canyon. East Rim Drive has numerous extraordinary views along its 25-mile route from Grand Canyon Village to Desert View—from which you can see all the way to the Painted Desert.

The North Rim's Cape Royal Scenic Drive will take you (follow the signs) to Point Imperial, which at 8,803 feet provides views of the Painted Desert, Vermilion Cliffs, and Navajo Mountain.

Buffalo Bill Cody takes time to tour the Grand Canyon in this 1889 photo. (Church of Latter-day Saints Archives)

■ HIKING

The best times to hike are morning and evening, when the air is cool and the colors enhanced by angled light. Easy walks and hikes along "maintained trails" are the best way for most people to get a sense of the canyon's majesty. Hiking to the bottom is memorable, strenuous, and best undertaken by people in excellent physical condition who take the precautions necessary in a desert landscape. The elevation change is dramatic, there is little or no water, and midday summer temperatures are often over 100 degrees.

Ambitious hikers should consult the hiking guides available in the stores, visitors centers, or the Backcountry Reservations Office. Talk to rangers and buy maps. Backpackers will need permits; day hikers do not.

The alternative to the busy maintained trails are the "secondary trails," which are not maintained by the National Park Service: Hermit, Grandview, Tanner, Boucher, New Hance, Thunder River, and others. They range from moderately difficult to very difficult; some may require route-finding skills. It goes without saying that they also are more rewarding. Hikers or mule riders staying overnight at Phantom Ranch may want to reserve an extra day for the lovely **Clear Creek Trail** (18 miles round trip), which passes Anasazi ruins and Cheyava Falls, the canyon's highest (usually a trickle, however, except during spring runoff). Clear Creek is relatively level and easy.

Many hikers prefer professionally guided overnighters. The **Grand Canyon Field Institute** offers three- and four-day educational programs on a variety of topics including geology, wildlife, and photography. *(520) 638-2485.*

❖

South Rim Hikes. An easy walk along the South Rim is via the **West Rim Trail**—a partially paved, fairly level trail that begins at Bright Angel Lodge (just to the west of Grand Canyon Village) and ends eight miles later at Hermit's Rest. The wonderful overlooks along the way aren't as crowded as those that can be driven to, and from May through September the road adjacent to the trail is closed to all vehicles but shuttle buses—which stop at various points along the way picking up anyone who wants to hop aboard. Many people walk to Hermit's Rest, get something to eat at the snack bar, and take the shuttle back to the Village.

South Kaibab Trail begins at Yaki Point four miles east of the Village. An excellent day hike is the three-mile round trip from Yaki Point to Cedar Ridge, which has magnificent views all along the way. The elevation drops 1,500 feet.

(previous pages) "It is impossible to conceive what the canyon is, or what impression it makes, from descriptions or pictures, however good. . . . The prudent keep silent." —John Muir

Early morning is the best time to go, when the air is still cool, and the colors, as the sun comes up, are magnificent. From Cedar Ridge you will get a sense of the depth and majesty of the canyon; the hike to the bottom of the canyon is six miles long, descends 4,620 feet, and is exceedingly hot, dry, and grueling.

Bright Angel Trail is the easiest and most overused rim-to-river trail in the canyon. One way it drops 7.7 miles and 4,420 feet. A strenuous day trip along this trail takes you to the magnificent river views at **Plateau Point.**

North Rim Hikes. Uncle Jim Trail is a fairly easy walk through forest with little elevation gain. It leads to several quiet canyon overlooks. Begin by following the Ken Patrick Trail at the North Kaibab trailhead (below).

North Kaibab Trail follows an exceedingly beautiful route, beginning in the forest on the North Rim and descending along Bright Angel Creek to the Colorado River. A good day trip on this route is to go as far as the Roaring Springs picnic ground—about 4.6 miles each way. The trail begins at a parking lot two miles north of Grand Canyon Lodge.

When hiking in the Grand Canyon, be sure to bring plenty of drinking water. Dehydration is one of the most common ailments to befall unprepared hikers. (photo below courtesy of Nevada Historical Society)

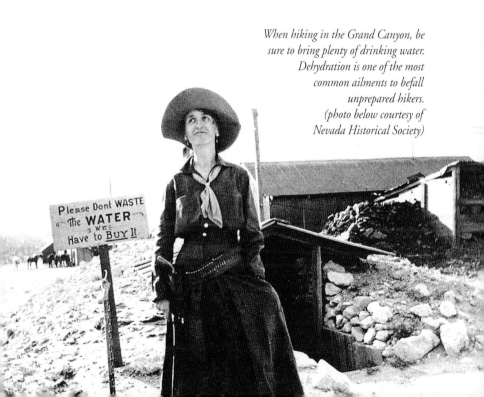

■ MULE TRIPS

Wrangler-guided trips ranging from seven hours to three days are available. The concessionaire requires that riders weigh less than 200 pounds and be fluent in English. Warns the brochure, "Those who are disturbed by heights or large animals should reconsider." Reservations are necessary up to 11 months in advance for the South Rim; for the North Rim, one day or two. Two-day trips include an overnight stay at Phantom Ranch near the bottom of the canyon. *For reservations call (303) 297-2757.*

■ RAFTING

The raft trip down the Grand Canyon is one of the great wilderness adventures in the world, but not for the faint of heart. Rapids such as the 19-foot drop at the Sockdolager are terrifying but, like other terrifying experiences, definitely unforgettable. Once you've done it, you'll probably spend the rest of your life hoping to run into other people who've done it so you can relive your experience with them.

Rafting from Lee's Ferry 277 miles to Lake Mead is about a 12-day trip. Shorter trips go to Phantom Ranch (three days, 89 miles) and to Bar 10 Ranch (seven to ten days, 188 miles). Along the way you can swim in turquoise pools, shower under waterfalls, and hike the side canyons. The canyon changes dramatically as you travel forward: cliffs rise thousands of feet overhead and it's possible to see bighorn sheep, beaver, mule deer, and peregrine falcons.

A half-day float trip (i.e. no rapids) can be taken on Zodiac rafts from Glen Canyon Dam to Lee's Ferry. *For float trips or whitewater rafting, make arrangements in the outdoor supply stores in Page, Arizona, just east of the dam, or call Wilderness River Adventures (800) 992-8022.*

■ STEAM TRAIN

Since 1989, South Rim visitors have had the intriguing option of driving to Williams, then riding a vintage steam locomotive to the South Rim. The Grand Canyon Railway ceased regular service in 1953 but now, after restoration and a very popular revival, it slices through 64 miles of scenic high plateau country and the Kaibab National Forest. Reservations are strongly advised. One big advantage to visitors who arrive by train is that they do not have to search for scarce parking spaces. *Grand Canyon Railway (520) 773-1976.*

Sunrise over the Colorado River from Toroweap Point.

■ HELICOPTER OR AIRPLANE TOURS

Grand Canyon Airport is now Arizona's third busiest, and the canyon's airspace is hazardous. Try **Scenic Airlines** *(702) 739-1900;* **Air Nevada** *(702) 736-2702;* **Sierra Nevada Airways** *(702) 631-3119;* or **Helicop-Tours Choppers** *(702) 736-0606.*

■ HAVASUPAI INDIAN RESERVATION

The Hualapais and Havasupais are the people of the Grand Canyon. The Hualapai, whose name derives from a Yuman word meaning "Pinetree People," live on 1,551 square miles of forest and high plateau land abutting the canyon's south rim. The Havasupais ("People of the Blue-Green Water") number only about 600 and are the most isolated of any Arizona tribe. To reach their village, **Supai,** from Grand Canyon Village, travel south on US 180 for 57 miles to Williams, then take I-40 west 44 miles to Seligman. Continue 34 miles west on AZ 66 until you reach Indian Route 18. Finally, head north 60 miles on AZ 66 through the Hualapai Reservation, park at Hualapai Hilltop, and either walk or ride a mule 11 miles further into Havasu Canyon. At the bottom of this Eden-like spot are the village and store, Havasupai campground, and a series of magnificent waterfalls that plunge 100 feet into a turquoise pool. Reservations at the campground and lodge must be made in advance. *Campground, (520) 448-2121 ; lodge, (520) 448-2111.*

■ LAKE MEAD AND HOOVER DAM

A vast, shimmering expanse that looms like a mirage, providing stark visual relief from the monochromatic landscape that surrounds it, Lake Mead is the largest man-made lake in the United States. It stretches for 110 miles, plunges to a depth of 500 feet, and has 822 miles of shoreline. This mighty reservoir irrigates two and a quarter million acres of land in the United States and Mexico, and supplies water for more than 14 million people. It is the centerpiece of the 1.5-million-acre Lake Mead National Recreation Area, which includes Lake Mojave, and the surrounding desert from Davis Dam to the south and Grand Canyon National Park in the east, all the way north to Overton, the largest Department of Interior recreational acreage in the country.

Like Lake Powell, it has a rather fantastic bleakness about it: red rock, little in the way of trees, wide stretches of water. Weatherwise, spring is fine but fall is the

Mooney Falls tumbles hundreds of feet into a turquoise pool on the Havasupai Indian Reservation. Hikers trek 11 miles to reach this idyllic spot.

best: the blistering summer heat's gone, the wind's steady, and the water's warm. Winter winds are fluky, characteristic of large inland bodies of water. In summer, ferocious storms can roar across the canyon with little mercy and less warning, only to disappear 30 minutes later. Power boats race across the surface, pulling water-skiers. Power skis race alongside them. Many visitors rent houseboats and pull up in hidden coves. Sailing and windsurfing are good year-round.

Fishing is eventful and changeable. Largemouth and striped bass, rainbow, brown, and cutthroat trout, catfish, and black crappie have been the mainstays for decades.

Boulder Beach, 30 miles from Las Vegas and just down the road from the Alan Bible Visitor Center (off US 93) is a good place to swim. Over a mile long, it's rarely crowded, and the water can reach 85 degrees in July.

Hoover Dam. Visiting this marvel of engineering that formed Lake Mead is a sobering experience. Built in 1935, Hoover Dam generates four billion kilowatt-hours of electricity each year, enough for half a million houses. The dam's statistics are all superlatives: it's 726 feet high, 1,244 feet across, and 660 feet thick at its base, and it holds back the force of 50 trillion pounds of water. *Located 34 miles southeast of Las Vegas on US 93/95.*

Hoover Dam construction in progress in 1934. The river's flow had to be diverted via two enormous man-made tunnels through the canyon walls on each side of the riverbed. (Underwood Archives, San Francisco)

■ LAKE MOJAVE

Created downstream by Davis Dam in 1953, Lake Mojave backs up almost all the way to Hoover Dam, like an extension of Lake Mead. The two lakes are similar in climate, desert scenery, vertical-walled canyon enclosures, and a shoreline digitated with numerous private coves. Lake Mojave, however, is much smaller, and thus not nearly as susceptible to Lake Mead's monsoons. It's narrower too, so the protection of shore is never too far away. Still, it offers excellent trout fishing at Willow Beach on the Arizona side, where the water, too cold for swimming, is perfect for serious angling. Marinas are found at Cottonwood Cove just north of the widest part of the lake and at Katherine Landing just north of Davis Dam. For all that, it's a much better-kept secret than exalted Lake Mead.

About 130 miles downriver from Lake Mojave is **Havasu City** with Arizona's most famous aberration, the **London Bridge.** Purchased in 1967 and reassembled to span a narrow arm of the 45-mile-long lake, the bridge has turned Lake Havasu into a year-round resort area.

■ LAS VEGAS

Whatever it isn't, Las Vegas is hard to forget—a booming, modern city, rife with malls, housing developments, schools, Bible classes, gambling, and big shows. The Las Vegas annual visitor count has now topped 30 million. Each year, tourists (and locals) lose more than six billion dollars inside the casinos and spend another six billion for food, lodging, and gas. Two million visitors attend conventions. Roughly 204,000 get married. Another 40,000 people—more than 1,000 a week—relocate to Las Vegas. The population has swelled to more than a million in the metropolitan area, making Las Vegas the fastest-growing city in the country and by far the largest American city to have been founded in the 20th century. The population is increasing so rapidly, in fact, that Las Vegas is the only city in the country which needs an updated Yellow Pages every six months.

Las Vegas claims more than 100,000 hotel rooms, more than any other city in the world by a mile. The 5,005-room **MGM Grand** is the largest hotel on the planet. It has 171,000 square feet of casino space, 93 elevators, a 33-acre amusement park, a monumental race and sports book, and a 15,000-seat arena for rock concerts and championship boxing matches (including the decade's most notorious fight, Tyson vs. Holyfield). **The Luxor,** the second largest hotel in Las Vegas

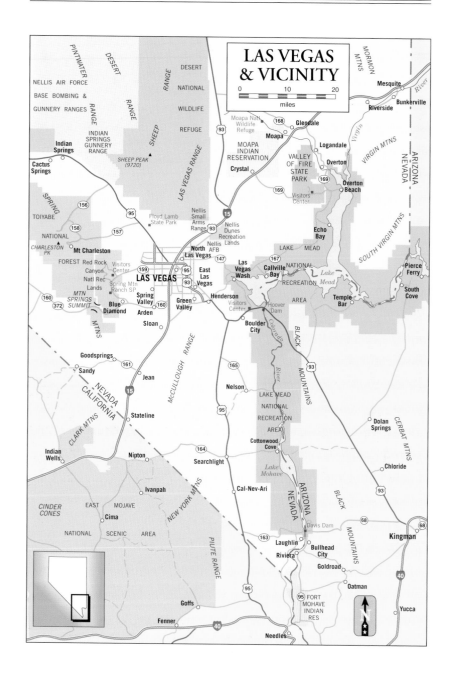

LAS VEGAS & VICINITY

0   10   20
miles

with nearly 4,500 rooms, is impossible to miss. The exterior of this giant pyramid encompasses 13 acres of glass in the form of 39,000 windows, and the spotlight, beaming through the apex, packs a 40-billion-candlepower punch. Other dazzlers include the **Mirage's** 54-foot "volcano" which erupts every half hour after dark; **New York–New York** with its astonishing replica of the Big Apple's skyline, Brooklyn Bridge, and Coney Island roller coaster; and the **Stratosphere Hotel, Tower & Casino,** which boasts the world's highest thrill ride and the tallest observation tower in the United States (ninth tallest building in the world). The **Las Vegas Hilton**, in partnership with Paramount, recently opened a multi-million dollar interactive attraction, "Star Trek: The Experience."

And there's no end in sight to the development of theme hotels, amusement parks, high-tech entertainment, and unabashed spectacle. At least 25,000 new rooms in 15 hotels have been announced and are slated to be built before the turn of the millennium. The luxury Bellagio Resort and Casino is due to open fall 1998 with 3,000 rooms and a 12-acre lake. Circus Circus is planning to open its new 3,600-room megaresort, Paradise, soon after. Las Vegas is on its biggest and fastest roll ever, still trying to live up to the challenge of simply fulfilling its destiny.

Luxor resort and casino in all its kitsch glory.

With a dozen arenas and concert halls hosting everything from headliners to prize fights and rodeos, floorshow extravaganzas, discos, nightclubs, comedy clubs, topless and bottomless joints, and country-western saloons, there's plenty to do.

The Thomas and Mack Center, MGM Grand Arena, Aladdin Theatre for the Performing Arts, Hard Rock Hotel, Bally's, Caesars, and the Desert Inn all have venues where star performers like Bill Cosby and Jerry Seinfeld (and Vegas types like Tom Jones and Julio Iglesias) draw large crowds. Unless the performer is a perennial sell-out, you should be able to get into any show that's in town. Check out the stars and revues as soon as you settle in, and make reservations immediately at the particular box office. About half the shows offer reserved seating, making it simple to call ahead and show up anytime. However, other venues still use the traditional Las Vegas system: you make reservations for general seating, which is first-come, first served. Seating begins hour or two before showtime. Be early and ready to tip the maitre d': generally $10 at revues. Some hotels prioritize reservations for their guests, so you might pick your hotel by the show you'd like to see—especially if it's included in a package deal. If you can't get reservations, you can show up at show time and hope for a no-show, or consult your bell captain for advice. *See page 251 for a list of 15 major hotels.*

■ RED ROCK CANYON

West of Las Vegas, stretching across the horizon and hemming in the valley, are the rugged Spring Mountains. Red Rock Canyon, a multicolored sandstone palisade lies a mere 10 miles from downtown Las Vegas on West Charleston Boulevard. The Mojave desert scenery—stands of Joshua trees, backdropped by the precipitous Spring Mountain walls, with Red Rock Canyon standing sentinel—has been known to leave even National Geographic photographers speechless.

Start with the enormity of the semicircular scenery, which swallows crowds and dwarfs climbers. Then superimpose the gorgeous colors of the sandstone—yellow, orange, pink, red, purple—all overlaid by the tempered gray of older limestone. The narrow, steep-walled canyons—moist, cool, lush gashes between the cliffs—have made Red Rock Canyon into a year-round climbing destination.

The BLM **Visitors Center** is nestled in the Calico Hills at the lower end of the wide oval that encompasses all this glowing Aztec sandstone. The center has excellent 3-D exhibits of geology, flora and fauna, and recreational opportunities; a short nature trail out back; and a 13-mile loop road with half a dozen overlooks, picnic sites, and trails leading to springs, canyons, quarries, and *tinajas* (tanks).

You can easily spend an entire day exploring the edges of the loop road. Be sure to stop at both Calico Vista points, with massive 6,323-foot Turtle Head Mountain leaning high and limy over the Calico Hills. A short trail from the second vista gets you into the territory. Another trail enters **Sandstone Quarry,** where red and white sandstone for Southwestern buildings was mined from 1905 to 1912. Absorb the view of the Madre Mountains, a dramatic limestone ridge line of the Spring Range, then swing around south past the White Rock Hills, Bridge and Rainbow mountains, and Mt. Wilson. Hikes enter Lost Creek, Icebox, and Pine Creek canyons. You could then spend another six days hiking around the 16- by 10-mile park, or devote a lifetime to climbing the 1,500 known routes up the red rock.

Spring Mountain Ranch. Watch for wild burros along the stretch between Red Rock Canyon and the state park. The ranch is nestled at the base of sheer, buff-colored sandstone bluffs of the Wilson Cliffs. The area's cooler temperatures, plentiful water, bountiful land, and gorgeous setting have attracted travelers since the 1830s. By 1869, a ranch had been established with a stone cabin and blacksmith shop (both still standing).

The long green lawns, bright white picket fences, and New England–style red ranch house make an idyllic setting. *Three miles west of Red Rock Canyon off US 159 (Charleston Boulevard); (702) 875-4141.*

■ VALLEY OF FIRE STATE PARK

The gods had miles of fire-red rock to carve at Valley of Fire State Park and 150 million years to fill in the details. Six miles long and three to four miles wide, this is another spectacular ancestral hall of the Navajo Formation, a continuum of Mesozoic sandstone that stretches from southern Colorado through New Mexico, Arizona, Utah, and Nevada. Its monuments, arches, protruding jagged walls, divine engravings, and human etchings, all in brilliant vermilion, scarlet, mauve, burgundy, magenta, orange, and gold are representative of the great American Southwest.

The highest and youngest formations in the park are mountains of sand deposited by desert winds 140 million years ago—the familiar Aztec sandstone. These dunes were petrified, oxidized, and chiseled by time, sun, water, and chemical reactions into their magnificent shapes and colors. *Approximately 55 miles northeast of Las Vegas off NV 169; (702) 397-2088.*

■ FOOD & LODGING

> *Restaurant prices:*
> Per person, not including drinks, tax, and tips:
> $ = under $10; $$ = $10–20; $$$ = over $20
>
> *Room rates:*
> Per night, per room, double occupancy:
> $ = under $50; $$ = $50–100; $$$ = over $100

Grand Canyon: North Rim

✕ **Grand Canyon Lodge Restaurant.**
South on AZ 67; (520) 638-2611 $$
Surprisingly good restaurant housed in
a historic lodge and overlooking the
canyon. Expertly prepared entrees
include steak, shrimp tempura, rainbow
trout, and lasagna.

✕ **Vermilion Cliffs Restaurant.** Lee's
Ferry Lodge, US 89A near Marble
Canyon Bridge; (520) 355-2231 $$
One of the only restaurants along US
89 en route to the North Rim.
Standard American fare in a rustic,
stone-walled dining room.

⌂ **Campgrounds.** Overnight camping
inside the canyon requires a permit, call
park headquarters (520) 638-7888.
Lee's Ferry Campground, 2 mi off US
89A rarely fills up and is a good place
to camp between the South and North
rims of the Grand Canyon. The sites
here have drinking water, but no
showers or hookups. (520) 645-2471.

⊤ **Grand Canyon Lodge.** Reservation
number: (303) 297-2757 $
Twelve miles from the park boundary

and overlooking the canyon is a 1930s-
vintage main lodge, built out of native
sandstone and ponderosa beams. Lodge
guest rooms are motel-like and moderately priced, or you can choose from
rustic to modern cabins.

⊤ **Jacob Lake Inn.** 40 miles from the
North Rim along US 89A.; (520) 643-
7232 $
Nothing fancy but this clean, no-frills
roadside motel is a good alternative to
the often crowded lodges closer to
Grand Canyon.

⊤ **Kaibab Lodge.** Five miles outside the
park on Kaibab Plateau, off AZ 67;
(520) 638-2389 $$
A lovely wooded setting surrounds
these 25 rustic cabins with motel-style
furnishings.

Grand Canyon: South Rim

⌂ **Grand Canyon National Park Lodges.**
Box 699, Grand Canyon, AZ 86023;
(303) 297-2757
Use the above address to reserve space
at all South Rim lodges, in addition to
Phantom Ranch on the canyon floor

(see below). Descending in cost are El Tovar ($$–$$$), designated a National Historic Landmark, dramatic and luxurious; Thunderbird and Kachina lodges ($$); Yavapai Lodge ($$); Bright Angel Lodge and Cabins ($–$$$); and Maswik Lodge ($) and Moqui Lodge ($). All except Yavapai, Maswik, and Moqui lodges are very close to the rim. Best value: Bright Angel.

Ψ **Phantom Ranch.** (303) 297-2757 $ Located at the bottom of Grand Canyon, the lodge is accessible only to hikers and mule riders. The dormitory is reserved for hikers; cabins are exclusively for mule riders.

Lake Havasu

Ψ **Nautical Inn.** 1000 McCulloch Blvd.; (520) 855-2141 $$$ Situated on a three-square-mile island in the center of Lake Havasu is this deluxe resort with a private dock. All units have patios and are on the water.

Ψ **Ramada London Bridge Resort.** 1477 Queen's Bay Rd.; (520) 855-0888 or (800) 624-7939 $$$ Luxurious Olde English theme resort, with golf course, tennis courts, pool, and modern guest rooms. Overlooks lake and London Bridge.

Lake Mead

⚓ **Campgrounds.** In addition to the campsites at Echo Bay (below), park service campgrounds are located on the south side of **Boulder Beach,** two miles from Hoover Dam off US 95; (702) 293-8906. Additional campgrounds are at **Overton Beach,** 9 miles south of Overton off AZ 169, and at **Valley of Fire State Park,** less than two miles west of the upper arm of Lake Mead, off AZ 169, (702) 397-2088.

Ψ **Echo Bay Resort and Campgrounds.** (702) 394-4000 $ This modest motel offers modern, inexpensive rooms, along with park service campgrounds, a restaurant, coffee shop, houseboat rentals, and an RV parking lot.

Ψ **Lake Mead Marina Lodge.** 322 Lakeshore Rd.; (800) 752-9669 $$ On the north side of Boulder Beach, this motel has hundreds of boat slips and a popular floating restaurant. Fine views of the lake.

Las Vegas

population 400,000   elevation 2,020

✗ **Andre's.** 401. S. 6th St., (702) 385-5016 $$$ An expensive French/Continental restaurant in a converted house downtown, with a world-class wine list and entrees. Lots of fish dishes with unusual sauces.

✗ **Battista's Hole In The Wall.** 4041 Audrie; (702) 733-3950 $–$$ The pizza here was voted Las Vegas's best. Family-style meals include

Grand Canyon ❖ Las Vegas Food & Lodging

Grand Canyon ❖ Las Vegas Food & Lodging

antipasto, garlic bread, minestrone, all-you-can-eat pasta on the side, and all-you-can-drink red wine. Classic Italian restaurant decor.

✗ **Cafe Michelle.** 1350 E. Flamingo Rd. near Paradise in the Mission Center; (702) 732-8687 $$
Very popular with Las Vegans, for its patio dining (overlooking the shopping center parking lot), eclectic American and European dishes (crepes, veal, spanikopita), and reasonable prices. Crowded at lunchtime; a bar next door has live music at night.

✗ **Carluccio's Tivoli Gardens.** 1775. E. Tropicana in the Liberace Plaza; (702) 795-3236 $$
The decor is straight out of Liberace —with good reason: Liberace opened this joint next door to his museum. Check out the grand-piano bar and the twinkling overhead lights. The food is good, workman-like Italian. Can't go wrong here.

✗ **Carnival World at the Rio.** 3700 W. Flamingo Rd.; (702) 252-7777 $$-$
The best buffet in this buffet-crazed town. You've got your choice of ribs, burgers, Chinese, fried fish, Italian, Mexican, Mongolian barbecue, salad bar, steaks, sushi, and a big dessert bar.

✗ **Cathay House.** 5300 Spring Mountain Rd.; (702) 876-3838 $$
One of the best Chinese restaurants in town, with a great view from big picture windows overlooking the Strip. Asian locals and visitors pack this place for the dim sum lunch.

✗ **Coyote Cafe.** MGM Grand, 3805 Las Vegas Blvd. South; (702) 891-7349 $-$$
An outpost of the famous Santa Fe restautant, the Coyote Cafe offers sophisticated Southwestern cuisine. There's a casual cafe in the front, too.

✗ **Lindo Michoacan.** 2655 E. Desert Inn Rd.; (702) 735-6828 $$
One of the most popular Mexican restaurants in Las Vegas—don't let the exterior fool you. Huge menu, big choice of combinations, and interesting cactus dishes.

✗ **Palace Station's Feast Buffet.** At Palace Station Hotel, 2411 W. Sahara; (702) 367-2411 $
The buffet line surrounds an open prep area, where cooks keep the food stocked, and prepare dishes to order (eggs, sandwiches, meat, and fish).

✗ **Pamplemousse.** 400 E. Sahara Ave.; (702) 733-2066 $$$
Housed in a converted house. There's no menu; the waiters recite the handful of available entrees of the day. This is the place to sit back, have them bring you the works, and savor each bite. Everything is superb.

✗ **Pasta Pirate.** California Hotel, 12 E. Ogden Ave.; (702) 385-1222 $-$$$
One of the best-value Italian restaurants in a hotel in Las Vegas. The decor is early rustic—vents, pipes, beams, neon. The pasta is plentiful and inexpensive (especially the kids' plate); the filet mignon dinner could be the best in town.

✕ **Primavera at Caesars Palace.** Caesars Palace; (702) 731-7731 $$–$$$
Overlooks the Garden of the Gods swimming pool. Poolside dining, too. The thing to have here, naturally, is the Caesars salad, but also try anything from eggs for breakfast and hamburgers for lunch to Maine lobster for dinner. Reservations a must for dinner. Casual (no shorts).

✕ **Seasons at Bally's.** 3645 Las Vegas Blvd. S.; (702) 739-4111 $$$
A true Continental gourmet room, run by the same European chefs who prepare the Sterling Sunday champagne brunch, long considered the top Sunday brunch in town. There's a large set menu in the $20-$50 range for entrees, but it changes a few times a year according to what's in season. Numerous nightly specials take advantage of the freshest ingredients the chefs can find. Reservations, jacket required.

✕ **Spago.** Forum Shops at Caesars, 3500 Las Vegas Blvd. South; (702) 369-6300 $$$
This counterpart to Wolfgang Puck's L.A. restaurant specializes in classsic California cusine—unusal pizzas and salads, stylish presentation. Reservations advised.

✕ **Steakhouse.** Circus Circus; (702) 734-0410 $$
The split-level dining area surrounds the grill, which lends an authentic, slightly smoky air to the room. Perfect for charcoal freaks.

✕ **Viva Mercado's.** 6182 W. Flamingo; (702) 871-8826 $$
Bobby Mercado has one of the most imaginative Mexican menus around: traditional Tex-Mex dishes are dressed in nouveau duds. Good ceviche (stick with the appetizer, not the salad), great grilled meats.

🛏 **Bally's.** 3645 Las Vegas Blvd. S.; (702) 739-4111 $$$
A massive single-story expanse, Bally's contains 3,000 guest rooms, a huge casino, a 40-store shopping mall, a comedy club, 10 tennis courts, two health spas, six good restaurants, and two showrooms. All the rooms are spacious and nicely decorated. If you decide to splurge on a mini-suite, expect a round bed, mirrored ceiling, and pink champagne on ice.

🛏 **Caesars Palace.** 3570 Las Vegas Blvd. S.; (702) 731-7110 $$$
A 20-foot statue of Caesar fronts the main entrance to this palace of opulence. Inside, stroll past Cleopatra's Barge dance lounge, and a replica of Michelangelo's "David." Make it a point to peak into the Bacchanal, Empress Court, Palace Court, and Primavera restaurants, and check out the Garden of the Gods pool area, modeled after the Pompeii baths with 8,000 inlaid tiles imported from Carrara, Italy. The Forum shopping mall features a sky that changes from dawn to dusk every hour or so and the most stores with Italian names this side of New Jersey.

Grand Canyon ❖ Las Vegas Food & Lodging

Grand Canyon ❖ Las Vegas Food & Lodging

☂ **Excalibur.** 3850 Las Vegas Blvd. S.; (702) 597-7777 $$$
One of the largest hotels in Las Vegas (no small accomplishment) is this King Arthur fantasy resort. Nightly, two dinner shows in the arena feature banquets where you eat with your hands and pound on the tables to root for your favorite knight. Jugglers and musicians stroll around the 23-store Medieval Village, and the hotel wedding chapel rents medieval attire for the ceremony. Despite the castle-like grandeur, the Excalibur often has decent rates on accommodations.

☂ **Golden Nugget.** 129 E. Fremont St.; (702) 385-7111 $-$$$
Spacious Victorian-style rooms (1,900 of them), formal lobbies with marble and red carpet, and gold detailing everywhere are the hallmarks of this downtown hotel and casino. Swimming pool, health spa, 5 restaurants, and showroom.

☂ **Las Vegas Hilton.** 3000 Paradise Rd.; (702) 732-5111 $$$
Adjacent to the Convention Center, this 3,000-or-so-room hotel offers a monumental Star Trek attraction, over a dozen restaurants, 6 tennis courts, swimming pool, a putting green, and Regular guest rooms are large—or stay in the Elvis Suite, where the King himself slept.

☂ **Luxor.** 3900 Las Vegas Blvd. S. (702) 262-4000 $$$
Named after an Egyptian city, the 30-story, pyramid-shaped Luxor is a traffic-stopper, displaying a 10-story sphinx and a full-scale reproduction of King Tut's Tomb. The nearly 4,500 rooms are done in a tasteful Egyptian theme; 7 restaurants, large lounge, showroom, resort spa, IMAX theater.

☂ **MGM Grand Resort Hotel and Theme Park.** 3799 Las Vegas Blvd. S.; (702) 891-1111 $$$
The MGM has 5,005 rooms and a casino space so big that it's divided into three separate themed casinos. This megaresort also houses an amusement park, mall, a mile-long monorail to Bally's, an arena for rock concerts and championship boxing matches, a 1,700-seat theater, restaurants, and a fast-food court.

☂ **The Mirage.** 3400 Las Vegas Blvd. S.; (702) 791-7111 $$$
A Polynesian/Fantasy Island resort featuring six white tigers, a dolphin pool, a shark aquarium, waterfalls, lagoons, tropical gardens, and a volcano—all against an opulent marble and gold background. Immaculately maintained guest rooms are decorated in bright, attractive colors.

☂ **New York–New York.** 3790 Las Vegas Blvd. South; (702) 740-6969 or (800) 693-6763 $$$
Just like its namesake, this joint is small (area-wise) and crowded (people-wise). Finding (and dodging) your way from the front desk to your hotel room can be an adventure. The rooms themselves are standard, but beware: the roller coaster noise, expecially in the front

lower rooms, is overwhelming.

- **Rio Suites Hotel.** 3700 W. Flamingo Rd.; (702) 252-7777 $$$
A red and blue Brazilian-theme all-suite hotel with casino, 6 restaurants, a gym, and a pool with its own sandy beach. Don't miss the "Show in the Sky," a year-round Mardi Gras extravaganza (daily between 1 and 11 PM).
- **Sahara.** 2535 Las Vegas Blvd. S.; (702) 737-2111 $$
Dubbed the "Jewel of the Desert" when it opened in 1952, the Sahara added an African style to the desert theme of the Las Vegas Strip. The hotel is still pretty intimate despite its 2,000 rooms. Health club, 2 pools, 5 restaurants.
- **Stardust.** 3000 Las Vegas Blvd. S.; (702) 732-6111 $$-$$$
Eighth, last, and largest hotel to go up on the Strip in the 1950s, the Stardust possesses the most outrageous and scandal-scarred history of them all. Today, the Stardust is known for its gorgeous race and sports book, popular low-limit poker room, and sizzling show, "Enter the Night."
- **Stratosphere.** 2000 Las Vegas Blvd. S.; (702) 380-7777 or (800) 998-6937 $$-$$$
Tower, 1,500 rooms, good gambling, fast food, thrill rides, Top of the World rotating restaurant, shopping. staying here can be surprisingly inexpensive.
- **Treasure Island.** 3300 Las Vegas Blvd. S.; (702) 894-7111 $$-$$$
Several times a day actors stage a pirates' battle at the hotel's front entrance. Inside, the restaurants, arcade, and casino are styled after Robert Louis Stevenson's swashbuckling book. Cirque du Soleil performs in the resort's showroom.
- **Tropicana.** 3801 Las Vegas Blvd. S.; (702) 739-2222 $-$$
The "Island of Las Vegas," carris off its Polynesian theme with totem poles, waterfalls, colorful birds, and rattan furniture. The water park includes a swim-up bar and blackjack table.

Laughlin

population 4,791   elevation 520

- **Colorado Belle.** 2100 S. Casino Dr.; (702) 298-4000 or (800) 458-9500 $-$$$
Along with its signature replica paddle-wheeler, the Belle has two outdoor pools, casino, and 24-hour coffee shop.
- **Golden Nugget.** 2300 S. Casino Dr.; (702) 298-7111 or (800) 237-1739 $-$$
This 300-room, tropical themed hotel on the river features a rainforest atrium, pool, restaurant, and shopping arcade.
- **Ramada Express.** 2121 S. Casino Dr.; (702) 298-4200 or (800) 2-RAMADA $-$$$
With its turn-of-the-century railroad motif, this 1,500-room hotel is a block from the river. Casino, 3 restaurants, bar, buffet, pool, and whirlpool.

Page

See Glen Canyon *in* "UTAH CANYON-LANDS," *page 222*

CENTRAL ARIZONA

■ HIGHLIGHTS

Petrified Forest
Flagstaff
Oak Creek Canyon
Sedona
Verde Valley
Sinagua Ruins
Jerome
Prescott
Mogollon Rim

■ LANDSCAPE

North-central Arizona from the Petrified Forest nearly to Flagstaff is high-desert country set astride the southern reaches of the Colorado Plateau. The plateau slopes gradually upward through piñon pine and juniper to the Mogollon Rim, a great escarpment southeast of Flagstaff that curves from the Verde Valley to Show Low. At the rim edge the land drops off sharply, and below it, to the south, sprawls a heavily forested series of interlocking serrated mountain ranges. Within it is the largest ponderosa pine forest in the world. The city of Flagstaff lies in the lee of the San Francisco Peaks, which can be seen for dozens of miles in every direction. Humphreys Peak at 12,643 feet is the highest point in Arizona. Below Flagstaff lie some of Arizona's loveliest red-rock canyons, and small towns decorate the landscape.

■ TRAVELERS ORIENTATION

Flagstaff is a growing city of 46,000 people at the intersection of two inter-state highways, I-40 and I-17. It has many adequate motels and restaurants, and it is a center for excursions to the Grand Canyon, the Four Corners, the Navajo reservation, Oak Creek Canyon, nearby Indian ruins, and the Petri-fied Forest.

Oak Creek Canyon, south of Flagstaff, is renowned for its beauty, as is Sedona—a little cousin of Santa Fe remarkable for its red rock rather than adobe. First discovered by artists, then embraced by affluent retirees, Sedona is pricey, oddly tacky in parts, but full of excellent resorts and first-class restaurants.

All along the Mogollon Rim, south of I-40, outdoorsmen will find lovely lakes, excellent fishing, and thousands of places to camp. There are also a wide variety of motels. Unfortunately, this area is now being heavily logged.

Food & Lodging appears on page 273.

This region of Arizona features the highest terrain in the state. Humphreys Peak, looming 12,600 feet above Flagstaff, and the Mogollon Rim and Plateau capture Pacific moisture moving eastward during the winter months, resulting in prodigious snows—Flagstaff is one of the snowiest cities in the United States. The climate of this area is similar to that found in the Rocky Mountains: cool summers with occasional thunderstorms, and cold, snowy winters. Elevation determines just how cold and how much precipitation any one location may receive. The Mogollon Rim, however, shields areas to its north and east from precipitation, and the deserts of the Colorado Plateau are the result. The difference between these two climate zones is illustrated by the statistics for Flagstaff (elev. 7,000) and Winslow (elev. 5,800), Winslow being only 60 miles east of Flagstaff but lying in the rain shadow of the Mogollon Rim. Also represented is Prescott (elev. 5,350).

TEMPS (F°)	AVG. JAN.		AVG. APRIL		AVG. JULY		AVG. OCT.		RECORD	RECORD
	HIGH	LOW	HIGH	LOW	HIGH	LOW	HIGH	LOW	HIGH	LOW
Flagstaff	42	15	57	25	82	50	63	30	101	-30
Prescott	49	22	65	33	90	57	70	37	105	-21
Winslow	46	19	70	38	94	62	75	38	107	-19

PRECIPITATION (INCHES)	AVG. JAN.	AVG. APRIL	AVG. JULY	AVG. OCT.	ANNUAL	SNOW
Flagstaff	2.1	1.4	3.1	1.5	20.9	100
Prescott	2.0	1.1	3.0	1.1	20.7	38
Winslow	0.5	0.5	1.5	0.5	8.3	28

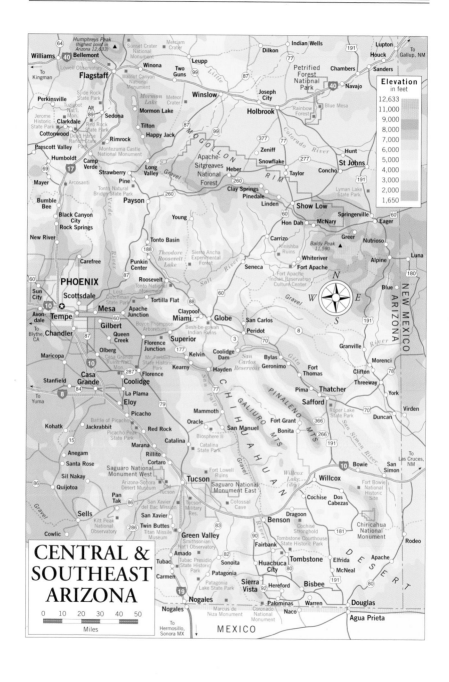

CENTRAL & SOUTHEAST ARIZONA

Elevation
in feet

12,633	
11,000	
9,000	
8,000	
7,000	
6,000	
5,000	
4,000	
3,000	
2,000	
1,650	

0 10 20 30 40 50
Miles

MEXICO

■ PETRIFIED FOREST

The southernmost appendage of the Colorado Plateau in Arizona is the **Painted Desert,** part of which is protected in the Petrified Forest National Park. It is strange, haunting country, scored by jagged canyons and punctuated by heroic sandstone skylines of cliffs, mesas, and buttes. Its exquisitely modulated colors change through the day and are most spectacular at sunrise and sunset. The visitor experiences a palpable, sometimes uncomfortable sensation of insignificance out here; the scale of everything seems too gigantic to comprehend.

The abundant petrified wood was formed 225 million years ago when trees were carried along in rivers from faraway mountains down to what was then vast, low-lying swamp. Over time, the cells in the wood were replaced by waterborn minerals that transformed the logs into brightly colored quartz and jasper crystals.

A scenic drive winds for 28 miles through this colorful landscape, with short, easy hiking trails branching off toward some of the more interesting sites—**Agate Bridge,** created when both ends of a petrified log became embedded in sandstone;

An enormous petrified log, photographed at Petrified Forest in the 1920s, is no longer at the site. (Underwood Archives, San Francisco)

ARIZONA FESTIVALS & EVENTS

The following are some of the better-known annual festivals in Arizona, but there are hundreds of smaller and more esoteric ones around the state. The best way to obtain information is to write or call a town's chamber of commerce. For the Phoenix metro area, contact the **Phoenix & Valley of the Sun Convention & Visitors Bureau,** 1 Arizona Center, 400 East Van Buren, Suite 600, Phoenix, AZ 85004, (602) 254-6500. For Tucson, contact the **Tucson Convention & Visitors Bureau,** 130 South Scott Avenue, Tucson, AZ 85701, (520) 624-1817.

JANUARY

Scottsdale: Phoenix Open
The PGA's best tee off at the Tournament Players Club.

Tempe: Fiesta Bowl
Nationally televised New Year's Day football game between two selected college teams.

FEBRUARY

Scottsdale: Jaycees' Parada del Sol Rodeo
Street dance, rodeo, and parade. (602) 990-3179/(602) 502-5600

Tubac: Festival of the Arts
Oldest arts and crafts fair in Arizona, featuring mostly visual arts. (520) 398-2704

Tucson: La Fiesta de los Vaqueros
Rodeo and parade. (520) 294-8896

MARCH

Phoenix: Jaycees' Rodeo of Rodeos
(602) 264-4808/(602) 272-6771

Tempe: Spring Festival of the Arts
Over 600 artists, crafters and food vendors. (602) 967-4877

Tucson: International Mariachi Conference
North America's largest festival of mariachi performances and workshops. Always a sellout; obtain tickets in advance. (520) 884-9920

MAY

Flagstaff: Native American Arts and Crafts Festival
The Museum of Northern Arizona celebrates the Zuni, Hopi, and Navajo cultures with dancing, artwork, and exhibits one weekend each month from May to July. (520) 774-5211

Phoenix: Jaycees' Rodeo of Rodeos
(602) 263-8671

JUNE

Flagstaff: Pine Country Rodeo
(520) 526-9926

Prescott: Bluegrass Festival. Big crowds turn out for this music festival held annually at Watson Lake Park. (520) 445-2000

Prescott: Territorial Days
Rodeo, golf tournament, 10k run, dancing, carnival. (520) 445-3103

J U L Y
Flagstaff: Festival of the Arts
Classical, jazz, and pops concerts. Late July to August. (520) 774-7750/ (800) 332-9444

Prescott: Bluegrass Festival
Watson Lake Park. (520) 445-2000

Prescott: Frontier Days
One of the world's oldest professional rodeos. (520) 445-3103

A U G U S T
Flagstaff: Summerfest
Arts and crafts, food booths. (520) 779-1213

S E P T E M B E R
Bisbee: Brewery Gulch Days
Mining contests, dancing, parade. (520) 432-5578

Flagstaff: Coconino County Fair
Pig races, lumberjack show, magicians, carnival, horse show tournament. Labor Day Weekend. (520) 774-3464

Grand Canyon: Chamber Music Festival
Evening concerts featuring many types of music from jazz to classical. (520) 638-9215

Phoenix: Music in the Garden
Concert series held at the Desert Botanical Gardens. Champagne

brunch also offered. Late September through November. (602) 941-1225

Sedona: Jazz on the Rocks
The state's top jazz festival, with a full day of outdoor performances. Always a sellout; request tickets months in advance. (520) 282-1985

Window Rock: Navajo Nation Celebration and Rodeo
One of the largest American Indian fairs and rodeos in the country. Intertribal powwow, concerts, parade, traditional singing, barbecue, arts and crafts. (520) 871-6478

O C T O B E R
Phoenix: Arizona State Fair
Rides, concerts, Native American and cowboy dancing, 4-H Club events. (602) 252-6771

Sedona: Fiesta Del Tlaquepaque
Mariachi bands, folklorico dance performances, piñatas, flamenco guitarists. (520) 282-4838

Tombstone: Helldorado Days
Shootouts, 1880s fashion show, rodeo, parade, entertainment. (520) 457-2211

Willcox: Rex Allen Days
Rodeo, county fair, concert. (520) 384-2272 or (800) 200-2272

D E C E M B E R
Tempe: Old Town Tempe Fall Festival of the Arts
Three-day fair of music, food, and local art. Downtown .(602) 894-8158

Newspaper Rock, covered with petroglyphs probably left by migrating Anasazi; and **Puerco Ruin,** a 75-room Anasazi site. More interesting than the ruins are extraordinary petroglyphs that can be seen nearby. Walk south from the ruin to the edge of the mesa and look among the rocks just below.

The 28-mile drive through the park can be accessed from either I-40 or US 180. The north entrance is off I-40, 25 miles east of Holbrook. The south entrance is off US 180, 19 miles southeast of Holbrook. There are no campsites here and hikers must obtain a park permit to stay overnight. Bring water and food with you. Call Petrified Forest National Park at (520) 524-6228 for more information.

■ SINAGUA RUINS OF WALNUT CANYON

A V-shaped furrow 385 feet deep, Walnut Canyon is lined with more than 300 Sinagua [SEEN-AH´-WAH] ruins built on a series of ledges halfway down the canyon walls. This is a perfect place to contemplate the question of whether the Southwest's prehistoric cultures, in the throes of a population boom after A.D. 1100, faced constant raids on their limited resources. Most of these dwellings were built during a short 30-year period between 1120 and 1150, at the same time that Chaco Canyon to the west was being abandoned. Walnut Canyon's settlements certainly look defensive; why else would they have been built in such preposterous locations? Tantalizingly, an archaeologist has found one "foreign" arrowhead in the rib cage of a Sinagua woman buried here—but just one. What became of them is unknown, but Hopis believe the Sinagua are among their ancestors.

A steep loop trail leads down from the rim of the canyon past some of these dwellings. *Located a few miles east of Flagstaff. Exit I-40 on exit 204, and travel south three miles. Call Walnut Canyon Visitors Center at (520) 526-3367 for more information.*

■ WUPATKI NATIONAL MONUMENT

The Sinagua people began to surge into this area about the year 600, then fled in 1064, after the volcano at nearby Sunset Crater erupted, spewing ash across the landscape. The Indians returned during a 100-year wet spell, when there was something of a land rush in this area. During these years the Sinagua constructed masonry buildings, a ball court, and terraced gardens, and made simple, undecorated pottery. Avid traders, they acquired Hohokam and Anasazi pots.

The San Francisco Peaks form a backdrop to Wukoki Ruin in Wupatki National Monument.

They apparently adopted Hohokam ceremonial ball games, and learned architecture from the Anasazi—or else welcomed immigrants from those cultures into their midst. The Sinagua left Wupatki for the last time between 1215 and 1225.

❖

Four major sites can be visited on the self-guided trails. **Wupatki Ruin** was once four stories high and had 100 rooms. At its far end is an oval ball court similar to those the Aztec and Maya built in Mexico and Central America and used for games with a rubber ball.

Wukoki is a three-story pueblo built of finely finished blocks of sandstone. **The Citadel** once had 30 rooms, and commanded a view of surrounding fields. At its foot are terraced gardens. At a fourth site, **Nalakihu Ruin**, storage jars have been found that were made 150 miles away.

North of Flagstaff about 27 miles on US 89. Or follow AZ 24 north from Sunset Crater Volcano National Monument. Call Wapatki National Monument Visitors Center at (520) 679-2365 for more information.

■ FLAGSTAFF

Except for the winter and spring winds, which can be ferocious, this town of 46,000 enjoys the best location in the state. It curls around the southern foot of 12,643-foot Humphreys Peak, a snow-capped landmark. In winter, people flock to Flagstaff to ski at Snow Bowl; in summer, perspiring lemmings swarm up from Phoenix and Tucson to escape the heat. So many geologic and prehistoric attractions cluster around Flagstaff that one suspects the town was founded as a tourist magnet (it wasn't). In addition to the Grand Canyon, the ruins of Walnut Canyon and Wupatki lie respectively 11 and 25 miles away, and Oak Creek Canyon creases into the plateau 10 miles south. Sunset Crater, looking like the mother volcano to a brood of baby cones, is 15 miles out of town; Meteor Crater, the best preserved such crater on the planet, is 45 miles due east.

Flagstaff will regret this spectacular setting only if a new or reactivated volcano someday appears on its horizon. It could happen; Sunset Crater last erupted in 1064—a few moments ago in geologic time. Like so many other Arizona settlements, Flagstaff hasn't made the best of its lovely physical setting. The main commercial arteries through town, Milton and Santa Fe (the old Route 66), are jammed with signs and billboards clamoring for attention. Off these streets, however, Flag's green, forested neighborhoods and cool, pine-scented air make it a wonderfully enticing place.

The **Museum of Northern Arizona** demands a visit. Guided tours of **Lowell Observatory** are conducted weekdays; (520) 774-2096. The **Flagstaff Festival of the Arts** consumes most of July and early August, offering classical music, art films, dance and professional theater. **Fairfield Snowbowl** on the San Francisco Peaks offers Arizona's highest-elevation skiing, with runs dropping from 11,200 feet.

■ OAK CREEK CANYON

As Highway 89A winds south out of Flagstaff, it descends into the leafy coolness of Oak Creek Canyon. Its top attraction, **Slide Rock State Park** (so named for a natural sandstone slide leading into a pool on Oak Creek), draws crowds like a Southern California beach on a warm summer afternoon. The U.S. Forest Service maintains about 10 hiking trails into Oak Creek's tributary canyons, all of which are spectacular. One deserves special mention: the **West Fork of Oak Creek,** four miles north of Slide Rock. Even in the daytime, West Fork can seem dark. Some of its walls are actually concave, sculpted by a creek into forms that look like frozen ocean waves. The trail crosses the creek repeatedly, so expect to get wet. *Slide Rock State Park; (520) 282-3034.*

❖

Red Rock State Park is a lovely riparian woodland along Oak Creek that abounds with wildlife. Located four miles southwest of Sedona off AZ 89A, it is best explored on foot. An excellent trail map, entitled "Experience Sedona," is available at local bookstores and boutiques. Fall is the best season in the canyon, because of the color show staged by its forests of oak, mountain mahogany, sycamore, and sumac. From mid-October to early November, Oak Creek Canyon near Sedona is the most colorful place in Arizona. *Red Rock State Park; (520) 282-6907.*

■ SEDONA

Scenic AZ 89A continues south to the towering red-rock formations of Sedona, famous as an art colony, a New Age "power spot," and one of Arizona's loveliest

retreats. Great red buttes tower 500 to 2,000 feet over the town—Bell Rock, Courthouse Butte, Capitol Butte, Bear Mountain—erosion-sculpted rocks that seem almost to be alive. They change color and character almost hourly. In a gray, woolly fog they seem to float eerily like velvet ghosts. Under a midmorning sun they can be a pale and cool violet; then as the day burns on they shift into the red and orange regions of the spectrum. After sunset, when the fire colors have burned out, the rocks turn the color of rust (which is what they are, on the surface) against a violet sky, and all their crevasses and canyons blacken into impenetrable, ominous mystery.

The town of Sedona has a short but intriguing history. It was founded in 1902 by a young Missouri couple, Carl and Sedona Schnebly. Beginning in the 1960s it became an art colony, and in the 1970s it exploded with retirees. In the early 1980s, Page Bryant, a psychic, claimed to have divined four metaphysical vortices in the red rocks around it, and Sedona also became a New Age mecca. In 1987,

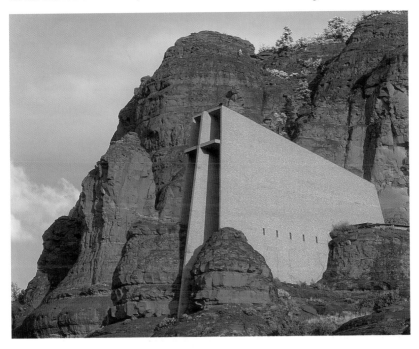

Sculptor and rancher Marguerite Brunswig Staude commissioned Sedona's Chapel of the Holy Cross (above) in 1953; she called it "a spiritual fortress so charged with God that it spurs man's spirit Godward!"

Cathedral Rocks (opposite) tower above Oak Creek in Sedona.

the Harmonic Convergence drew at least 5,000 people to town, a few of whom willingly paid $75 for tickets to go sit on Bell Rock at the moment that it was supposed to depart for the galaxy of Andromeda.

Art remains Sedona's prime industry. Out of a population of 11,000 there are an estimated 300 professional artists in town, some 40 galleries, and an annual outdoor sculpture exhibition on the banks of Oak Creek. In some inexplicable way, the Red Rocks are involved in all this. Touring the galleries, the visitor will notice that, although there is a plentiful variety of art, there is seldom anything combative, confrontational, or unyieldingly baffling. The Red Rocks seem not to tolerate dark emotions.

An essential stop is **Tlaquepaque**, a fetching collection of art galleries and boutiques built in the fashion of an 18th-century Spanish colonial village on the bank of Oak Creek where it crosses under AZ 179. Sedona firms also offer balloon rides and jeep tours. Jazz aficionados who think their music is naturally a creature of the night, properly played only in smoky nightclubs, invariably are converted by Sedona's Jazz on the Rocks festival. It's a day-long September lawn party, and in the years since its 1982 inauguration it has become Arizona's premier music festival. Tickets always sell out; order early. *(520) 282-1985.*

■ VERDE VALLEY

South of Sedona, the edge of the Colorado Plateau extends to the Verde Valley, former home of the dry-farming Sinaguas. While the Verde River that traverses the valley is home to some of the last remaining riparian vegetation in the state, the greenness of this plant life did not inspire the name. The "green valley" instead takes its name from the deep-green malachite—a copper mineral found in the surrounding hills. Copper was abundant here long before Anglo settlers turned it into a billion-dollar mining district.

Among the many mysterious ruins left in the region by the Sinaguas, **Montezuma Castle National Monument** is the most engaging, an astonishingly graceful pueblo with smooth, concave façades that fill in much of a huge cave high in a limestone cliff. It does not, by the way, have anything to do with Montezuma; 19th-century Verde Valley settlers gave it this name, blithely assuming that the Aztecs had preceded them. The nearby **Montezuma's Well** was formed when the roof of a large limestone cavern collapsed. Fed by perennial springs, it was used as a water source by both the Hohokam and Sinagua tribes, and ruins of ancient dwellings still surround the well. *From I-17 take exit 289 and follow the signs for three miles; (520) 567-3322.*

Nearby **Tuzigoot National Monument** is a very different sort of development, demonstrating Sinagua adaptability; its 86 rock-walled rooms flow over the crest of a low hill to the north of Mingus Mountain. Built around 1200 by the skilled masons of the Sinagua culture, it once housed more than 200 people. *Off US 89A, three miles east of the town of Clarkdale; (520) 634-5564.*

■ JEROME

Indians were mining Mingus Mountain for its copper when the Spanish arrived in the area over 300 years ago, but the first American town was not founded here until 1876. For the next 60 years the town was assaulted by floods, fires, and epidemics, but the wealth buried under it in Mingus Mountain kept it booming. Finally the tormented mountain responded. A combination of abnormally wet weather, continuous blasting, and a honeycomb of more than 100 miles of mine shafts under the town caused a piece of the mountain to collapse in a colossal mud slide that swept away hundreds of structures. A quaint fraction of Jerome, some 300 buildings, still hugs the mountainside. At its peak, Jerome had been home to 15,000 people.

Today, Jerome numbers only a few hundred citizens, but they are a colorful lot. The former estate of mining magnate James S. Douglas has been converted into **Jerome State Historic Park and Museum.** Douglas's home is the only mansion remaining in the town. *The park is just outside of town off AZ 89A; (520) 634-5381.*

The rest of the homes, many of them abandoned and deteriorating, others restored and well-kept, are a jumble of cottages and Victorian-style houses clinging to the steep slopes of Cleopatra Hill. The free-wheeling spirit of Jerome's old mining days prevails, and tourists now visit the former jailhouse, a brothel-turned-restaurant, and an array of funky shops, art galleries, and cafes.

■ PRESCOTT

Prescott, a small city of 26,000, is indeed a gentle, civilized, and picturesque place, and its collection of prim Victorian homes gives it a wistful air. Add a near-perfect mile-high climate with four distinct seasons, none of them harsh, and Prescott seems like everyone's choice for an ideal place to live. Of course, there is a catch: no industry. It's tough to earn a living in Prescott.

The town was founded, curiously, as a consequence of the Civil War. President Lincoln had designated Arizona a territory in 1863 and dispatched his appointed governor, John G. Goodwin, to set up a government. En route, Goodwin heard that there was a nucleus of Confederate sympathizers at Tucson, the presupposed capital. The gubernatorial party went instead to Fort Whipple, an army post in northern Arizona, and in 1864 wisely founded the capital of Prescott on politically virgin ground.

Prescott lost the capital to Tucson just three years later (eventually it migrated yet again to Phoenix), but nearby gold mining and ranching delivered a boom to the town anyway. It became as legendary for drinking as Tombstone for gunfighting; by the early 1900s there were about 40 saloons lining Montezuma Street, still known today as "Whiskey Row." There remain a few token historic bars on

Jerome has become a magnet for artists and art galleries.

Whiskey Row, and on Saturday nights they sound boisterous enough to convince passersby that at least a sliver of the tradition endures.

❖

To understand the enduring charm of Prescott, simply walk the Victorian neighborhoods that stretch about six blocks in each direction from downtown. In these neighborhoods, domestic life still spills from house out to street; people lounge on their cool porches, greeting strangers as well as neighbors. On a winter evening, as a light snow slowly blankets the town, families walk downtown under umbrellas to stroll and throw snowballs in the park surrounding the county courthouse.

Prescott also is the antique capital of Arizona. Most of the shops are clustered on Cortez Street downtown and Montezuma Street a few blocks south of downtown.

The excellent **Sharlot Hall Museum** sprawls through several historic buildings and details the history of Prescott and Arizona Territory. *415 W. Gurley Street at corner of McCormick; (520) 445-3122.*

New Age guru Paolo Soleri built Arcosanti about 70 miles north of Phoenix as a social experiment in "living with the Earth."

Prescott National Forest. The forest surrounding Prescott is laced with delightful mountain hiking trails; ask for a map at the Forest Service office in town. No other Arizona town of its size seems to have as many festivals and annual events as Prescott. A sampling: Territorial Days (crafts, entertainment and historic home tours) in June, Frontier Days and World's Oldest Rodeo in July, Bluegrass Festival also in July, and the horse racing season at Prescott Downs from late May to late August.

■ MOGOLLON RIM

Running southeast of the Verde Valley and northwest of the White Mountains, the Mogollon Rim [MUG'-GY-OWN] is a weird and spellbinding escarpment that plunges 2,000 feet in one vertical slash from the undulating mountain country to the Tonto Basin. Spectacular and vertiginous views are best from the **Rim Drive** (Forest Route 300), a good but lonely gravel road closely paralleling the rim for 43 miles. To enjoy this area you'll want to consult maps and ranger stations.

Forty-two miles south of Winslow on AZ 99, the Chevelon Ranger District in the **Apache-Sitgreaves National Forest,** provides maps and information. Campgrounds and lakes are in the area, and the **Rim Lakes Vista trail** is a fairly easy three-mile hike with lovely views that follows the Mogollon Rim. The upper trailhead is two miles in on Forest Route 300 from AZ 260.

The town of **Show Low**—named for a winner-take-all poker game—resides at an elevation of 6,400 feet and is near many of the best outdoor areas of the Rim. Nearby you can fish, hike, camp, ride, and take scenic drives. Go by the Chamber of Commerce at West Deuce of Clubs Street and South Eighth Avenue, or call (520) 537-2326 for advice on campgrounds, ranger stations, motels, and many other sights of interest.

For a slow, lonely, and wonderfully scenic route south from the Rim country, take US 60 from Show Low to Springerville, then turn south on US 191. This corkscrewing mountain highway is also known as the **Coronado Trail** because it may have been near the route the Spanish explorer Francisco Vásquez de Coronado followed in his foray into Arizona and New Mexico in 1540. Elk, deer, raccoon, wild turkey, and even black bear can often be sighted from the car, and side excursions on gravel logging roads will take you to pristine streams and canyons that aren't seen by more than a few dozen people in a season.

■ FOOD & LODGING

> *Restaurant prices:*
> Per person, not including drinks, tax and tips:
> $ = under $10; $$ = $10–20; $$$ = over $20
>
> *Room rates:*
> Per night, per room, double occupancy:
> $ = under $50; $$ = $50–100; $$$ = over $100

Flagstaff

population 45,900   elevation 6,910

X **Cafe Espress.** 16 N. San Francisco St.; (520) 774-0541 $
All the food at this trendy cafe/bakery is homemade, natural, and dished out in generous portions. Try the Greek salads, pita pizzas, or one-of-a-kind veggie burgers.

X **Chez Marc Bistro.** 503 N. Humphreys St.; (520) 774-1343 $$–$$$
Owner/chef Marc Balocco describes his country French cuisine as "classic but modern, with a flair." Indeed: ravioli stuffed with lobster and bathed in a sun-dried tomato sauce; duck breast bathed in juniper berry-sauce or whatever occurs to maestro Marc on a given day. Refreshingly informal.

X **Macy's European Coffee House and Bakery.** 14 S. Beaver St.; (520) 774-2243 $
Gourmet café food.

X **New Delhi Palace.** 2700 S. Woodland Village; (520) 556-0019 $–$$
Superb East Indian cuisine.

🏨 **Best Western Woodlands Plaza Hotel.** 1175 W. Rte. 66; (520) 773-8888 or (800) 528-1234 $$$
Near downtown with 183 nicely furnished rooms and two restaurants.

🏨 **Embassy Suites.** 706 S. Milton Rd.; (520) 774-4333 $$$
Includes breakfasts in sunny dining room, adjacent to Northern Arizona University.

🏨 **The Inn at Four Ten.** 410 N. Leroux St.; (520) 774-0088 $$$
Bed and breakfast in a splendidly restored 1907 home. The nine guest suites are decorated in varying themes from southwest to turn-of-the-century. Some rooms have fireplaces, some have hot tubs. Marvelous breakfasts and friendly hosts.

🏨 **Little America.** I-40 at Butler Ave.; (520) 779-2741 or (800) 352-4386 $$–$$$
Flagstaff's premier motel: large unexpectedly luxurious rooms with comfortable sitting areas. Pool, tennis courts, golf and many other amenities. Set in a ponderosa pine woods.

Central Arizona Food & Lodging

Central Arizona Food & Lodging

Jerome

population 500   elevation 5,246

✗ **House of Joy.** 416 Hull Ave.; (520) 634-5339 $$$
Lots of eccentricities lurk around Jerome, but none is odder than this highly regarded Continental restaurant installed in (what used to be) a bordello. There are just seven tables, it's open only on Saturday and Sunday nights, and you'll need reservations months in advance. No credit cards. (What did you expect in a cathouse?)

🛏 **Rose Garden Bed and Breakfast.** 120 Juarez St.; (520) 634-3270 $$
Built around 1900, this small old miner's home features period antiques. Friendly and helpful innkeepers.

Prescott

population 26,500   elevation 6,910

✗ **Murphy's.** 201 N. Cortez.; (520) 445-4044 $$
This has been the hot dining-and-drinking spot in town since it opened in 1984. Part of the appeal is the setting, an 1890 mercantile building, beautifully renovated. American menu: prime rib, steaks, shrimp. Big room, often noisy.

🛏 **Hassayampa Inn.** 122 E. Gurley St.; (520) 778-9434 $$$
Built in 1927 and listed on the National Historic Register, this elegant downtown hotel, now nicely renovated in period style, features a lovely lobby and guest rooms with private baths and antiques.

🛏 **Marks House Inn.** 203 E. Union St.; (520) 778-4632 $$
A Queen Anne Victorian mansion built in 1894, now a four-room B&B. Family-style breakfasts.

🛏 **Prescott Pines Inn.** 901 White Spar Rd.; (520) 445-7270 $$-$$$
A pleasant B&B, where some of the 13 rooms have fireplaces or kitchens. Impressive full breakfasts.

Sedona

population 7,700   elevation 4,400

✗ **The Coffee Pot.** 250 West Hwy. 89A; (520) 282-6626 $
A friendly omelette parlor, bustling with business weekend mornings.

✗ **Garland's Oak Creek Lodge.** Eight
🛏 miles north of Sedona on US 89A; (520) 282-3343 $$$
Fixed menu with eclectic gourmet fare changes nightly. Superb dining. Overnight reservations at the lodge must be made a year in advance. Open April through November.

✗ **The Heartline Cafe.** 1610 W. Hwy. 89A; (520) 282-0785 $$-$$$
Charming and private, away from the bustle of shoppers and red-rock gawkers. Lunches are wonderfully eclectic: unusual salads, sandwiches, and entrees. For dinner choose between pastas and other vegetarian dishes, fish, and a variety of grilled or roasted red meats.

✗ **L'Auberge de Sedona.** 301 L'Auberge Ln.; (520) 282-1667 $$$
Pining for Paris? Superb French cuisine (and stratospheric prices) in a secluded

creekside setting, reminiscent of an elegant French country inn.

X **Loaves and Some Fishes II.** Bell Rock Plaza on AZ 179. (520) 204-2461 $ Homemade, soups, salads, vegetarian dishes, pasta, desserts, and gourmet coffee. Breakfast and lunch only.

X **Pepe Muldoon's Beachside Cantina.** 2620 W. US 89A; (520) 282-4849 $$ Despite the corny name and the Hacienda Disney atmosphere, Muldoon's has one of the more ambitious Mexican menus in Arizona.

X **Pietro's.** 2445 W. US 89A; (520) 282-2525 $$–$$$. Arizona's most attractive resort town has become a real mecca for foodies, as exemplified by this excellent little Italian restaurant.

Canyon Villa. 125 Canyon Circle Dr.; (520) 284-1226 or (800) 453-1166 $$$ Six miles south of town, this modern B&B rivals Sedona's big resorts for luxury. Attractive library; some rooms are done in Victorian, others in Santa Fe style.

Forest Houses Resort. Oak Creek Canyon; (520) 282-2999 $$-$$$ Thirteen rustic cabins 10 miles north of Sedona in Oak Creek Canyon. The Lower Sycamore cabin cantilevers dramatically over the creek.

Junipine. 8351 N. US 89A; (520) 282-3375 or (800) 742-7463 $$$ Condo-like resort nine miles north of Sedona in Oak Creek Canyon. Wood and stone "creekhouse" units have full kitchens and redwood decks overlooking the canyon.

L'Auberge de Sedona. 301 L'Auberge Ln.; (520) 282-1661 or (800) 272-6777 $$$ Lovely resort beside Oak Creek in a sycamore forest. Rates include six-course dinner at L'Auberge's excellent French restaurant (see above).

Los Abrigados Resort and Spa. 160 Portal Lane; (520) 282-1777 or (800) 521-3131 $$$ A deluxe resort set on 22 acres in the heart of town. The charming, modern architecture is a delightful twist on the standard hacienda-style. Luxurious suites include fireplace and patio or balcony. Tennis courts, swimming pool.

Winslow and Vicinity

X **Casa Blanca Café.** 1201 East 2nd St., Winslow; (520) 289-4191 $ Known for tacos, chimichangas, cheese crisps, and burgers. Ceramic-tiled establishment with booths and tables.

Adobe Inn. 1701 North Park Drive, Winslow; (520) 289-4638 $$ A two-story Best Western motel with 72 rooms and modern decor. Cafe and an indoor pool on the premises.

Best Western Arizonian Inn. 2508 East Navajo Blvd., Holbrook; (520) 524-2611 $$ Pleasantly decorated, English-style motel with all of the modern amenities. Pool and coffee shop on the premises.

Wigwam Village #6. 811 West Hopi Dr., Holbrook; (520) 524-3048 $$ Much more fun than a chain motel but just as accommodating: each stucco teepee has a TV and air conditioning.

Central Arizona Food & Lodging

SOUTHEAST ARIZONA

■ HIGHLIGHTS
Sonoran Desert
Phoenix
Tucson
Tubac
Bisbee
Chihuahuan Desert
Tombstone

■ LANDSCAPE
Between Flagstaff and Phoenix the elevation drops 6,000 feet in 138 miles, and the landscape changes from red rock and forest to the Sonoran Desert. The most common misconception about the Sonoran Desert is that it is a desolate place. In fact, it teems with life—weird, colorful, perfectly adapted, interdependent, fiercely obstinate life. More species of birds, some 300, make their homes in it than in any other arid region on the continent, and there are forests here—called *bosques*—of mesquite. In spite of the Sonoran Desert's low rainfall, between 4 and 12 inches, plant life is abundant. The desert's signature plant is the giant saguaro cactus.

Due south of Tucson along I-19, the Santa Cruz River Valley stretches 63 miles to Nogales on the border of Mexico. Here the view is of desert and grassland, punctuated by low mountain ranges. About 40 miles southeast of Tucson, the Sonoran and Chihuahuan deserts merge, the Chihuahuan being higher, cooler and more monochromatic—a landscape dotted with ocotillo, yucca, and mesquite. Due east of Tucson are the spectacular boulders of Texas Canyon, and beyond that, irrigated farmland in which grow pistachios, apples, peppers, pumpkins. Further south are horse ranches, rolling hills, vineyards, and recently established wineries.

■ TRAVELERS ORIENTATION

Most people speed across Arizona's deserts on major highways. A more immediate desert experience can be had on side roads, but don't undertake trips into isolated country without maps, compasses, extra water, and extra gas.

Within the desert are two burgeoning cities. Metropolitan Phoenix, the commercial hub of the Southwest, has more than two million people and metropolitan Tucson has 700,000 people. Both cities have excellent golf courses and luxury resorts.

In the far southeastern corner of the state lie several towns worth visiting—Tubac, Bisbee, and Tombstone—and Chiricahua National Monument, a garden of fantastic rock formations in the Chiricahua Mountains.

Food & Lodging appears on page 302 and golf courses on page 307.

For a map of Southeast Arizona see page 258.

The low desert of southwestern Arizona ranks as one of the hottest regions in the world, and Phoenix rests on its northerly edge. On average, Phoenix endures 91 days of +100° F readings per year. Buckeye, Gila Bend, and Casa Grande all have been brutalized by 100-degree marks in March. The first 100-degree-day usually strikes Phoenix by mid-April, Tucson by early May.

The winter months are generally very pleasant throughout this area, and the best time to visit is October through April. Statistics for Phoenix (elev. 1,100), Tuscon (elev. 2,600), and Tombstone (elev. 4,600) illustrate the effect the elevation of the deserts has on climate.

TEMPS (F°)	AVG. JAN. HIGH	LOW	AVG. APRIL HIGH	LOW	AVG. JULY HIGH	LOW	AVG. OCT. HIGH	LOW	RECORD HIGH	RECORD LOW
Phoenix	65	39	82	53	106	80	88	60	122	16
Tombstone	61	34	82	56	94	65	84	58	110	6
Tucson	63	38	80	50	99	74	83	57	117	6

PRECIPITATION (INCHES)	AVG. JAN.	AVG. APRIL	AVG. JULY	AVG. OCT.	ANNUAL	SNOW
Phoenix	0.7	0.3	0.8	0.6	7.1	0
Tombstone	0.8	0.3	3.6	0.7	14.7	2
Tucson	0.9	0.3	2.5	0.9	11.1	1

■ HISTORY

The key figure in the Spanish settlement of southern Arizona was a Jesuit missionary not from Spain but from the Italian mountain town of Segno. Padre Eusebio Kino, an indefatigable explorer and solicitor of souls, pushed into what is now Arizona as far as the Gila River, just south of Phoenix, and established the two missions of Tumacácori and San Xavier del Bac. (The two buildings standing today are successors of Kino's more modest originals; he died in 1711.) Kino, whom many Mexican and Arizona Catholics think a candidate for sainthood, was described thus by a contemporary:

> When he publicly reprimanded a sinner, he was choleric. But if anyone showed him personal disrespect, he controlled his temper to such an extent that he made it a habit to exalt whosoever maltreated him. . . . He never had more than two coarse shirts, because he gave everything as alms to the Indians. . . .

A trickle of miners and ranchers followed the missionaries, and in 1752 the Spanish crown established the first presidio at Tubac, 20 miles north of the present-day Mexican border. In 1776, the garrison was moved to Tucson. Indian raids and attacks were a chronic threat, and atrocities were committed on both sides—foreshadowing the ugly war between the Anglos and Apaches a century later.

In 1821, Spanish Arizona became a piece of Mexico, and treaties with that nation in 1847 and 1854 made it a U.S. Territory. It was a violent, lawless frontier. "If the world were searched over," wrote passing journalist J. Ross Browne in 1869, "I suppose there could not be found so degraded a set of villains as then formed the principal society of Tucson. Every man went armed to the teeth, and street-fights and bloody affrays were of daily occurrence." For at least the next generation, much the same could be said of the silver-rush town of Tombstone and copper-mining capital of Bisbee.

Arizona won statehood from a somewhat reluctant Congress in 1912, but it wasn't until the advent of air conditioning in the 1930s and 1940s that Arizona's two principal settlements, Phoenix and Tucson, began to become cities. Phoenix, founded as a farm community in 1867, had a population of 11,000 in 1910; 40 years later it was 10 times that size. If it were not for refrigeration, Phoenix and Tucson would still be farm towns and winter resorts. If it were not for a vast but now dwindling aquifer and the Central Arizona Project, a canal that drags water *uphill* more than 300 miles from the Colorado River, they would be ghost towns.

■ PHOENIX

Big, sophisticated Phoenix (along with its brood of suburbs, collectively called the Valley of the Sun) has never looked like a desert city. Unlike its downstate rival, Tucson, Phoenix was conceived as an oasis. Agriculture was its original raison d'être, and when in 1911 Roosevelt Dam walled off the Salt River 60 miles to the east, the combined watersheds of the Salt and Verde rivers became a 13,000-square-mile catchment—an area larger than Belgium—to make Phoenix verdant.

The engine that drives the Phoenix boom is the city's raw youth—as an urban entity it is less than 50 years old, and buildings constructed in the early 20th century are considered "historic." People grouse that there's nothing much to do in Phoenix except drive around on freeways trying to reach another place with an air conditioner, but slowly, that's changing. Nevertheless, you'll need to plan ahead and have an excellent map if you plan to go sightseeing in Phoenix. Resorts and golf courses are listed at the end of this chapter.

Heritage and Science Park. This square block encompasses three important Phoenix institutions, all connected by a tree-lined walkway that runs from Monroe Street south to Washington. **Heritage Square** features more than a half-dozen restored turn-of-the-19th-century homes, some of which house museums and are open for tours. **Phoenix Museum of History** shows what life was like in early Phoenix. Adjacent **Arizona Science Center** is a massive complex that includes a plantarium, an Iwerks theater, and a waterplay exhibit.

Shopping. The open-air **Arizona Center,** is a wonderfully inviting shopping mall and office complex with a spectacular (and typically thirsty) three-acre terraced garden. **Biltmore Fashion Park** at 24th Street and Camelback, another upscale outdoor shopping area, features a flower-lined promenade, an excellent bookstore, and some very good restaurants.

Heard Museum. The world-class Heard Museum has a staggering collection of more than 75,000 artifacts and art works that document both prehistoric and modern Native American cultures. The changing exhibits are consistently first-rate. *22 E. Monte Vista Rd.; (602) 252-8840.*

Phoenix Art Museum. The permanent collection consists of 19th-century European and 19th- and 20th-century American paintings, drawings, and

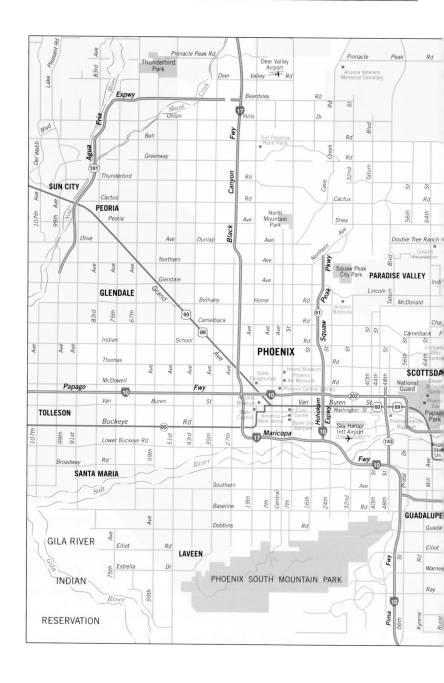

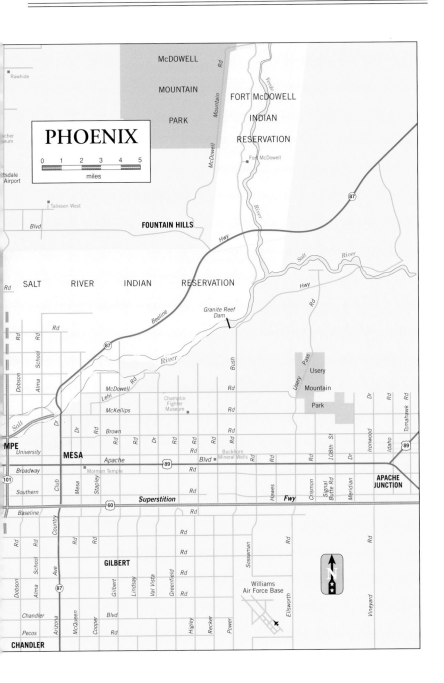

PHOENIX

0   1   2   3   4   5
miles

clothing. Every October the museum hosts the Cowboy Artists of America sale; Western art collectors come in droves. *1625 N. Central Ave.; (602) 257-1222.*

Desert Botanical Garden. Located in east Phoenix, the garden is a tribute to desert flora that boasts 10,000 different plants, including half the world's cactus species. At Chrismastime, visitors come at night and walk paths lit by the glow of thousands of luminarias. During spring, many of the desert plants bloom in glorious colors. *1201 N. Galvin Pkwy. in Papago Park; (602) 941-1217.*

■ SCOTTSDALE AND TEMPE

About 15 suburbs huddle around Phoenix; the exact number is hard to establish because some towns that qualify geographically as suburbs are not at all related culturally to the mother city. One example is the little town of **Guadalupe,** squeezed between Tempe and Phoenix's South Mountain Park. It is a Yaqui Indian settlement, founded in 1904 as a refugee camp. The Yaquis, indigenous to Mexico, were around that time being conscripted into forced labor by Mexican President Porfirio Díaz, and thousands gained sanctuary in Arizona. Another sanctuary on the opposite corner of the valley is **Sun City,** manufactured in 1965 as one of the first retirement villages in the nation. Sun City's population is now about 38,000, its statutes still prohibit home ownership by anyone younger than 55, and 80 percent of its registered voters are Republican. It has its own professional symphony orchestra. **Mesa,** as Arizona's third-largest city, seems almost too big to be called a suburb. Founded by Mormons, and 15 miles east of Phoenix, it's a place where people raise families.

Scottsdale. This suburb has wealth, resorts, sophisticated art galleries, and the most progressive community in the state with regard to preserving its natural beauty. For **shopping and restaurants** try the following areas: (1) along Fifth Avenue, four blocks north of Old town between Scottsdale Road and Indian School Road; (2) west of the Civic Center around Brown Street, and on Main Street west across Scottsdale Road to 69th Street; (3) 6166 N. Scottsdale Road a few miles north of Old Town—a pricey, faux-Italian shopping center called The Borgata.

A small but exquisite space, the **Fleischer Museum** in Scottsdale, showcases more than 200 paintings from the California Impressionist school. *17207 N. Perimeter Dr.; (602) 585-3108.*

Set into the foothills of the McDowell Mountains in northeast Scottsdale is Taliesin West, founded in 1937 as the winter home of Frank Lloyd Wright and his school of architecture. Tours daily. *13201 N. 108th St. at Cactus Road—from Shea Boulevard turn left on Frank Lloyd Wright Boulevard; (602) 860-8810.*

Tempe. Thanks to **Arizona State University,** the state's largest with 45,000 students, Tempe has a more animated nightlife and more entertainment options than the other Valley suburbs. It also has a compact downtown district with more life in it than all the other suburbs combined. Tree-lined Mill Avenue has a number of restored 19th-century commercial buildings converted into quaint shops and restaurants. The city is currently preparing to turn the Salt River and its flood plain, which cuts off downtown on the north, into a five-mile linear park that is to include wildlife refuges, bike paths, water sports, and even "urban fishing."

On the northwestern corner of the campus stands the **Nelson Fine Arts Center at Arizona State University.** Housed in a building that is itself a work of art, the extensive collection includes American paintings and crafts, and works from Africa and Latin America. *Nelson Fine Arts Center (602) 965-2787.*

■ Out of Doors

Hiking. Phoenix's several mountain ranges aren't as high as those surrounding Tucson, but they offer entertaining hiking and great views.

Climb the well-used trail to the top of **Squaw Peak** in Scottsdale, for instance, 1,500 feet above the valley floor, to watch the sunset turn the city below into a horizon-to-horizon blaze of light. Urban hiking enthusiasts also highly recommend the four-mile roundtrip **Echo Canyon Trail** up **Camelback Mountain** (north of Camelback Road on 48th Street). For a much easier hike try the **Hidden Valley Trail** (three miles) at the splendid **South Mountain Park** (10919 S. Central Avenue). South Mountain's 16,000 acres of undeveloped desert make it the largest city-owned park in the world. Well-marked hiking and mountain bike trails cover over 40 miles. *Call the South Mountain Ranger's Office at (602) 495-0222 for information and group hiking reservations.*

Water Sports. A traditional warm-weather pastime is **tubing the Salt,** meaning floating down the gentle Salt River east of Phoenix in an inner tube. Boating and jet skiing also are popular on the chain of lakes created by the dams on the Salt;

Roosevelt Lake, 50 miles east of Phoenix, is the largest. Avoid it on weekends. In the city, there are several surfing waterparks with wave machines. *Salt River Recreation Inc (602) 984-3305.*

Golf. Unquestionably the Valley's most popular winter sport. A few of the best, and most scenic, golf courses in Phoenix include the **Arizona Biltmore**, *24th Street and Missouri Avenue;* **Encanto Park**, *2705 North 15th Avenue;* **Papago Golf Course**, *5595 E. Moreland Street;* and **Wigwam Gold**, *Litchfield Park; (602) 935-9414.* Call the **Arizona Golf Association at** *(602) 944-3035* for more information. *Also see page 307 for telephone numbers and additional listings.*

Scenic Drive. A scenic drive from Phoenix that can be undertaken in a day is the Apache Trail, which loops past the Superstition Mountains. The 164-mile drive today has nothing to do with the Apache—it doesn't even quite reach the San Carlos Indian Reservation in the White Mountains to the east. During the Apache wars, however, U.S. Army troops and Indian scouts combed the desert and mountains around here, trying to track down bands of Apache guerrillas. The loop

Frank Lloyd Wright's Taliesin West school of architecture (above) in Scottsdale is the counterpart to his Taliesin in Spring Green, Wisconsin.

The skyline of the hottest city in the United States. Phoenix averages a high of 106° F in July.

offers great views of the Superstitions, three of the lakes devised by damming the Salt River in the early 1900s, a lovely Salado Indian ruin, and the Boyce Thompson Arboretum. Best time to make the drive is October through April.

■ TUCSON

Nature has created few such spectacular settings for a city. Metropolitan Tucson's 780,000 people sprawl across a desert basin defined by four mountain ranges, each lying in a cardinal direction from the city's midpoint and each exuding a distinctive character. The 9,157-foot Santa Catalinas on the north are heroic and craggy, a late Beethoven sonata of gneiss and granite. The Rincons, to the east, appear smooth and rounded, as if they have been buffed. The twin peaks of the Santa Ritas, to the south, often wear caps of snow; the summit of Mount Wrightson towers to 9,453 feet. The small Tucson Mountains close off the western horizon like randomly sized sawteeth.

The city has not lived up to its stage setting. Strip-zoned arteries six, eight, ten miles long, choked with billboards and shopping centers, carry rivers of traffic between the mountains. There is little distinguished public architecture.

The city's two oldest neighborhoods, El Presidio and Barrio Histórico, huddle immediately north and south, respectively, of downtown's modern towers. The oldest houses, dating from the 1860s and 1870s, are pure Sonoran: simple, boxlike shapes with plastered adobe walls two feet thick, a wide entry hall called a *zaguán,* and ceilings fashioned of saguaro or ocotillo ribs. By 1880, some of these adobes began to sport porches and peaked roofs of corrugated steel, the Anglo newcomers' stopgap efforts to make traditional Mexican architecture into something that felt more like home to them.

Compared with Phoenix, Tucson is more liberal, more cosmopolitan, more intellectual, more conceited—and less affluent. The university is the city's largest employer, and the backbone of its economy.

Tucson differs markedly from Phoenix in its attitude toward the Sonoran Desert. Phoenix repudiates the desert; Tucson embraces it. There is relatively little agriculture in Tucson's history, no irrigation, and no river comparable to the Salt. Tucson's "rivers" are its network of arroyos, dry most days out of the year, but periodically tearing through town on a muddy, rain-swollen rampage. Even when dry, however, these arroyos nourish what biologists call a xeroriparian habitat, a word marrying Greek and Latin roots for "dry" and "riverbank." These are linear forests

RAILROAD TO THE CHRISTIAN WORLD

When the railroad arrived in Tucson on March 20, 1880, the city's very proud Mayor Leatherwood was unable to contain his excitement. After dispatching a number of celebratory drinks and a greater number of telegrams to dignitaries all over the United States, he and his cronies felt compelled to telegraph Pope Leo XII the following message:

> To His Holiness, the Pope of Rome, Italy
> The mayor of Tucson begs the honor of reminding Your Holiness that this ancient and honorable pueblo was founded by the Spaniards under the sanction of the Church more than three centuries ago, and to inform Your Holiness that a railroad from San Francisco, California, now connects us with the entire Christian World.
> —R. N. Leatherwood, Mayor

Before the message was wired, a few more temperate locals got wind of Leatherwood's potentially embarrassing idea. They raced to the telegrapher's office and begged the fellow not to send it. After some palm-greasing, the telegrapher complied. But perhaps because he didn't want to spoil Tucson's party, he wrote his own "response" to the boastful city fathers. The note was delivered to Leatherwood, and before looking it over, he read it aloud to the gathered Tucsonians:

> His Holiness the Pope acknowledges with appreciation receipt of your telegram informing him that the ancient city of Tucson at last has been connected by rail with the outside world and sends his benediction, but for his own satisfaction would ask, where the hell is Tucson?
> —"Antonelli"

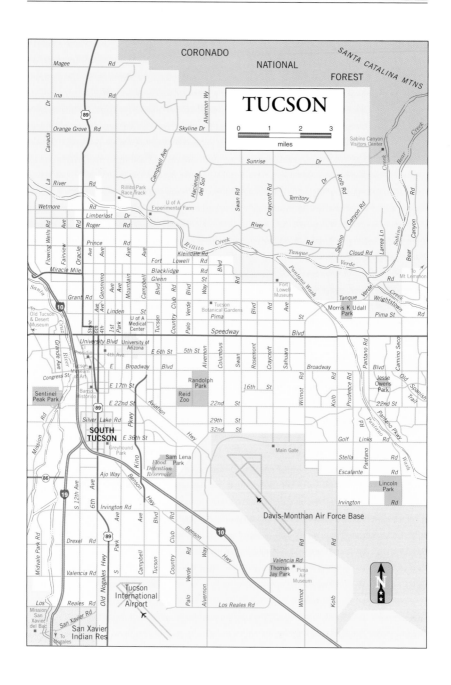

of mesquite and paloverde trees and bird habitats, and they have the effect of extending tendrils of the lushest imaginable desert through the urban landscape. Reminded so frequently of the desert they live in, Tucsonans tend to be more respectful of it.

❖

Historic Tucson. Two tiny slices of Tucson as it was in the 1870s and 1880s have survived into the present as historic districts: the **Barrio Histórico,** 13 square blocks just south of downtown on Main, Meyer, and Convent avenues; and **El Presidio,** just north of downtown in the area encompassed by Franklin and Pennington streets and Main and Church avenues. Barrio Histórico has some wonderful adobe Sonoran row houses; El Presidio illustrates, in the space of one block from Meyer to Main, the transformation of Tucson from a Mexican to an American village.

Shopping. Tucson's most unusual shopping street is **Fourth Avenue,** a five-block stretch of galleries, custom furniture builders, restaurants, and oddball shops where stepping inside seems to whisk one into a time warp back to the sixties. There certainly is no better place to buy hippie clothes in Arizona.

Street mural in Tucson's Barrio Historico.

University of Arizona. Located near N. Park Avenue and University Boulevard, the university opened for business in 1891 with one building, 36 students, and six professors. Its curricula tilted heavily in the direction of mining and agriculture, the two sciences that had immediate application in 19th-century Arizona. At this point there was still no high school in the territory, so the professors had to teach prerequisites as well as college courses. In this crude frontier town, Tucson citizens had little pride in their university. It was a decade or two before Tucson began to feel the influence of its frontier university.

The University of Arizona today has more than 35,000 students, a massive research establishment, and a major intercollegiate sports program. It shapes the city's character as pervasively as the mountains have shaped its geography. To explore the campus, stop by the visitors center on the southeast corner of University Boulevard and Cherry Avenue. From here pick up a map or join one of the free tours led by student volunteers. University Boulevard, on the north edge of the campus, is a lively street lined with student-oriented stores, cafes, and burger joints.

Several of Tucson's most interesting museums are found at the University of Arizona, including the **Flandrau Planetarium,** *Cherry Avenue and University Boulevard; (520) 621-4515,* the **University Museum of Art,** *at the junction of Speedway and Olive Roads; (520) 621-7567,* the **Center for Creative Photography,** *1030 North Olive Road; (520) 621-7968,* and the **Arizona State Museum,** *Park Avenue and University Blvd.; (520) 621-6302.*

City Museums. Elsewhere in Tucson are several other museums worth a visit. A great collection of 200 historic aircraft can be found at the **Pima Air Museum.** The most recent addition is an SR-71 Blackbird—the fastest jet ever built. *6000 E. Valencia Rd., (520) 574-9658.*

The only place in the world where the public can tour a disarmed ICBM in its underground silo is the **Titan Missile Museum.** *20 miles south of Tucson via I-19, exit 69. 1580 W. Duval Mine Road; (520) 625-7736.*

The permanent collections at the **Tucson Museum of Art** includes pre-Columbian art, 20th-century Western art, and a block of restored historic buildings. The changing exhibits are often quite good. *166 W. Alameda; (520) 624-2333. Free on Tuesdays.*

The International Wildlife Museum, endlessly controversial locally, displays the vast big-game animal collection of hunter C. J. McElroy. The collection is housed in a rebarbative building modeled on a French Foreign Legion fort in sub-Saharan Chad. *4800 W. Gates Pass Road; (520) 617-1439.*

■ TUCSON AREA SITES

Arizona-Sonora Desert Museum in Tucson regularly appears on lists of the world's ten best zoos. Its world is the animals, plants, and natural history of the Sonoran Desert, but its exhibits also encompass this desert's forested mountains, rivers, and seacoast on the Gulf of California. The full range of Sonoran Desert animals is on display here, from the one-tenth-ounce calliope hummingbird to the black bear. Docents work the grounds, continually giving demonstrations on topics such as the differences between the jaws of herbivores and carnivores. Allow three hours for a complete visit. *2021 N. Kinney Rd.; (520) 883-2702.*

Saguaro National Park. The park is split into two units: the more popular one is 15 miles west of Tucson; the other is on the city's eastern edge in the foothills of the Rincon Mountains. The east unit offers a paved eight-mile loop road popular with runners and cyclists, and off the road, wildlife such as javelina and even deer are abundant. The West Unit has a dense saguaro forest. *West Unit: 2700 N. Kinney Road; (520) 733-5158. East Unit: East on Broadway, then southeast on Old Spanish Trail. 3693 S. Old Spanish Trail; (520) 733-5153.*

Santa Catalina Mountains. Situated on Tucson's north edge, these are one of the few major Arizona ranges to be probed by a paved road, the **Mt. Lemmon Highway.** Picnic grounds, campgrounds, and awesome geologic spectacles occur every couple of miles along the two-lane road, which climbs 5,293 feet in 25 miles. At the end is Ski Valley, the southernmost developed ski area in the United States, and Summerhaven, a community with a few unpretentious inns and boutiques. On holiday weekends in summer, the Mt. Lemmon Highway is best avoided. A road also curls to the summit of 6,882-foot **Kitt Peak** 55 miles southwest of Tucson. This is the nexus of astronomical research in Arizona, with more than a dozen telescopes clustered on the mountaintop. There is a visitors center and small museum open daily (free) with guided tours of the observatories given on weekends and holidays.

Mission San Xavier del Bac. One of the loveliest examples of Spanish Colonial architecture anywhere in the Southwest is the mission San Xavier del Bac, just south of Tucson. Built some 200 years ago "to attract by its loveliness the unconverted [Indians] beyond the frontier," according to the Spanish captain of the presidio at Tucson in 1804, its lavish scrolls, curlicues, arches and spires continue to impress visitors. *Located on the Tohono O'odham Reservation nine miles southwest of Tucson via I-19; (520) 294-2624.*

■ TUBAC

This lovely unincorporated village in the lee of the Santa Rita Mountains is charming, slow-paced, and unpretentious, with some 50 galleries and boutiques and a state historical park with exhibits on the settlement's long history. Prices for art are substantially lower than in Arizona's other major art centers, Scottsdale and Sedona.

The oldest non-Indian settlement in Arizona, Tubac is redolent with history. Several times in its first 150 years of existence it was a locus of the conflict between

Mexican dancers (above) perform at an event in Tumacácori National Historic Park near the Mexican border south of Tucson.

Mission San Xavier del Bac (opposite) is considered one of the finest examples of Spanish colonial architecture in the United States.

European and Native American civilization in the New World. Tubac was established as a *visita*—a chapel served by an itinerant priest—around 1726; that, at any rate, is the date of the first recorded baptisms by one Fr. Agustín de Campos. The next generation was a time of increasing tension in the upper Pima Indian lands (the Pimería Alta), however, with not only more Jesuit missionaries but also Spanish silver miners flooding in. The European attitude was summed up in the term *gente de razón*—"people of reason"—which the Spanish used in census documents to describe themselves, as opposed to the unenlightened (even if freshly baptized) native *bárbaros*.

In 1751, the Pimas revolted, killing two priests and more than 100 ranchers and miners, and burning churches, including the one at Tubac. The following year the Spanish established the presidio of Tubac, their first permanent military presence in Arizona.

The fifty soldiers stationed with their families at Tubac succeeded in quieting the Pimas, but the Apache proved to be the presidio's doom. In 1774, Tubac's commander, Juan Bautista de Anza, made his famous expedition to open a route to California, where he established the settlement that would become San Francisco. Two years later the Tubac garrison was moved to Tucson, where it could more effectively protect the route. Thus disarmed, Tubac was repeatedly raided, abandoned, and resettled.

Eventually Tubac did rise again, phoenix-like; the grasslands of the surrounding Santa Cruz Valley seemed ideal for ranching. Then in 1948, a nationally known artist named Dale Nichols established an art school in Tubac, and even though it lasted only a year, it placed Tubac on the map as an art center.

Important events are the Cinco de Mayo (May 5) fiesta and the Tubac Festival of the Arts in February. Many shops close in the summer. Four miles south lies the ruin of the 1822 **mission of San José de Tumacácori,** now a national monument.

■ ORGAN PIPE NATIONAL MONUMENT

The organ pipe cactus occurs naturally in only one place in the world: Organ Pipe National Monument, a 516-square-mile preserve on the Mexican border. The cactus is a spectacle sprouting a cluster of huge vertical arms up to 12 feet high that resemble—vaguely, at least—the pipes of an organ. Quitobaquito Spring, a historic natural watering hole, attracts more than 260 species of birds. *Take AZ 85, 22 miles south of Why; (520) 387-6849.*

■ NOGALES, MEXICO

Tourists in southern Arizona invariably visit Nogales, the industrial Mexican border city 60 miles south of Tucson. Generally they travel nowhere else in Sonora, which is a mistake.

Nogales ("Walnuts") is neither historic, charming, nor quaint, but the sheer variety of shops and stalls is almost entertainment enough. In any given shop visitors may find leather duffel bags, wool rugs and blankets, ornamental tiles, leather jackets, silver jewelry, fake Toltec icons, margarita glasses, religious statues, and musical instruments from the guitar to the double bass. Most of the tourist shops are along the first three blocks of Calle Obregón, up to its intersection with Calle Aguirre. Obregón continues south for about five miles, however, with shops mainly serving Mexican clientele. These are interesting, too.

MEXICAN MANNERS

*T*he Mexicans, like the French, are remarkable for their politeness and suavity of manners. You cannot visit a friend but he assures you that, *"Está V. en su casa, y puede mandar,"* etc. (You are in your own house, and can command, etc.), or, *"Estoy enteramente á su disposicion"* (I am wholly at your disposal), without, however, meaning more than an expression of ordinary courtesy. Nor can you speak in commendation of any article, let its value be what it may, but the polite owner immediately replies, *"Tómelo, V. Señor; es suyo"* (Take it, sir; it is yours), without the slightest intention or expectation that you should take him at his word.—Mr. Poinsett observes, "Remember, when you take leave of a Spanish grandee, to bow as you leave the room, at the head of the stairs, where the host accompanies you; and after descending the first flight, turn round and you will see him expecting a third salutation, which he returns with great courtesy, and remains until you are out of sight; so that as you wind down the stairs, if you catch a glimpse of him, kiss your hand, and he will think you a most accomplished cavalier." Graphic as this short sketch is, it hardly describes the full measure of Mexican politeness; for in that country, when the visitor reaches the street, another tip of the hat, and another inclination of the head, will be expected by the attentive host, who gently waves, with his hand, a final *'á dios'* from a window. —Josiah Gregg, *Commerce of the Prairies,* 1844

SAGUARO CACTUS

The saguaro inhabits a more-or-less horseshoe-shaped chunk of southern Arizona that includes Tucson, Phoenix and the 4,335-square-mile Tohono O'odham Reservation. They then march south into the Mexican states of Sonora and Baja California. But even though their range is tightly restricted by climate, they have come to serve as a symbol of the entire frontier West. So essential is their emblematic value that in *Broken Arrow,* the classic 1951 western, the film crew scattered plaster-of-Paris saguaros among the red rocks of Sedona. A saguaro would no sooner grow in cool Sedona than in San Francisco!

An average human lifetime, about 75 years, expires before it occurs to a saguaro to perform the act that makes it so impressive to humans, which is to grow its first arm or two. Thus outfitted, the still-adolescent cactus takes on an anthropomorphic character. Some individuals seem to raise their arms in surrender, others in supplication, a few in bewilderment. One monster in the foothills of the Santa Catalina Mountains currently sports 21 arms curling in a swirl around its trunk. The sentient human, wandering about a forest of these 30-foot creatures, feels like an explorer in the midst of a race of strangely still and silent alien beings. This eerie sensation is multiplied tenfold in the moonlight.

This most prominent living object in the Sonoran Desert is a good citizen, serving the biological community in several remarkable ways. Gila woodpeckers chisel apartments in mature saguaro trunks and nest in them, staying both cool and safe from climbing predators. After the woodpecker moves on, any of several other species will move in—screech and elf owls, purple martins, Wied's crested flycatchers. The saguaro's flower, which grows only at its top on the ends of its arms, provides bats with an energy-rich nectar; the bats reciprocate by pollinating other saguaro. Spanish and Mexican settlers, Tohono O'odham and Pima Indians, and probably their prehistoric ancestors as well, harvested the fruit to make jelly and wine, and employed ribs from dead saguaros as roofing material.

Yet people also abuse the saguaro. As early as 1854, a pioneer explorer, J. R. Bartlett, found arrows sticking into saguaros in the Yuman Indian lands of far west Arizona. In the early 1980s, a Phoenix man fired a shotgun into a saguaro until it toppled, killing him. Sometimes even good intentions doom the plants. Mature saguaros, which landscape architects love to use in their designs, usually die when transplanted. The Arizona-Sonora Desert Museum has seen a 95 percent mortality rate among transplanted saguaros 12 or more feet high, and has quit moving them.

Landscapers haven't, because they don't connect the transplant with the cactus's demise. A mature saguaro, perfect symbol of both the desert's perseverance and fragility, takes three to five years to die.

A forest of saguaro cactus at Sabino Canyon in Tucson.

■ CHIHUAHUAN DESERT OF COCHISE COUNTY

East of Tucson along Interstate 10, a gradual change marks the transition from Sonoran into Chihuahuan Desert. The saguaro give way to yucca, the elevation rises some 1,500 feet, and the shrub cover changes to rolling hills of straw-colored grass. This edge of the Chihuahuan Desert receives only eight to 10 inches of rain a year, which is less than Tucson gets, but because it is higher, it is also cooler, and that makes the rain more efficient. Hence the grass.

Two remarkable features mark the edge of the Chihuahuan Desert: **Texas Canyon,** a mountain range literally made of boulders, and the **Willcox Playa.** The playa looks like a vast lake shimmering in the distance, but it is a permanent mirage, a cruel optical joke surrealistically imposed on a 50-square-mile basin that used to be a lake. Now it is one of the strangest places in Arizona, a parched, table-flat wasteland where absolutely nothing grows from one horizon to another, as far as the eye can see. Yet even this most desolate region of the desert supports life. Eggs of three species of miniature shrimp lie dormant below the lake bed for as long as 30 years, and then after an extravagant summer rain, when water puddles into a soupy mud on the playa, the crustaceans hatch. If the water holds out they may last two weeks, which is just long enough to mate, deposit more eggs and then die, having miraculously assured, a shrimp's eon later, the eventual appearance of their offspring.

Throughout the year but during the hot summer months especially, some of the most elaborate mirages ever seen in the desert have been spotted at the playa. Reported sights include a group of women dancing and a speeding freight train.

■ CHIRICAHUA MOUNTAINS

In Arizona's southeastern corner lie mountains rich in both history and scenery. These were the ancestral homelands of the Chiricahua Apache, and when their leader, Cochise, negotiated peace with the Army in 1872, he was promised the mountain range as a reservation. Cochise died two years later, and in 1875 the promise evaporated and his people were herded north to the San Carlos Reservation. In 1924, President Calvin Coolidge designated the most spectacular part of the range as a national monument. The **Chiricahua National Monument** has a number of hiking trails that can fill anywhere from a half-day to several days.

■ TOMBSTONE

No newspaper ever wore a more memorable masthead than the famous *Tombstone Epitaph*. Tombstone, in its silver-boom prime of the early 1880s, was the West's most notoriously violent town. While its history has been embellished by Hollywood as well as popular historians, it was undeniably a place in which men lived fast and died in trivial quarrels. The killing was common enough that the *Epitaph* ran its accounts of the everyday grim-reaping under a standing headline: "Death's Doings." Lawlessness was so rampant that in 1882 it even attracted the notice of President Chester Arthur, who threatened to send in the Army. Hearing that, the *Epitaph,* in the finest tradition of Arizona boosterism, ran an editorial ridiculing Arthur and insisting that "We were never in a more peaceable community than Tombstone and law and order is absolute." In the three months preceding that editorial, the *Epitaph* had chronicled eight killings.

It was a uniquely colorful town, a melange of adventurers, drunks, whores, rustlers, honest working stiffs, and wealthy sophisticates. The silver mines were throwing off enough money that Tombstone built ambitious show halls and imported vaudeville and serious theater. At one point there were 110 liquor licenses in town, but Tombstone also boasted, according to historian John Myers, "the best food between New Orleans and San Francisco."

But Tombstone has secured enduring fame not for its culture, but for all that flying lead. The shootout at the OK Corral in 1881 remains the most notorious gunfight of all time.

On one side were Sheriff Johnny Behan and the Clanton clan, ranchers who moonlighted as cattle rustlers and harbored stagecoach robbers. On the other were the relatively good guys: U.S. Marshal Wyatt Earp, his brothers Virgil and Morgan, and the infamous alcoholic gunfighter "Doc" Holliday. On the afternoon of October 26, the Earps and Holliday strode purposefully into the vacant lot at Fremont and Third Street, where five young members of the Clanton gang were rumored to be looking for a fight.

According to later testimony by Ike Clanton, Wyatt Earp shoved his pistol into Clanton's belly and growled, "You son of a bitch, you can have a fight." Clanton turned white and fled, pistols and shotguns began blazing, and in about 30 seconds—Wyatt Earp's estimate—three of the Clanton gang lay dying and Virgil and Morgan Earp had been seriously wounded.

The story doesn't end there, and the aftermath tells much about the nature of life and justice in frontier Tombstone. The Earps and Holliday faced a hearing on murder charges and were cleared. Two months later, a midnight marksman tried to take out Virgil Earp but succeeded only in crippling his left arm for life. Three months after that, an assassin did kill Morgan Earp. Wyatt, operating well outside the law on the trail of vengeance, gunned down three of the men he suspected of killing his brother. He then left Cochise County for good and ended his days in Hollywood, helping in the production of early Western movies.

❖

This is a tourist town today, making a living from its historic infamy. The restored **Crystal Palace Saloon,** among others, is open for business. **Helldorado Days** every October includes a parade, gunfight reenactments, and in several recent years, visits by Edward Earp, cousin of Wyatt. **Allen Street,** once lined with bars, casinos and cathouses, has been beautifully restored; it has served as a set for Japanese crews filming samurai Westerns. The original **Cochise County Courthouse,** built in 1882, is now a state historic park. It is the most sophisticated piece of Victorian neoclassical architecture in the state—an anomaly to ponder while listening to the reenacted gunfights echoing in the street two blocks away.

■ BISBEE

Serious copper mining began in these hills and gulches six miles north of the Mexican border in 1880. By 1900, Bisbee was the largest, most prosperous settlement in Arizona Territory. It was crude but at the same time remarkably cosmopolitan. The copper mines had attracted immigrants from Germany, Serbia, Italy, Ireland, Mexico, even Russia. Each ethnic group clustered in its own "town" or neighborhood. Some longtime Bisbee folk recall the charm of it all—the Germans making wine, the Serbs raising goats (their neighborhood was called "Goat Grove"), the Irish raising hell.

Underground, in the mines, these people depended on each other for their lives, so they got along well. Above ground, cosmopolitan Bisbee was tense with ethnic rivalries. "You never went to the show by yourself; you always took someone with you," said Les Williams, a retired miner. "Each 'town' had its own gang. We stole burros from each other, we'd play baseball with each other, then we'd fight after the games."

Today the town has many serious artists, wonderful Italianate Victorian architecture, no industry, and an utterly seductive, delightful spirit. Bisbee is Aspen turned inside-out, kicked into a time warp and trapped in a happy reverse universe devoid of traffic lights, designer labels, or pretentious boutiques. Bisbee is a town where one can walk the narrow, decaying, mountainside streets in the evening and hear someone practicing Bach fugues on a piano in questionable tune. Bisbee, more than any other town in Arizona, is a place in which to re-invent oneself; the presence of 6,207 people doing just that makes it the most fascinating small town to visit in Arizona.

Tours are available underground into the **Copper Queen Mine** or around the edges of the enormous **Lavender Open Pit Mine.** Bisbee also hosts an impressive number of annual events. The town's steep hills make April's **La Vuelta de Bisbee** one of the world's most harrowing professional bicycle races. Visitors to Bisbee at any time should bring a camera; the colors, textures, and historic buildings of the town are a photographer's dream.

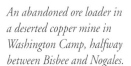

An abandoned ore loader in a deserted copper mine in Washington Camp, halfway between Bisbee and Nogales.

Southeast Arizona Food & Lodging

■ FOOD & LODGING

Restaurant prices:
Per person, not including drinks, tax and tips:
$ = under $10; $$ = $10–20; $$$ = over $20

Room rates:
Per night, per room, double occupancy:
$ = under $50; $$ = $50–100; $$$ = over $100

Bisbee/Tombstone

✕ **Cafe Roka.** 35 Main St.; (520) 432-5153 $$
It used to be impossible to find a decent dinner in this quirky old mining town, but no more. A few years back Rod Kass, the sous-chef at Phoenix's swank Registry Resort, opened this contemporary Italian/eclectic cafe here, serving delectable concoctions such as shrimp in angel hair pasta with brown garlic, sweet peppers and cream. "We're just trying to keep ourselves from getting bored," says Kass. Dinner only.

🛏 **Bisbee Grande Hotel.** 61 Main St.; (520) 432-5900 or (800) 421-1909 $$
Elegantly furnished 11-room Victorian hotel, with red carpeting and brass beds. Downstairs is an old saloon, a theatre for melodramas, and a billiards room. Light breakfast included.

🛏 **Bisbee Inn.** 45 OK St.; (520) 432-5131 $-$$
Overlooking Brewery Gulch is this nice renovation of a historic miners' rooming house, with sinks and homemade quilts in the 18 rooms. Guests must share baths, but an all-you-can-eat breakfast is included.

🛏 **Copper Queen Hotel.** 11 Howell Ave.; (520) 432-2216 or (800) 247-5829 $$-$$$
This five-story brick building has been Bisbee's swankiest hotel since the Copper Queen Mining Company opened the doors in 1902. Some rooms are cramped but baths are spacious. Dining room and saloon are on the premises.

Phoenix

population 983,400   elevation 1,090

✕ **Christopher's/The Bistro.** 2398 E. Camelback Rd.; (602) 957-3214 $$$
Two superb restaurants under the direction of the highly regarded Chris Gross: the less formal Bistro has Mediterranean-American food; Christopher's is contemporary French.

✕ **El Bravo.** 8338 N. Seventh St.; (602) 943-9753 $
Unassuming Sonoran-style Mexican food that's won every media award in

town. The succulent *chile colorado* tastes as if it's been simmered for a week. Green corn and chicken tamales braid the prickly flavor of green chiles with sweet corn masa. Prices are barely higher than fast food.

✗ **Eliana's.** 1627 N. 24th St.; (602) 225-2925 $
Never had El Salvadoran food? It's delicate and delicious, and this is one of the few places save El Salvador where you're sure to encounter it. Small, friendly, very informal.

✗ **Greekfest.** 1940 E. Camelback Rd.; (602) 265-2990 $$
Sophisticated Greek cuisine such as *exohiko,* a melange of lamb, cheese and vegetables baked in phyllo. Pleasant surroundings, good service.

✗ **Havana Cafe.** 4225 E. Camelback Rd.; (602) 952-1991 $$
The fare here is "pre-Castro" Cuban cuisine, in which every region of Spain is filtered through Caribbean influences. Small and informal.

✗ **Lombardi's.** Arizona Center, 455 N. Third St.; (602) 257-8323 $$
A convivial but very noisy downtown place with big crowds and excellent pasta, pizza, veal and seafood. Try the cioppino Livornese, an Italian-accented bouillabaisse.

✗ **Pizzeria Bianco.** 623 E. Adams St. (7th St.); (602) 258-8300 $
Outstanding pizza baked in a brick oven, wonderfully fresh salads,and irritatingly long lines.

✗ **Roxsand.** 2594 E. Camelback Rd.; (602) 381-0444 $$$

It's called "New American fusion cuisine," which means dishes like "Confit of African pheasant with Evil Jungle Prince sauce." What?! Nevertheless, it's superbly conceived and executed. One of the best restaurants in Phoenix.

✗ **San Carlos Bay Seafood**. 1901 E. McDowell; (602) 340-0892 $$
Authentic Mexican seafood. Beware any dish with the word "diablo" in the title—that means "devil," and the sauce will indeed be satanically spicy.

✗ **Steamers.** Biltmore Fashion Park, 2576 E. Camelback Rd.; (602) 956-3631 $$$
Seafood in Arizona used to be shrimp trucked up from the Sonoran coast and not much else, but that's ancient history now. Steamers has some 20 different fresh fish on the menu, plus eight shellfish entrees—and, of course, an oyster, clam and mussel bar.

✗ **Such is Life.** 3602 N. 24th St.; (602) 955-7822 $$
One of the best Mexican restaurants in Arizona. Forget tacos and enchiladas —try the shredded lamb wrapped in the leaves of a maguey cactus, roasted for six hours, and served with a pasilla chile sauce. The upstairs kitchen has an authentic Spanish menu. There's a Scottsdale location also: 7000 E. Shea; Blvd.; (602) 948-1753.

✗ **Vincent on Camelback.** 3930 E. Camelback Rd.; (602) 224-0225 $$$
Exceptional and imaginative New Southwestern cuisine such as roasted veal chops with *chipotle chile beurre blanc* or grilled sea bass with chimayó chile or duck tamales.

Southeast Arizona Food & Lodging

Southeast Arizona Food & Lodging

⊟ **Arizona Biltmore.** 24th and Missouri; (602) 955-6600 or (800) 950-0086 $$$ Built in 1929 and designed by Frank Lloyd Wright's colleague Albert Chase McArthur, this remains the Valley's most beautiful resort. The lobby is decorated in gold leaf, teak, and marble. Several good restaurants, as well as a dozen tennis courts, two full golf courses, and five pools.

⊟ **Best Western Executive Park Hotel.** 1100 N. Central Ave.; (602) 252-2100 or (800) 528-1234 $$ This eight-story hotel boasts spacious and quiet rooms, as well as a pleasant restaurant, pool, and health club. It's centrally located a half-mile north of downtown, yet outside the most congested area. Good value.

⊟ **Westcourt in the Buttes.** 2000 Westcourt Way, Tempe ; (602) 225-9000 or (800) 843-1986 $$–$$$ Luxury 350-room hotel dramatically built into the top of a small mountain. Tennis courts, pools, and two restaurants. Located near Arizona State University and airport.

Scottsdale

population 130, 000   elevation 1,250

✗ **La Tache.** 4175 Goldwater Blvd.; (602) 946-0377 $$-$$$ For a romantic dinner, settle in on the patio with a view of Camelback Mountain and enjoy dishes like pot roast Provençal or Thai curry prawns. There's also a wine bar with some 70 wines available by the glass.

✗ **Marquesa at the Scottsdale Princess.** 7575 E. Princess Dr.; (602) 585-2723 $$$ A destination resort restaurant with a Catalonian menu? Bold idea, but it certainly works. The paella is sheer art. Very expensive and rather formal.

⊟ **Marriott's Camelback Inn Resort.** 5402 E. Lincoln Dr.; (602) 948-1700 or (800) 24-CAMEL $$$ Very deluxe resort , with over 400 spacious and luxurious rooms in casitas, many of them two-story, with patios, fireplaces, and even private pools. Set on 125 acres with three pools, with poolside dining; saunas, 36-hole golf course, spas upon spas, concierges.

⊟ **The Phoenician.** 6000 E. Camelback Rd.; (602) 941-8200 $$$ Covering 130 acres of Camelback Mountain and heavily landscaped with tiers of waterfalls and pools (one is tiled with mother-of-pearl), this ultra-deluxe resort offers over 440 lavish rooms, suites and casitas. Golf, tennis courts and health spas.

Tucson

population 405, 000   elevation 2,386

✗ **AZ Stixx.** 3048 E. Broadway Blvd. 520-323-3701 $$ Asian cuisine was slow to come to Tucson, but the wave has finally begun. A great spot for a casual dinner, this tastefully decorated restaurant serves charred ahi sashimi, ginger-smoked duck, and other such specialties from across the Pacific.

✕ **Boccata.** 5605 E. River Rd.; (520) 577 9309 $$

A wonderful menu combining southern French and northern Italian cuisines. If you're lucky, fettuccine Genovese with pesto and grilled scallops and shrimp will be on the menu. Dine on the deck to get a lovely view of the city lights.

✕ **Cafe Terra Cotta.** 4310 N. Campbell Ave.; (520) 577-8100 $$

The fountainhead of New Southwestern cuisine in Tucson and a favorite with locals and visitors. An excellent place to graze on appetizers, which sometimes are more intriguing than the mains. There's a Scottsdale location also: 6166 N. Scottsdale Rd.; (602) 948-8100.

✕ **Daniel's.** 4340 N. Campbell Ave.; (520) 742-3200 $$-$$$

This northern Italian restaurant is very expensive, very sophisticated, and very good. Superb wine list and even an extensive single-malt scotch list.

✕ **El Charro.** 311 N. Court Dr., (520) 622-1922 $

Located in a historic downtown house, this Mexican restaurant is famous throughout Tucson for its succulent *carne seca* (sun-dried beef).

✕ **Janos.** 150 N. Main Ave.; (520) 884-9426 $$$

Tucson's best restaurant, no matter that Mobil gives the venerable Tack Room one more star. They're wrong. Owner-chef Janos Wilder presides over kitchen and dining rooms in a tastefully but not pretentiously decorated 1865 adobe home. Cuisine is eclectic and imaginative, drawing on French, Mexican and American traditions and techniques. Inexpensive summer specials are a startling bargain.

✕ **Kingfisher.** 2564 E. Grant Rd.; (520) 323-7739 $$

New American menu. Good grilled seafood, spit-roasted chicken. Mashed potato infused with rutabaga may be an idea whose time hasn't come, however.

✕ **Le Bistro.** 2574 N. Campbell Ave.; (520) 327-3086 $$

Somehow overlooked in some travel guides, this pretty but unassuming place offers very good classic French bistro cuisine. Great desserts.

✕ **Mi Nidito.** 1813 S. Fourth Ave.; (520) 622-5081 $

A local institution since 1954 and the best Mexican food in town. Most tourists never hear about it because of its location in mostly Hispanic South Tucson. Always jammed at normal mealtimes; go at an odd hour or be prepared for a long wait. Try the green chile enchiladas and a Bohemia, Mexico's best beer.

✕ **Ventana Room at Loews Ventana Canyon Resort.** 7000 N. Resort Dr.; (520) 299-2020 $$$

This is an aerie with a view—the night lights of Tucson, sprawling halfway to Mexico. The very expensive New American cuisine presents itself elegantly, and service is formal and professional. Male patrons must wear a jacket and tie.

Southeast Arizona Food & Lodging

✕ **Vivace.** 4811 E. Grant Rd.; (520) 795-7221 $$
Owner-chef Daniel Scordato, who hails from a venerable Tucson restaurant family, serves up four-star food at two-star prices in this contemporary trattoria. Fabulous seafood soup.

▦ **Arizona Inn.** 2200 E. Elm St.; (520) 325-1541 $$$
Cypress and orange trees cover the 14-acre lawns of this 1930s-vintage resort. The 80 guest rooms are decorated in period style, all have patios, many have fireplaces. Pool, tennis courts, and restaurant. Conveniently located.

▦ **Elkhorn Guest Ranch.** Sasabe Star Route; (520) 822-1040 $$–$$$
Accommodation in cabins, with meals included. Horseback riding, pool, tennis. Open November through April.

▦ **Elysian Grove Market.** 400 W. Simpson; (520) 628-1522
A former grocery store, this 1920s adobe in the Barrio Histórico has been lovingly rennovated and filled with folk art and antiques. Four rooms, skylights, garden.

▦ **El Presidio Bed & Breakfast.** 297 N. Main Ave.; (520) 623-6151 $$
Lovely B&B in an 1879 Victorian adobe.

▦ **La Posada Del Valle.** 1640 N. Campbell Ave.; (520) 795-3840 $$
This Southwest-style adobe, ca. 1920, offers five guest rooms, each named after a famous woman from the '20s (many guests prefer "Zelda's Room"). Afternoon tea is served in a common room furnished with art deco antiques.

▦ **Lazy K Bar Ranch.** 8401 N. Scenic Dr., 85743; (520) 744-3050 $$–$$$
The adobe main house (built in 1933) is set on 160 acres of beautiful desert and mountain trails. Meals are served family-style, or at picnics and cookouts. Guests enjoy mountain bikes, hayrides, rodeos, and trapshooting; there's also a library, a pool, and a whirlpool. Open September through mid-June; lower rates from late spring to fall.

▦ **Loews Ventana Canyon Resort.** 7000 N. Resort Dr.; (520) 299-2020 or (800) 234-5117 $$$
Tucson's most beautiful destination resort: 93 acres nestled in a saguaro forest at the foot of the Santa Catalina Mountains. The 400 Southwest-style rooms feature private balconies, dark pine furniture, and artwork. In addition to restaurants, tennis courts, pools, and quiet paths through mesquite and blue palo verde is an 80-foot waterfall spilling into a picturesque lake.

▦ **Tanque Verde Ranch.** 14301 Speedway; (520) 296-6275 $$$
This super-deluxe ranch, dating from the 1880s, offers 70 adobe casitas and main lodge rooms, furnished with antiques and beehive fireplaces. Swim indoors or out, go horseback riding, play tennis, and take a course in nature studies. Open year-round.

▦ **White Stallion Ranch.** 9251 W. Twin Peaks Rd., 85743; (520) 297-0252 $$$
An informal ranch on 3,000 acres, with 29 rooms in cottages and lodge. Family-style meals; tennis, golf, trap and target shooting. Hayrides, rodeos, bonfires. Open September through May.

Southeast Arizona Golf Courses

■ GOLF COURSES

Listed below are a few of the top-ranked golf courses in Southeast Arizona.

PHOENIX/SCOTTSDALE

Ahwatukee Country Club. Phoenix; (602) 893-1161. Public.

Arizona Biltmore Country Club. Phoenix; (602) 955-9655. Public.

Arizona Golf Resort. 25 miles from Phoenix in Mesa; (602) 832-1661. Resort.

Boulders Club. About 30 miles from Phoenix in Carefree; (602) 488-9028. Resort.

Dobson Ranch Golf Club. 15 miles from Phoenix in Mesa; (602) 644-2291. Public.

Encanto Park. Phoenix; (602) 253-3963. Public.

Gainey Ranch Golf Club. Scottsdale; (602) 951-8051. Resort.

Hillcrest Golf Club. 10 miles from Phoenix in Sun City West; (602) 584-1500. Resort.

Karsten Golf Course. Tempe; (602) 921-8070. Public.

Legend Golf Course at Arrowhead. Glendale; (602) 561-0953. Resort.

Marriot's Camelback Golf Club. Scottsdale; (602) 596-7050. Resort.

McCormick Ranch. Scottsdale; (602) 948-0260. Public.

Ocotillo Golf Club. Chandler; (602) 917-6660. Resort.

Papago Golf Course. Phoenix; (602) 275-8428. Public.

Sedona Golf Resort. 90 miles from Phoenix in Sedona; (602) 258-1443. Resort.

Scottsdale Country Club. Scottsdale; (602) 948-6911. Public.

Superstition Springs Golf Club. Mesa; (602) 985-5622. Public.

Tournament Players Club. Scottsdale; (602) 585-3939. Resort.

Troon North Golf Club. Scottsdale; (602) 585-5300. Public.

Wigwam Gold Resort. 15 miles from Phoenix in Litchfield Park; (602) 272-4653. Resort.

TUCSON AREA

Canoa Hills Golf Course. Green Valley; (520) 648-1880. Public.

El Conquistador Country Club. Tucson; (520) 544-1900. Resort

Randolph Golf Course North. Tucson; (520) 325-2811. Public.

Tucson National Golf Resort. Tucson; (520) 297-2271. Resort.

Starr Pass. Tucson; (520) 670-0300. Public.

San Ignacio Golf Club. Green Valley; (520) 648-3468. Public.

Ventana Canyon Golf & Racquet Club. Tucson; (520) 577-1400. Resort.

Westin La Paloma. Tucson; (520) 742-6000. Resort.

SOUTHERN NEW MEXICO

■ HIGHLIGHTS
Mogollon Mountains
Silver City
Gila Cliff Dwellings
Columbus
Las Cruces
Ghost Towns
Socorro
White Sands
Ruidoso
Cloudcroft
Carlsbad Caverns

■ LANDSCAPE

The vast, arid expanses of southern New Mexico virtually define the word "desert"—but that doesn't mean the land is barren or devoid of interest for the passerby. Mountain ranges such as the Mogollon, Ánimas, and Guadalupes powerfully define the horizons, and Las Cruces is surrounded by the majestically sawtoothed Organ Mountains bursting out of the desert to its east.

Several national treasures are scattered over this land: Gila Cliff Dwellings, built by the prehistoric Mogollon culture around 1276 and abandoned just 30 to 40 years later; White Sands National Monument, with its ghostly, wavelike dunes of almost pure white gypsum; and Carlsbad Caverns, one of the largest cave systems in the world. NM Highway 152, corkscrewing across 63 miles of forests, mountains, and canyons from Silver City to Interstate 25, is one of the most beautiful drives in the Southwest. Bisecting the state north to south is the placidly flowing Rio Grande and a wide ribbon of irrigated farmland straddling it. North of Hatch—chile capital of New Mexico and therefore of the United States—is Elephant Butte Lake, manufactured by a dam across the Rio Grande. Framed by dry desert buttes, its considerable length —43 miles—offers water skiing and endless coves for sailboats.

■ TRAVELERS ORIENTATION

Towns in southern New Mexico seem to lie just about 60 miles apart, and while the pace of traffic between them is fast, the pace of life within them is blessedly slow. It's a good place to tune the car radio to some mournful country station—which, more than likely, will be your only choice anyway—and let the uneventful miles pass in a contemplative blur of desert, clouds, and distant mountains.

The land here may seem harsh to an outsider, but the people are not. They are generally unpretentious, plain-spoken, friendly, and helpful—whether it's a gas station attendant in Silver City or a librarian at New Mexico State University in Las Cruces. Mexican culture flows north across the border; in some towns you may hear more Spanish than English.

Food & Lodging appears on page 333.

Elevation is the key factor determining climate in southern New Mexico. Mountains and plateaux above 5–6,000 feet tend to receive two or three times as much precipitation as those regions between 2,000 and 4,000 feet and temperatures drop about 4° or 5° F for every increase of 1,000 feet in elevation. Silver City (elev. 5,900) rests in the mountainous region near the Arizona border and is indicative of the weather one might encounter at the Gila Cliff Dwellings. Las Cruces (elev. 3,900) is in the Rio Grande basin, while Carlsbad (elev. 3,100) is in the southeast corner of the state and has a climate similar to that of the southern plains. The region may be visited comfortably at any time of the year, the high summer temperatures offset by extremely low humidity.

TEMPS (F°)	AVG. JAN. HIGH	AVG. JAN. LOW	AVG. APRIL HIGH	AVG. APRIL LOW	AVG. JULY HIGH	AVG. JULY LOW	AVG. OCT. HIGH	AVG. OCT. LOW	RECORD HIGH	RECORD LOW
Carlsbad	59	31	82	56	96	68	84	58	112	-7
Las Cruces	63	38	80	50	99	74	83	57	109	-10
Silver City	48	19	69	34	85	56	70	43	105	-17

PRECIPITATION (INCHES)	AVG. JAN.	AVG. APRIL	AVG. JULY	AVG. OCT.	ANNUAL	SNOW
Carlsbad	0.3	0.9	2.2	1.4	12.4	6
Las Cruces	0.3	0.2	1.6	0.7	8.7	3
Silver City	0.8	0.6	3.3	1.2	16.8	14

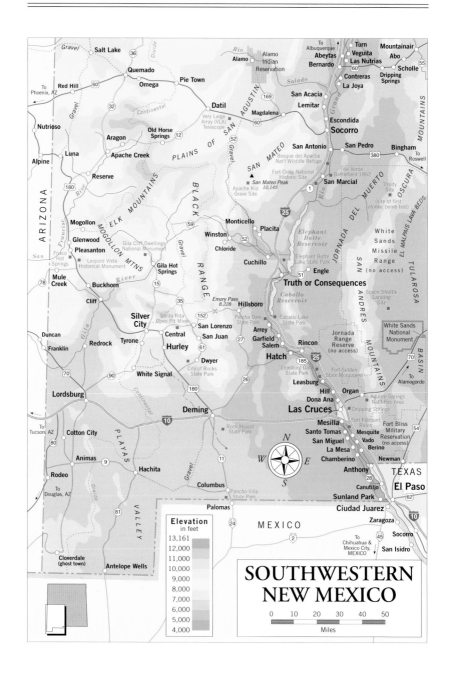

SOUTHWESTERN
NEW MEXICO

Elevation
in feet
13,161
12,000
11,000
10,000
9,000
8,000
7,000
6,000
5,000
4,000

0   10   20   30   40   50
Miles

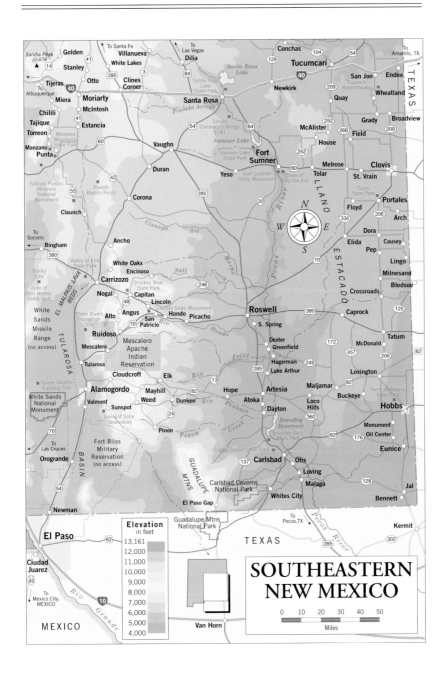

SOUTHEASTERN
NEW MEXICO

Elevation
in feet

13,161
12,000
11,000
10,000
9,000
8,000
7,000
6,000
5,000
4,000

0   10   20   30   40   50
Miles

■ HISTORY

The most famous event in southern New Mexico's past occurred on the morning of March 9, 1916: the first and only military invasion of the United States mainland in this century. While most of the residents of the little border village of Columbus lay sleeping, Mexican revolutionary Pancho Villa led his guerrilla band across the border, torching the town and killing 18 American citizens. The provocation: 3,000 miles away, U.S. President Woodrow Wilson had recognized the government of Mexican president Venustiano Carranza. The day after the attack, Wilson sent 10,000 troops storming into Mexico after Villa. They never found him, but Villa never returned to the United States, either.

At the time of the Villa raid, New Mexico had been a state for only four years. The southern end of it was still thinly populated. Ranchers and farmers, many of Hispanic descent, wrested a living from the desert where they could. But in Silver City, the land had already proven that it could provide prosperity; in 1870 a farmer/prospector named John Bullard stumbled across a phenomenally rich vein of silver just behind the present Grant County Courthouse. Typically, it became an overnight boom town; atypically, a decade later, the town passed an ordinance that every new building was to be constructed of brick. This spared Silver City the disastrous fires that periodically ravaged most of the jerry-built mining towns in the West, and bequeathed a large cluster of sturdy, handsome Victorian architecture to today's visitors.

The precious metals that had eluded the Spanish *conquistadores* in New Mexico for centuries weren't the only riches of southern New Mexico. In 1901 a young cowboy discovered Carlsbad Caverns, which 30 years later became the region's premium tourist attraction. In 1928 a vast pool of oil was discovered in the far southeastern corner of the state, which turned Hobbs into another boom town.

The most portentous boom of all came on July 16, 1945, when a team of scientists who had been feverishly laboring in secret at Los Alamos detonated the world's first atomic bomb at what is now called the Trinity Site, 60 miles northwest of Alamogordo. J. Robert Oppenheimer, director of the team, somberly quoted the *Bhagavad Gita*: "Now I am become Death, the destroyer of worlds."

COCHISE AND GERONIMO

Two great warriors were born to separate bands of the Apache in the Southwest in the early 19th century. The first was Cochise, who along with four other chiefs, was interrogated by the U.S. army after Indian raiders rustled cattle and abducted a white child. The chiefs maintained they were innocent, but one was shot, three were hanged, and Cochise escaped only after cutting his way out of a tent, bleeding from the wounds of three bullets. After that, Cochise waged war against whites and was successful in part because U.S. Army units in Arizona were called east to fight in the Civil War, leaving much of the frontier undefended. Eventually, the army led a war of extermination against the Apache, but Cochise and 200 followers disappeared into the Dragoon Mountains, where they continued to fight. After Gen. George Crook forced the relocation of 4,000 Apache to the Chiricahua Apache Reservation, a barren wasteland in east-central Arizona, Cochise joined them, dying there in 1874.

A younger chief, Geronimo, remained unsatisfied with reservation life and refused to stay within its confines. A veteran of many battles, he had been admitted to warrior councils at 17. After his wife, mother, and children were killed by the Mexicans, he led raids of vengeance against them. In 1874, he left the Chiricahua reservation with 35 men, 8 boys, and 101 women, and again began leading raids against white settlers. He was captured after being stalked by 5,500 U.S. troops. Exiled to Florida, then Fort Sill, Oklahoma, Geronimo tried farming, and he joined the Dutch Reformed Church. He found both unsatisfying, and was expelled from his church for gambling. Geronimo died in 1909, never having seen Arizona again.

Geronimo (right) and his warriors in 1886. (Arizona Historical Society)

■ SILVER CITY

In the Mogollon Mountains of southwestern New Mexico, at the end of the 19th century, rumor had it that silver was everywhere. Soon the pine-covered hills were covered with tents and makeshift shacks that became known as Silver City. Banks, saloons, restaurants, billiard halls, and meat markets popped up on the dirt streets, along with the offices of doctors, lawyers, dressmakers, and tailors. These people apparently were eager to know of the larger world, for by the end of 1882, six newspapers were being published in the mining district.

Prior to the arrival of the railroad in 1881, 12- and 14-horse teams hauled ore from the Mogollon Mountains to town, where it was shipped off by stagecoach and wagon train. Stacks of gold and silver bricks stood outside freight offices.

The original townsite looks much the same as it did in the old days. Silver City, like so many other cities in New Mexico, lays claim to Billy the Kid. As a pre-teen then known as Henry McCarty, the outlaw attended school and worked as a waiter at the Star Hotel. He moved there with his mother and stepfather, who had a burning desire to strike it rich in the silver mines. You can follow the outlaw's brief presence in the mining district on a self-guided Billy the Kid tour that takes you past the site of his boyhood home (since torn down), the Star Hotel, his mother's grave, and the site of the jail from which he made his first escape.

Silver City's mines are still producing, though copper has replaced silver as the primary metal extracted. Thirteen miles east of town, the village of Santa Rita has been swallowed up by a massive open-pit copper operation. From an observation deck, you can peer into the 1,000-foot-deep mine that stretches more than a mile across.

North of Silver City is the small mining town of Pinos Altos, home to the time-trapped **Buckhorn Saloon** with its creaky wooden floor, and the **Opera House**, which stages a comic-western melodrama every weekend.

■ GILA CLIFF DWELLINGS

Past Pinos Altos, NM 15 ends at the Gila Cliff Dwellings, where Mogollon Indians lived from the 1270s into the early 1300s. These people cultivated squash, corn, beans, and tobacco on nearby mesas and along the West Fork of the Gila River. They also hunted deer and gathered wild berries and nuts in the nearby forest. For generations their voices had echoed throughout the canyon, but by the

Harlan Webb, leather artist from White Oaks north of Alamogordo.

early 1300s, the only sounds remaining came from birds and the river. No one knows for certain why they left, but many think they joined other Pueblo Indians to the north and south. The monument is adjacent to the 438,360-acre Gila Wilderness, promoted by conservationist Aldo Leopold and established in 1924 as the first designated wilderness in the country. A one-mile loop trail takes you up and through 42 rock-walled rooms built into the side of a volcanic cliff. You can climb ladders to explore the dark interiors.

■ HIDEOUTS AND RANCHING TOWNS

Northwest of Silver City, US 180 skirts the 2.7-million-acre Gila National Forest and passes through a few small ranching communities. At **Glenwood**, the Catwalk, a two-and-a-half-mile steel walkway anchored to a rock wall above the rushing waters of Whitewater Creek, is open to the public. Before gold and silver were discovered in the Mogollon Mountains above the creek, the box canyon served as a hideout for Geronimo and for Butch Cassidy, who carefully picked a path along the creek bed. A few miles past Glenwood is the turnoff to **Mogollon**, population nine, an old mining town wedged into a narrow canyon in the Mogollon Mountains. In 1890, it was a bustling mining camp that boasted 20 saloons and 2,000 residents, including Ben Lilly, one of the West's most adept mountain lion hunters. Lilly charged ranchers $50 for each dead mountain lion he brought them. He bagged 110 during his career. Silver and gold ore was processed at nearby mills, which produced 18 million ounces of silver before the mines closed at the outbreak of World War II. The town clock still reads 4:00, the time the last shift ended in the mines.

■ MESILLA VALLEY

When New Mexico was being colonized by the Spanish empire via Mexico, wagons of Spanish colonists passed this way following the lush banks of the Rio Grande below the dry, rugged Organ Mountains. They were frequently ambushed by Apaches, and in 1787, the bodies of several oxcart caravan drivers were found and crosses were erected atop their graves. Forty-three years later, a party of 30 travelers from Taos met the same fate and more crosses were raised. What began as an eerie graveyard known as La Placita de Las Cruces, "The Little Square of the Crosses," eventually became a town.

The Mesilla Valley is flanked by the Rio Grande beginning just north of Las

Cruces. *Travelers on Interstate 10 between Las Cruces and El Paso may want to take the smaller roads through the Mesilla Valley via NM 28.*

Las Cruces. "The Little Square of the Crosses," has grown to become the second largest city in New Mexico. In the mid-1800s, colonists began putting down roots, cultivating crops along the banks of the Rio Grande. They lived in *jacales,* created by placing poles vertically in a ground trench. The poles were lashed together and coated with mud plaster, forming walls that could be whitewashed. Vigas and latillas supported dirt roofs. Adobe bricks were used in later homes, brick copings topped parapets, and square wooden columns supported porches. Many of these houses are still visible in the Mesquite Street area, east of downtown, Las Cruces's oldest neighborhood. Homes are stuccoed in pastel pink, green, blue, and shades of brown that range from tawny to deep chocolate. An occasional shrine graces a front yard.

After the Santa Fe Railroad reached Las Cruces in 1881, farm lands between the Mesquite district and the depot were transformed into homes that reflected the styles of the town's new residents, who came from the East Coast.

Mesilla. Nearby Mesilla lost out to Las Cruces in population and prestige when the railroad chose the latter, but it retained its 19th-century character. From miles away, the white crosses atop two steeples of the **San Albino Church** can be seen towering above the tree-shaded town. This block-long brick church anchors the northern end of a quiet central plaza that has a whitewashed gazebo in its center. The Confederate flag flapped above the plaza for a year between 1861 and 1862, and 20 years later in a stuffy courtroom, a shackled Billy the Kid was sentenced to die for the murder of Lincoln County Sheriff William Brady.

Away from the plaza on Mesilla's narrow back streets, residents still live in old adobe homes, some displaying brightly painted wooden window casings.

South of Mesilla, with the jagged peaks of the Organ Mountains a distant backdrop, NM 28 follows the bends of the Rio Grande, passing beneath a three-mile-long canopy created by thick groves of pecan trees. This 3,850-acre pecan orchard is one of the largest in the world. Farmers who tend these fields live in small hamlets with names like San Miguel, Chamberino, and La Mesa. They meet to share a beer and discuss local politics at Chope's Bar and Cafe in La Mesa. The green chile that smothers plates of enchiladas and burritos served here is for palates accustomed to fire. If yours isn't, expect to leave with a runny nose and perspiring brow.

NOTORIOUS PERSONALITIES OF THE OLD SOUTHWEST

BILLY THE KID

William H. Bonney, a.k.a. Billy the Kid, was born in a New York City tenement on November 23, 1859. At an early age, he moved to Coffeyville, Kansas, with his mother and father and then moved further west to Silver City, New Mexico, following his father's death. Legend has it that the Kid killed 21 men by his 21st birthday. His criminal career began in earnest in 1878 with the Lincoln County War, when he recked vengeance on a group of hired guns (including a crooked sheriff) who had murdered his boss and mentor, rancher John Tunstall. A former friend-turned-sheriff, Pat Garrett, finally tracked down the Kid and shot him to death in 1881.

DOC HOLLIDAY

Perhaps the most famous gunfight in American history, the shootout at the OK Corral in Tombstone, Arizona, took place on October 26, 1881. On the side of law and order were lawmen Wyatt Earp, his two brothers, Virgil and Morgan, and former dentist John H. "Doc" Holliday; on the other side were the two Clanton brothers, two McLowery brothers, and Billy Clairborne. Doc and the Earps killed both McLowery brothers and Billie Clanton. Virgil and Morgan Earp were injured. Following the shootout, Doc Holliday and Wyatt Earp were arrested for having fired the first shots, but they were soon exonerated. Wyatt Earp went on to kill several other notorious outlaws including Curly Bill Brocious and Johnny Ringo. He eventually retired to California and acted as a consultant to Hollywood filmmakers producing Westerns. Doc Holliday died of tuberculosis at the age of 35 just five years after the gunfight at OK Corral.

PANCHO VILLA

Francisco Villa, born to a poor Mexican family in 1878, fought against the regimes of Porfirio Díaz in 1909 and Victoriana Huerta during the Mexican Civil War of 1914. A talented military tactician, he defeated the army of Huerta in 1913 and entered Mexico City as one of the victorious leaders of the revolution. In 1916, he torched the American town of Columbus, New Mexico. Woodrow Wilson sent 10,000 troops into Mexico to capture Villa, but he disappeared into the Chihuahuan Desert. The Mexican government eventually gave Villa a ranch near Parral, where he was murdered three years later.

LA DOÑA TULES

A notorious *monte* dealer-player dominated Santa Fe's social and gambling scene during the 1830s and 1840s. Born Gertrudis Barceló, she became infamous as La Doña Tules. She traveled long distances to gamble at trade fairs and *bailes* (balls), dealing *monte* to trappers, soldiers, governors, generals, women, and clergy. In appreciation for a loan of $1,000, a U.S. officer escorted La Doña to a play at the Palace of the Governors. In 1852, Bishop Jean Baptiste Lamy officiated at La Doña's funeral after Tules paid $2,000 to be buried in his church.

THE APACHE KID

Born about 1867, the Apache Kid grew up on the San Carlos Indian Reservation in New Mexico, where he became a prized sergeant of scouts. When his father was killed by a renegade, the Kid swiftly slayed the murderer. Pardoned by President Cleveland, he soon got into trouble again, and with a $5,000 bounty on his head he roamed the New Mexico territory terrorizing settlers. In 1894 a prospector claimed to have killed the Kid and his wife when they tried to rob his camp.

Dripping Springs. At first glance, the jagged Organ Mountains outside Las Cruces appear as dry as the desert around them. And for the most part, they are, except at Dripping Springs. There, a trickle of water seeps from the volcanic rock, forming a few refreshing pools. During and after a rainstorm, the drip becomes a waterfall, sending a roaring river through nearby Ice Canyon. In 1988, this 2,852-acre spread of cactus-laden foothills and rugged rock outcroppings was acquired by the Nature Conservancy, which then transferred title to the Bureau of Land Management. Now that it's in the public domain, the main ranch house has been turned into a visitors center. A one-and-a-half mile trail leads you to the remnants of the old Dripping Springs resort—a turn-of-the-century in-spot which attracted such notables as Pancho Villa and Pat Garrett. *To reach the ranch, take University Boulevard east off I-25, heading toward the mountains. When the pavement ends, you are on Dripping Springs Road. Most of the 10-mile trip is on gravel, and it takes about 30 minutes. Call the Bureau of Land Management in Las Cruces for more information, (505) 525-4300.*

■ GHOST TOWNS

The road north from Las Cruces to Socorro and on to Albuquerque follows the Rio Grande and several reservoir/recreational lakes. Off the main road there are a few ghost towns, their once-busy streets now deserted, their bustling mercantile stores now reduced to wooden skeletons. Northwest of Truth or Consequences, NM 52 passes through **Cuchillo**, a Hispanic hamlet tucked into an abrupt outcropping. During the 1860 gold rush days, prospectors and suppliers changed horses here, and stagecoaches let their passengers off to stretch their legs. Cans of soup and small jars of spices line the walls of the general store, which has doubled as a bar since opening its doors in 1850.

Gently rising hillsides dotted with piñon pines give way to a broad meadow of pale green and yellow grasses amid which the mining district of **Winston** sits. Silver attracted prospectors here in the 1880s. Today, cattle graze in the valley, and tall weeds and grass are what prosper, jutting up between the false-fronted and mostly abandoned wooden buildings. Beyond this almost nonexistent town, the road turns to gravel, ending two miles closer to the looming mountains at **Chloride.** In 1879, Henry Pye, a muleskinner and prospector, discovered veins of silver chloride in a nearby rock outcropping. He established a claim, but a few months later, before he could enjoy the wealth, he was killed in an Apache raid.

At the southern end of the Black Range and southwest of Truth or Consequences, NM 152 crosses rugged mountains, winding among steep, pine-covered slopes. But first, it bisects the old mining district of **Hillsboro**, its tin roofs hidden underneath giant cottonwoods. Once a gold- and silver-mining boom town and Sierra County seat, Hillsboro turned into a ranching center after the minerals were depleted. Today, a collection of novelty shops, art galleries, and antique stores lines the main street. Eccentric artists, solitary writers, and slow-moving retirees share star-filled evenings and quiet days with rough-riding ranchers and diehard miners.

Every Labor Day weekend, the village comes alive during the **Hillsboro Apple Festival.** People gather in the streets and along sidewalks lined with arts and crafts booths, food stalls, and apples harvested from nearby orchards.

Nine miles farther into the mountains, **Kingston** is the last stop before NM 152 climbs over 8,228-foot Emory Pass on its way to the Mimbres Valley. In its 1880s heyday, 7,500 fortune hunters flocked to Kingston's pine-covered slopes, which surrendered more than $10 million worth of silver in fewer than 15 years. For a short time the town boomed. Twenty-two saloons lined the broad sidewalk on the main street, and Lillian Russell performed at the town's theater. Kingston had no church until a hat was passed in the saloons one night to raise money for one. Today, several dozen resourceful people live here and hold regular meetings of the Spit and Whittle Club.

■ JORNADA DEL MUERTO

Interstate 25 from Las Cruces to Socorro and on to Albuquerque follows the Rio Grande. The first Spanish explorers to enter this region came this way as well, but the river route curved back and forth, wagons bogged down in its flood plain, and they were ambushed by Indians in the wooded curves along the river. In 1598, when Spanish explorer Juan de Oñate led a group of adventurers north toward Santa Fe, he thought a less difficult route for wagons, and one less prone to Indian attack, would be a shortcut east across a 90-mile expanse of sandy prairie strewn with spiny mesquite trees and black grama grass. The day before Oñate headed into the unknown desert, one of his men, Pedro Robledo, died and was buried at the base of a mountain that today bears his name. Undaunted, the explorer and his entourage left behind the Rio Grande Valley as scheduled. Oñate was hoping the route would soon curve back to the Rio Grande. It didn't. Water ran short and animals began to die. The party crept along, spread out for miles. On the evening of the second day, a resourceful dog returned to camp with mud on its paws and muzzle, and probably saved the expedition. One of the soldiers followed paw prints in the sand to a nearby spring, which he named Los Charcos del Perrillo (the Pools of the Little Dog). This site became a regular stop on the trail for future travelers, and its name was shortened to **Perrillo.**

Refreshed, the settlers continued, and Oñate and a few horsemen pushed on ahead. A few days later, they arrived at present-day Socorro, exhausted, dehydrated, and certainly dispirited. Oñate spied the sun-dried adobe walls of Pilabo, a Piro pueblo where he found long-haired men and women planting their fields. They were probably startled at his unkempt appearance, but he nevertheless persuaded them to provide corn and water for himself and the other hungry travelers who were behind him.

By 1610, the route between Chihuahua, Mexico, and Santa Fe was an established trade route, and Oñate's shortcut, called the Jornada del Muerto, became the most dreaded portion of the trip. Countless Spaniards died within its God-forsaken expanse, including Oñate's son, who was killed by Apaches.

Jornada del Muerto, *a painting by George Brewerton done in 1853. (Oakland Museum, Kahn Collection)*

Three Rivers petroglyph site overlooks a desolate southern New Mexico landscape.

You can't cross the Jornada now even if you wanted to, because a portion of it is within the confines of White Sands Missile Range, but as you drive along I-25 toward Albuquerque, you'll pass the sleepy community of **San Antonio**, which sits on a drainage ditch along the Rio Grande. Stop by the Owl Bar, for a green chile cheeseburger.

A few miles to the north is **Socorro**, where Oñate's party—and many afterwards—found succor. Today, this quiet town has a small historic district, a tree-shaded plaza, and the 19th-century **San Miguel Mission Church.**

■ BOSQUE DEL APACHE WILDLIFE REFUGE

Sandhill cranes, pure white snow geese, and ducks fly overhead along NM 1 (old US 85), which winds south past fields of wheat, corn, and millet—a lavish banquet for these birds, who spend their winters at the nearby Bosque del Apache. The refuge was established in 1939 to provide a winter home for the whooping crane, then threatened with extinction. A handful of the rare white birds still winter at the refuge. While birdwatching is best at dawn and dusk from October to February, in the summer more than 3,000 ducks, hundreds of Canada geese, and scores of wading birds such as herons and egrets take over the wetlands. *From Socorro travel 12 miles south on Interstate 25, then east on NM 380; (505) 835-1828.*

■ WHITE SANDS NATIONAL MONUMENT

A span of glimmering white desert dunes lies west of US 70. The site was once an enormous lake formed at the end of the last ice age by water from melting glaciers. These windswept dunes look like ocean sand, but they actually are fine granules of gypsum. Only one-half of the extensive rolling hills are included in the White Sands National Monument's 230 square miles. The sweet fresh smell of gypsum permeates the atmosphere, and the fine-grained sand swirls in the wind. The undulating expanse of white is interrupted only by an occasional yucca shooting skyward. At the edge of the 50-foot-tall dunes, animals have taken on the protective shade of gypsum: there are white mice, white lizards, and light-colored insects. This soft, silent, ghostly world of grit seems like an odd oasis in the surrounding harsh desert of sharp cactus and cracked earth. On nights when the moon is full,

A FORM OF PARADISE

*B*rightest New Mexico. In that vivid light each rock and tree and cloud and mountain existed with a kind of force and clarity that seemed not natural but supernatural. Yet it also felt as familiar as home, the country of dreams, the land I had known from the beginning.

We were riding north from El Paso in my grandfather's pickup truck, bound for the village of Baker and the old man's ranch. This was in early June: the glare of the desert sun, glancing off the steel hood of the truck, stung my eyes with such intensity that I had to close them now and then for relief. And I could almost feel the fierce dry heat, like that of an oven, drawing the moisture from my body; I thought with longing of the cool water bag that hung from the hood latch over the grille in front, inaccessible. I wished that Grandfather would stop for a minute and give us time for a drink, but I was too proud and foolish to ask him; twelve years old, I thought it important to appear tougher than I really was.

When my eyes stopped aching I could open them again, raise my head and watch the highway and fence and telephone line, all geometrically straight and parallel, rolling forever toward us. Heat waves shimmered over the asphalt, giving the road far ahead a transparent, liquid look, an illusion which receded before us as fast as we approached.

Staring ahead, I saw a vulture rise from the flattened carcass of a rabbit on the pavement and hover nearby while we passed over his lunch. Beyond the black bird with his white-trimmed wings soared the western sky, the immense and violet sky flowing over alkali flats and dunes of sand and gypsum toward the mountains that stood like chains of islands, like a convoy of purple ships, along the horizon.

Those mountains—they seemed at once both close by and impossibly remote, an easy walk away and yet beyond the limits of the imagination. Between us lay the clear and empty wilderness of scattered mesquite trees and creosote shrubs and streambeds where water ran as seldom as the rain came down. Each summer for three years I had come to New Mexico; each time I gazed upon the moon-dead landscape and asked myself: what is out there? And each time I concluded: *something* is out there—maybe everything. To me the desert looked like a form of Paradise. And it always will.

—Edward Abbey, *Fire on the Mountain*, 1962

the glistening sands reflect an eerie glow. From May to September, the dunes are open until midnight on full-moon nights.

White Sands Missile Range is off-limits to the public, but as the highway runs through it, travelers on this road are occasionally stopped at one of the roadblocks erected during missile firings. In 1982, another group of bystanders witnessed the graceful landing of the Space Shuttle Columbia when it descended onto the missile range's hard-packed sand at Northrop Strip.

But very few people were on hand in the early morning hours of July 16, 1945. The explosion vaporized everything in its path and created a blinding flash of light, followed by a shock wave that shattered windows 120 miles away in Silver City. Even early-rising Albuquerque residents noticed a flash on the southern horizon and felt the shock waves. The explosion left a crater 400 yards in diameter and eight feet deep, and intense heat fused sand in the crater into a glasslike solid the color of jade. This substance was called trinitite after the code name of the top-secret project, Trinity.

■ LINCOLN

Along the Rio Bonito, in a narrow valley at the edge of the Capitán Mountains, is the town of Lincoln, settled in 1849 by a small group of Hispanic farmers. Mescalero Apaches chased them out three times, but the settlers kept returning. The village was known as Las Placitas del Rio Bonito until 1869, when the townsfolk renamed it after Abraham Lincoln.

In 1878, a feud between two competing shopkeepers—Alexander McSween and Lawrence Murphy—escalated into the Lincoln Country War. When Murphy's men gunned down McSween's business partner, John Tunstall, a group of avengers formed the "Regulators," and killed several of Murphy's supporters, including Sheriff William Brady and the three men who shot Turnstall. One of the "Regulators" was an affable, wavy-haired 19-year-old ranch hand named William Bonney (a.k.a. Henry McCarty) whose nickname was **Billy the Kid.** Even though Billy caused a lot of trouble, he's as much fun to tell stories about as Pancho Villa. So, once a year, residents honor Billy the Kid in a folk pageant that dramatizes his last escape from the Lincoln County Courthouse. **Lincoln Days** is usually held the first weekend of August, and features a fiddler's contest, arts and crafts fair, and a

(previous pages) Twilight over the gypsum sands of White Sand Dunes National Monument.

42-mile Pony Express race that begins at the ghost town of White Oaks and ends at Lincoln.

East of Lincoln, bushy piñons and junipers give way to the orchards of the **Hondo Valley** as the Rio Bonito joins the Rio Ruidoso to become the Rio Hondo. The tiny communities of San Patricio, Hondo, Tinnie, and Picacho hide among corn and bean fields that mix with cherry and apple orchards across this narrow, fertile valley.

■ CAPITAN AND SMOKEY THE BEAR

A few miles farther west along US 380 is Capitán, a village where the original Smokey the Bear was found after a devastating forest fire destroyed 17,000 acres in the Capitán Mountains in 1950. In its smoky aftermath, firefighters discovered a badly singed black bear cub clinging to the side of a charred pine tree. The frightened cub was given the name "Hotfoot," because of his severely burned feet. His burns were treated at the nearby Flatley Ranch, then Game Warden Ray Bell flew the cub to a veterinary hospital in Santa Fe. Hotfoot soon became Smokey. Bell

The original Smokey the Bear, a cub found after a forest fire in New Mexico.
(U.S. Forest Service)

later kept the bear in his home, where the cub ran roughshod over the family's other household pets. Once healed, Smokey was flown to Washington, D.C., where he lived out his life at the National Zoo. The fire proved fortunate for the U.S. Forest Service, which had invented Smokey Bear six years earlier as its fire-prevention symbol. The charred bear cub brought life to this campaign. When Smokey died in 1976, he was replaced by Smokey II, who also came from the Capitán Mountains.

■ RUIDOSO AND MOUNTAIN TOWNS

Texans come to Ruidoso hoping to cool off in the hot summer months or to ski the slopes of Sierra Blanca in the winter. Next door is the Mescalero Apache Reservation. The Mescaleros didn't take well to their incarceration at Bosque Redondo in 1862, but they have adjusted quite well to the tenets of capitalism. One of the most financially successful tribes in the country, the Mescaleros operate Ski Apache on the flanks of the 12,000-foot Sierra Blanca and run a timber operation, as well as a fish hatchery that supplies trout to a number of nearby lakes. The tribe's Inn of the Mountain Gods sits alongside Lake Mescalero and is regarded as one of the prettiest resorts in the country. Golf, tennis, horseback riding programs, and hunting expeditions are available. See **Food & Lodging** on page 335.

❖

The friendly, rustic village of **Cloudcroft** caters to tourists. In summer there are arts and crafts fairs or music festivals nearly every weekend. But the natural beauty of 215,000 acres of the Lincoln National Forest is enough to make a visit worthwhile most times of the year: spectacular views of the white swath of gypsum sands laid out below in the Tularosa Basin, along with the fresh smell of tall pines and a profound quiet.

Farther south of Cloudcroft is **Sacramento Peak Observatory**, one of the world's largest solar observatories. Open to the public from May to October, it offers self-guided tours daily, and guided tours on Saturday. Down the road from here, amateur astronomer Alan Hale first caught a glimpse of what became the century's brightest celestial show, Hale-Bopp Comet.

The only natural entrance to Carlsbad Caverns, the most extensive cave complex in the country.

■ CARLSBAD CAVERNS

One of New Mexico's major waterways, the Pecos River, bisects the southeastern part of the state, carrying the crucial resource of water to a number of tiny farming and ranching communities. The best known of these is Carlsbad, famous for an underground environment of other-worldly limestone formations.

One of the largest cave systems in the world, Carlsbad Caverns comprises a three-mile maze of concert-hall rooms whose floors and ceilings are blanketed with house-size stalagmite statues and stalactite icicles. Filling these massive vaults are grandiose obelisks and pagodas laced with delicate tracery. A paved winding path descends through a black opening in a limestone ridge into the eerily lit bowels of the earth, leading you past dripping, pale-green limestone walls and into rooms that seem as if they belong in a science-fiction movie, or on another planet. The names of the most spectacular formations bear witness to the lifelike shapes created by the limestone deposits: Whale's Mouth, King's Palace, Hall of Giants, Queen's Chamber Draperies. The Big Room, aptly if unimaginatively named for an expanse that could hold 14 Astrodomes, makes you feel as insignificant as an ant on a sidewalk. Its ceiling curves 256 feet above the damp floor. The temperature of 56° F never varies here.

The cave remained unnoticed until 1901, when a young cowboy, James White, spotted what looked like a cloud of smoke spiraling upward near the foothills of the Guadalupe Mountains. The cloud turned out to be thousands of bats heading off to a night of hunting. Using a rope ladder, White descended into the damp cave and saw for the first time what thousands of people now see each year. By 1930 his discovery had become a national park.

Each August, Carlsbad hosts its annual **Bat Flight Breakfast,** during which visitors eat scrambled eggs and sausage just as the world's only flying mammal, satiated after a night of hunting, swoops into its daytime haven of dark.

Carlsbad Caverns National Park is 27 miles southwest of the town of Carlsbad off US 62/180; (505) 785-2232.

Southern New Mexico Food & Lodging

■ FOOD & LODGING

Restaurant prices:
Per person, not including drinks, tax, and tips:
$ = under $10; $$ = $10–20; $$$ = over $20

Room rates:
Per night, per room, double occupancy:
$ = under $50; $$ = $50–100; $$$ = over $100

Alamogordo and Vicinity

✗ **Angelina's Italian Restaurant.** 415 S. White Sands, Alamogordo (US 54/70/82); (505) 434-1166 $$
Casual Italian restaurant with a good assortment of pastas and pizza, and a salad bar. Dinner only.

✗ **Rebecca's at the Lodge.** 1 Corona Pl., Cloudcroft; (505) 682-2566 $$–$$$
Never mind if you see a redheaded ghost floating above your head—that's Rebecca, often an uninvited dinner guest. She may be jealous of that salmon dish you ordered: the nouvelle American cuisine here is delightful.

✗ **Sí Señor.** 1480 N. White Sands (US 54/70/82); (505) 437-7879 $
Traditional Mexican fare: enchiladas, chiles rellenos, burritos.

🛏 **Holiday Inn.** 1401 White Sands Blvd., Alamogordo (US 54, 70, 82); (505) 437-7100 $$
Basic hotel amenities.

🛏 **The Lodge.** 1 Corona Pl., Cloudcroft; (505) 682-2566 $$–$$$
A luxurious hunter's lodge where a long-horned eland stares down from over the copper fireplace and a stuffed bear eyes guests from one of the lobby's corners. Elegantly furnished with floral carpeting and antique furniture.

Artesia

population 10,600   elevation 3,380

✗ **La Fonda.** 210 W. Main; (505) 746-9377 $-$$
One of the state's finest New Mexican restaurants, where you'll get large helpings of enchiladas, chimichangas, and burritos.

🛏 **Heritage Inn.** 209 W. Main St.; (505) 748-2552 or (800) 594-7392 $$
Located above a Main Street storefront, this Victorian B&B is a hidden gem. Continental breakfast.

Carlsbad

population 25,000   elevation 3,110

✗ **The Flume Room in the Motel Stevens.** 1829 S. Canal; (505) 887-2851 $-$$
Prime rib, steaks, seafood, and a bountiful salad bar.

Southern New Mexico Food & Lodging

X **Lucy's.** 701 S. Canal; (505) 887-7714 $–$$

Try a Gold Margarita with a plate of fajitas, enchiladas, or chimichangas.

⌐ **Best Western Motel Stevens.** 1829 S. Canal; (505) 887-2851 or (800) 528-1234 $$

There are 151 rooms at this centrally located motel. Outdoor pool and playground are also on the premises.

Columbus and Vicinity

X **Pancho Villa Restaurant.** Across the border in Palomas, Mexico $$

This pink building houses the best restaurant in these parts. You'll be treated to bottled water and first-rate chiles rellenos. U.S. currency accepted.

⌐ **Martha's Bed and Breakfast.** 32 Lima St., Columbus, off NM 11; (505) 531-2467 $$

In a small town where historic buildings prevail, this adobe inn offers an alternative to camping at Pancho Villa State Park. If you're lucky, your visit will coincide with a performance by the Tumbleweed Theater, a cadre of local actors who occasionally put on musical melodramas.

Las Cruces and Vicinity

X **Dick's Cafe.** 2305 S. Valley, Las Cruces; (505) 524-1360 $

The waitresses know their business at this local hangout where you'll find hearty New Mexican food and a good cup of strong coffee.

X **Double Eagle.** Mesilla Plaza, Mesilla; (505) 523-6700 $$–$$$

This upscale steakhouse offers hearty specialties such as juicy steaks, duck á l'orange, and quail. The choice of seafood is also extensive and includes red snapper, lobster, shrimp, and crab.

X **Guacamole's Outdoor Eatery.** 3995 W. Picacho; (505) 525-9115 $

Enjoy a house-specialty hamburger in this al fresco setting.

X **La Posta.** Just off the Plaza in Mesilla; (505) 524-3524 $$

Originally built as a stagecoach mail station, La Posta is a lively and popular New Mexican restaurant, festively decorated with stagecoach artifacts, fountains, plants, and live parrots.

X **Mesilla Valley Kitchen.** 2001 E. Lohman; (505) 523-9311 $

Locals favorite place for green chile cheeseburgers and breakfast burritos. Breakfast and lunch only.

X **Mesón de Mesilla.** 1803 Avenida de Mesilla, Mesilla; (505)525-2380 $$$

Chateaubriand for two is the specialty of this stylish southwestern dining room. The menu also features more innovative dishes such as seared sturgeon in pesto.

X **Nellie's Cafe.** 1226 W. Hadley; (505) 524-9982 $

In a town brimming with great, cheap New Mexican food, this cozy diner stands out.

⌐ **Las Cruces Hilton.** 705 Telshor, Las Cruces; (505) 522-4300 $$

Across from the Mesilla Valley Mall,

the Hilton is nicely situated on a bluff-side, affording spectacular views from some of the rooms.

☂ **Mesón de Mesilla.** 1803 Avenida de Mesilla, Mesilla; (505) 525-2380 $$-$$$
Southwestern colors adorn this quiet adobe inn on the edge of Mesilla. A full gourmet breakfast, served inside the glass-enclosed atrium, is one of many charming details.

Lincoln and Vicinity

✕ **Cafe Rio.** 2547 Sudderth Dr., Ruidoso; (505) 257-7746
A small, casual Midtown restaurant with great pizza, interesting European specialities, ice cream, and espresso.

✕ **Cattle Baron Restaurant.** 657 Sudderth Dr., Ruidoso; (505) 257-9355 $-$$
This popular steakhouse also has fresh seafood and a good salad bar. Great lunch specials.

✕ **The Deck House.** 202 Mechem Rd. in the Adobe Plaza, Ruidoso; (505) 257-3496 $
All the Mexican and New Mexican standards are here: carnitas, green chili, enchilidas. Also open for breakfast. Closed Wednesdays.

✕ **Hotel Chango's Restaurant.** 103 Lincoln, Capitán (505) 354-4213 $$-$$$
Nouveau continental cuisine, artistically arranged, in a romantic 19th-century setting.

✕ **La Lorraine.** 2523 Sudderth Dr., Ruidoso; (505) 257-2954 $$$

Classic French cuisine, including veal and seafood in a cozy country-French setting. Patio dining in summer months.

✕ **Wortley Hotel.** Lincoln; (505) 653-4300 $$
Omelettes take star billing on the breakfast menu. Dinner fare includes chicken-fried steak and other standard American entrees. Cobbler is baked fresh daily.

☂ **Casa de Patrón.** Lincoln; (505) 653-4676 $$
Three smallish guest rooms located inside the B&B's main house. Two casitas, more generously sized, are a short walk from the main house. Citrus-pecan waffles for breakfast and handmade soaps in the baths are two of the thoughtful touches provided by the friendly innkeepers.

☂ **Dan Dee Cabins.** 310 Main Rd., Ruidoso; (505) 257-2165 $$
Cozy cabins tucked away in the tall pines near the Rio Ruidoso. Cabins include fireplaces, kitchen, and special ski packages.

☂ **Inn of the Mountain Gods.** Carrizo Canyon Rd., Mescalero; (800) 545-9011 or (505) 257-5141 $$$
Situated on the Mescalero Apache Indian Reservation, this resort is one of the loveliest in the state. Nice golf course.

☂ **Shadow Mountain Lodge.** 107 Main Rd., Ruidoso; (505) 257-4886 or (800) 441-4331 $$
Fireplaces keep you warm in the winter, and in the summer guests cool off on

Southern New Mexico Food & Lodging

Southern New Mexico Food & Lodging

the veranda at this adults-only lodge. Each room has a kitchenette.

⊡ **Story Book Cabins.** 410 Main St., Ruidoso; (505) 257-2115 **$$**
Nestled amid the pines in a secluded canyon a mile from downtown. Each cabin includes fireplaces and kitchen.

⊡ **Wortley Hotel.** Off NM 380, Lincoln; (505) 653-4300 **$$**
Rebuilt 19th-century hotel where Deputy Bob Olinger ate his last meal before being gunned down by Billy the Kid. Brass beds and simple adornments remind you of yesteryear. Rocking chair on the hotel's front porch.

Silver City

population 10,700   elevation 5,895

✕ **Corner Cafe.** Corner of Bullard and Broadway; (505) 388-2056 **$**
The giant cinnamon rolls here are one of the town's highlights. Other breakfast specialties include crepes, pancakes, and French toast. For lunch the cafe has assorted sandwiches and "quiche of the day."

✕ **The Red Barn.** 708 Silver Heights Blvd.; (505) 538-5666 **$$**
Informal steakhouse with friendly service and a family atmosphere. Salad bar.

⊡ **Bear Mountain Guest Ranch.** Bear Mountain Road off NM 180; (505) 538-2538 **$$-$$$**
Three miles north of Silver City amid a flat expanse of piñons and junipers sits this two-story Pueblo Revival bed-and-breakfast inn that caters to naturalists. The 160-acre ranch backs up to the Gila Wilderness—prime country for bird watching and native plant excursions led by innkeeper Myra Mc-Cormick. She also offers archaeology and Indian pottery workshops as part of weekend and week-long packages.

⊡ **Carter House.** 101 N. Cooper; (505) 388-5485 **$$**
A five-room B&B housed in a three-story 1906 Colonial Revival-style mansion. Located in the town's historic district, the inn is only a short walk to galleries and shops. Lovely mountain views from the front porch.

Socorro and Vicinity

✕ **Owl Bar and Steakhouse.** NM 380, San Antonio; (505) 835-9946 **$**
Drivers traveling between Albuquerque and Las Cruces eagerly anticipate a stop at the Owl Bar for their green chile cheeseburgers. Other New Mexican entrees are also available. Owls of all varieties, including macramed and painted, adorn the walls.

✕ **Val Verde Steak House, Socorro.** 203 E. Manzanares; (505) 835-3380 **$$-$$$**
Housed in a Spanish Mission Revival building, this restaurant was once the main dining room of the Val Verde Hotel and hasn't changed much since it was built in 1919. The specialties are ribs and sirloin steaks.

☂ **Casa Blanca.** 13 Montoyas St., San Antonio; (505) 835-3027 **$$**
This Victorian bed-and-breakfast was built in 1880 as a farmhouse for Socorro's Territorial Sen. Eutimio Montoya. Only a few miles from the Bosque del Apache Wildlife Refuge.

☂ **Eaton House.** 403 Eaton, Socorro; (505) 835-1067 **$$-$$$**
Over one hundred years old, Colonel Eaton's house is a charming B&B and an idyllic retreat for birdwatchers. The innkeeper prepares a scrumptious breakfast table and even provides pastry-filled baskets for morning birding excursions.

Truth or Consequences

population 6,200   elevation 4,240

☂ **Elephant Butte Resort Inn.** NM 195; (505) 744-5431 **$$**
Recently remodeled full-service motel with views of Elephant Butte Lake. Golf, volleyball, and tennis facilities.

✕ **Blue Note Cafe.** 407 Broadway; (505) 894-6680 **$**
Soups, sandwiches, and pasta in downtown storefront.

✕ **K-Bob's.** 2260 N. Date St.; (505) 894-2127 **$-$$**
Steaks, New Mexican food, and a large salad bar in a casual and friendly atmosphere.

The living room of the Stratford Hotel in Shakespeare oozes old world charm. Bring your own bedding and a six-shooter for the snakes.

Southern New Mexico Food & Lodging

TEXAS TRANS-PECOS

■ HIGHLIGHTS
El Paso
Guadalupe National Park
Big Bend National Park

■ LANDSCAPE
The Trans-Pecos is some 30,000 miles square, defined by the Rio Grande, which forms its western border, and the Pecos River, which marks it to the east. Excluding this area's only city—El Paso, which sits on its western edge—fewer than 60,000 people inhabit the place. While measuring the American West, the U.S. Census Bureau determined that an area was "settled" when its population density exceeded six persons per square mile. By those terms, the Trans-Pecos is still frontier, a great empty expanse of caliche and rock surrounded by dry mountains.

The Guadalupe Mountains, east of El Paso, mark the southeastern tip of the Rocky Mountains and the northern limit of the Chihuahuan Desert. Further south, the smooth-crowned Davis Mountains reach an elevation of 5,000 to 6,000 feet. As the Rio Grande turns east, it forms an arc that now makes up Big Bend National Park, a desert sanctuary larger than Rhode Island.

■ TRAVELERS ORIENTATION
The Trans-Pecos is as isolated as any area in the United States. It's a long way from El Paso, the major city of this area, to anywhere, or from anywhere to El Paso. Two roads lead east from the city: US 180/62, to the north, and Interstate 10, the more southerly highway. The northern route is usually taken by travelers headed to New Mexico's Carlsbad Caverns. It's a five-hour drive south from El Paso to Presidio, a town of 3,000 people who drive 90 miles to pick up a pizza, 60 miles to play golf, and 230 miles to attend a football game.

The drive over Texas Farm-to-Market Road 170, from Presidio to Lajitas through Redford, is one of the prettier ones in the state. The pavement snakes, climbs, and dives. On one side stand red, rocky canyon walls; on the other, steep banks lead down to the Rio Grande.

For a stretch of more than 250 miles along the Rio Grande, from the roadless space between Candelaria and McNary on the west, to Langtry on the eastern edge of the Trans-Pecos, settlement is sparse. The long boundary line with Mexico has only one international bridge, complete with customs house and immigration offices, connecting Presidio with the Mexican town of Ojinaga. Elsewhere along the empty stretch, border crossings are strictly unofficial. At the end of FM 2627, for example, lies a blacktop-covered concrete bridge—but there's nothing on the other side except the mining camp at La Linda, in the Mexican state of Coahuila. Over the rest of the Trans-Pecos border span, footbridges cross the Rio Grande, which is only yards wide in this part of the state.

❖

This region of Texas is climatically the same as the mountainous areas of Southern New Mexico. El Paso (elev. 3,900) has a climate very similar to that of Las Cruces, which also rests on the banks of the Rio Grande. Big Bend National Park is represented by two stations, Chisos Basin (elev. 5,300) typifying the higher mountain zones and Panther Junction (elev. 3,700) representing the valley bottom locations such as the town of Presidio. The region may be comfortably visited virtually anytime of the year although summer temperatures at the lower elevations will be oppressive.

TEMPS (F°)	AVG. JAN. HIGH	LOW	AVG. APRIL HIGH	LOW	AVG. JULY HIGH	LOW	AVG. OCT. HIGH	LOW	RECORD HIGH	RECORD LOW
Chisos Basin	57	35	76	52	85	64	73	51	106	-2
El Paso	58	30	79	49	95	70	79	50	116	-8
Panther Junction	61	35	83	54	93	68	79	53	112	11

PRECIPITATION (INCHES)	AVG. JAN.	AVG. APRIL	AVG. JULY	AVG. OCT.	ANNUAL	SNOW
Chisos Basin	0.6	0.6	3.1	1.9	19.2	3
El Paso	0.4	0.2	1.6	0.8	7.8	6
Panther Junction	0.5	0.3	1.9	1.5	14.0	0

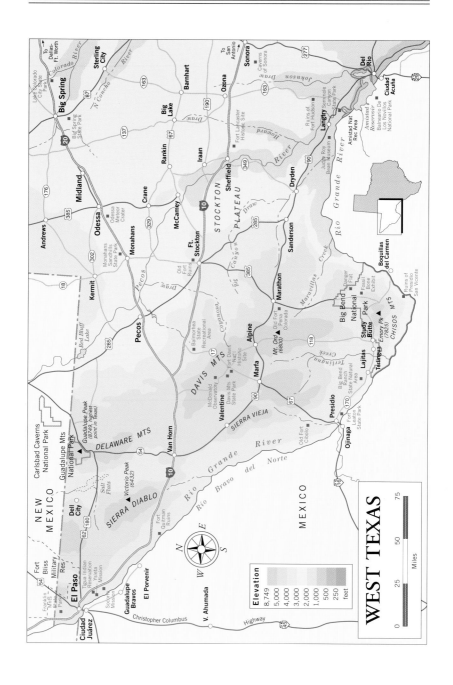

WEST TEXAS

■ THE PEOPLE

Most of the people who live in the Trans-Pecos were born there and wouldn't complicate their lives by going elsewhere. But a fair share of non-natives, both tourists in Lajitas and the Big Bend area and urban expatriates, are scattered here and there. Contrasts among the three groups are sometimes significant. Tourists spend surplus income, natives strive to earn it, and expatriates try to ignore it, groaning that they've given up the getting-and-spending lifestyle. Many visitors to this empty region might enjoy a copy of the *New York Times,* or of *USA Today,* but they can't, because national newspapers are sold only at Alpine's Front Street Books where, due to its late arrival, *USA Today* is known as *USA Yesterday.* Most of the area's expatriates came to the Trans-Pecos to get away from the news—and most of the locals, having never seen a copy of either publication, don't know what they're missing. The differences among the area's three types of inhabitants preclude much meaningful contact—and as long as it's that way, tourists and expatriates will continue to aid the region's economy, spending money to get to a place where there's little to buy but much peace and quiet to be had for free.

A QUIET PLACE IN THE COUNTRY

*O*f course, real scouting skills were superfluous in a place as tame as Lonesome Dove, but Call still liked to get out at night, sniff the breeze and let the country talk. The country talked quiet; one human voice could drown it out, particularly if it was a voice as loud as Augustus McCrae's. Augustus was notorious all over Texas for the strength of his voice. On a still night he could be heard at least a mile, even if he was more or less whispering. Call did his best to get out of range of Augustus's voice so that he could relax and pay attention to other sounds. If nothing else, he might get a clue as to what weather was coming—not that there was much mystery about the weather around Lonesome Dove. If a man looked straight up at the stars he was apt to get dizzy, the night was so clear. Clouds were scarcer than cash money, and cash money was scarce enough.

—Larry McMurtry, *Lonesome Dove,* 1985

■ EL PASO

In 1886, the town of El Paso inventoried one saloon for every 232 residents. As local historian Leon C. Metz wryly observed, "The chances of dying of thirst [were] not alarming."

But unlike other rough-and-tumble frontier watering holes of the time, El Paso was no embryonic boom town. It traced its beginnings back to 1659, when Spaniards heaped up a modest adobe mission and called it Nuestra Señora de Guadalupe de los Mansos del Paso del Norte. The church was on the south bank of the Rio Grande, which would place it in present-day Ciudad Juárez, Mexico, but until 1848, and the end of the U.S.–Mexican war, there was no political division between the two border towns. Ciudad Juárez, now El Paso's Mexican sister, didn't receive its present name until 1868.

Throughout the 1600s and 1700s El Paso del Norte ("The Pass of the North") served as a vital staging area for Spanish incursions into New Mexico.

It is difficult to imagine, surveying the parched surrounding desert today, but in the 1700s and early 1800s it also became the viticultural capital of New Spain. "The vineyards produce such excellent sweet wines," wrote a traveler in 1822, "that they are even preferred to the wines of Parras in New Biscay. The gardens contain in abundance all the fruits of Europe, figs, peaches, apples and pears."

After the United States acquired Texas in 1848, El Paso fought off Apache raids and slowly began developing what it calls its five "C" industries today: copper, cotton, cattle, climate, and (most recently) clothing.

With its half-million residents, El Paso is the anchor of the Trans-Pecos, yet in some ways El Paso has more in common with cities like Monterrey, Chihuahua, and Hermosillo than with any city to its north or east. The downtown streets appear to be cobbled with squarish black stones, rather than paved with asphalt or cement. As in Mexican cities, this street-surfacing is a contemporary, not a rustic touch: black cement is poured onto the streets and a roller is passed over them, leaving the cobblestone-like imprint.

El Paso has in recent years been under federal orders to improve its air quality, which has been rated the worst in the nation. The city can't do much about the situation: its air is the air of its Mexican industrial sister city, Juárez.

If El Paso shares a certain quaintness with other Mexican towns, however, parts of it reveal the impact of the border close by. El Paso's shopping malls are gargantuan, three and four times the size they'd be in a Midwestern city of the same population, because half or more of their customers come from the Mexican side of the border. Middle-aged women hang out in the city's downtown San Jacinto plaza, hawking Marlboros at about 25 percent below the American price. The cigarettes are Mexican-made, and the women, residents of Juárez who cross the river each morning, carry their wares as contraband in handbags.

Despite its Spanish, Mexican, and borderlands influences, El Paso is in other ways sufficiently American, even Midwestern, to make some Texocentrics cringe. A series of downtown streets is named after other states, and while other cities in Texas have a street here or there named in honor of Illinois or Oregon, none has shown such a systematic sense of nationhood as El Paso has. The city's sports obsession is the Miners, the basketball team of the University of Texas at El Paso, despite the fact that football is the rest of the state's favorite sport. No other town in Texas—not even Austin, home of the champion Lady Longhorns—cares for basketball as much as El Paso does.

■ EL PASO POINTS OF INTEREST

Border Patrol Museum. Exhibits include uniform, canine, and weapon displays. The memorial room commemorates agents killed on duty. Gift shop. *North-South Freeway to 4315 Transmountain Road; (915) 759-6060.*

Chamizal National Memorial. This memorial celebrates the 1968 resolution of century-long boundary disputes between Mexico and the United States. Both sides converted their land into national parks. El Paso's side houses a border history museum, theater, and graphic arts gallery. The Mexican side has been developed into acres of botanical gardens and an interesting archaeological museum. *800 South San Marcial Street; (915) 532-7273.*

Concordia Cemetery. Originally divided by ethnicity, religion, and status. Behind one walled-off section are the remains of 19th-century Chinese laborers who built railroads in the region. Just outside that wall, in the "Boot Hill" area, lie infamous desperados such as John Wesley Hardin, a Texas thug who claimed to have killed 40 people with his six-shooter. *Just north of I-10 at the Gateway North and US 54 interchange.*

El Paso Museum of History. Life-size dioramas depict the people of El Paso, past and present: Indians, Spanish explorers, cowboys, and cavalrymen. *I-10 East at the Avenue of the Americas, about 15 miles from downtown; (915) 858-1928.*

Fort Bliss. Site of the largest air-defense establishment in the nation and headquarters for the U.S. Army Air Defense. The post also houses four military museums. The **Air Defense Artillery Museum** in Building 5000 displays anti-aircraft weapons from around the world. Located in Building 2407 is the **Cavalry Museum,** illustrating the history of the U.S. Cavalry with paintings, photos, and a collection of vehicles used since the Cavalry's founding in 1856. The **Fort Bliss Replica Museum** in building 600 is a reconstruction of the original fort as it stood 1848 to 1948. The **Museum of the Non-Commissioned Officer** in Building 1133 traces the changing role of the non-commissioned officer from combat soldier to military bureaucrat. *Main Post, east of US 54 and a half mile north of the El Paso International Airport; (915) 568-8646.*

The Plaza and Church of El Paso, *an 1857 chromolithograph from the Report on the United States and Mexican Boundary Survey. (Library of Congress)*

Fort Davis in the Davis Mountains is an historic site about halfway between El Paso and Big Bend National Park.

The Mission Trail. A 12-mile drive past El Paso's oldest Mexican and Indian districts—neighborhoods filled with notable restaurants, craft shops, and antique stores—leads to the missions of Ysleta and Socorro, and the presidio of San Elizario. *The drive begins at the Zaragosa exit off I-10, southeast of downtown El Paso, and ends at FM 1110.*

Magoffin Homestead. Completed in 1875 by Joseph Magoffin, son of James Wiley Magoffin, one of El Paso's founders. Filled with ornate Victorian furnishings dating back to the original owner and adobe walls scored to look like stone, this hacienda is a remarkable combination of eastern style and southwestern construction. *1120 Magoffin Avenue; (915) 533-5147.*

Socorro Mission. Originally built in 1681 by now-extinct Piro Indians, the structure was destroyed by the Rio Grande, as was its successor. The present church was built in 1843, but several of the features, particularly the bell tower, are said to be the best representation of Spanish colonial architecture in West Texas. *FM 258 (Socorro Road) at Nevarez, about 25 minutes from downtown; (915) 859-7718.*

Tigua Indian Reservation. A living history pueblo. The reservation museum and cultural center hosts a number of demonstrations including ceremonial dancing, weaving, pottery, and bread-baking. The grounds also house two restaurants and **Ysleta Mission,** the oldest mission in Texas. Built by Franciscans and Tigua Indians in 1681, the present structure was erected in 1908 on the original foundation. *119 South Old Pueblo Road., exit I-10 at Zaragosa, 15 miles east of downtown; (915) 859-7913.*

Wilderness Park Museum. A 17-acre, indoor-outdoor museum tracing the evolution of the region's climate and recreating the Pueblo Indian life. Outdoor trails lead visitors past replicas of a Pueblo ruin and a pithouse. *4001 Transmountain Road and Gateway South, about 30 minutes from downtown; (915) 755-4332.*

■ HUECO TANKS STATE PARK

According to Indian lore, this land is the site of Tigua Indian creation. Tribesmen say that some of the ancient pictographs found in Hueco Tanks State Park were the work of Tigua, although scholars believe that passing Apache, Comanche, and Kiowa produced most of them. There are more than 2,000 pictographs throughout this 860-acre park. Most visitors to the park, though, come for the rock climbing. The park's 300-foot boulders are pocked with small hollows, or *huecos,* important in the past because they held rainwater, important today as hand- and footholds. The hollows, along with the cracked and uneven surfaces of the park's outcroppings, provide challenges for experienced and novice climbers alike. The best season for climbing is October to May; in summer months the rocks can become too hot to handle. *To reach the park travel east from El Paso on US 62/180 about 25 miles, then eight miles north on FM 2775 (Hueco Tanks Rd.); (915) 857-1135.*

■ GUADALUPE MOUNTAINS NATIONAL PARK

With elevations of 8,749 feet and 8,085 feet respectively, Guadalupe Peak and El Capitán are the highest patches of land in Texas. Snowfall is common in the mountains even in springtime, and windsocks affixed to road signs warn of invisible hazards. Camping is permitted, but overnight and auto facilities in the park are scant; it's a place for either the Sunday driver or the serious outdoor buff, not for a family vacation.

In winter people visit the park to see snow, in fall to see the changing foliage, and in spring and summer to glimpse the smooth red wood of the madrone tree, which grows wild nowhere else in the state. A word of advice is in order, however: take water when you go. Once you step outside your auto in the Guadalupe Mountains, even in chilly months, you'll soon feel thirsty: these mountains, however green, stand above the driest climate in Texas. *About 110 miles east of El Paso on US 62/180. Headquarters at (915) 828-3251.*

■ ROAD TO BIG BEND

The southern road out of El Paso goes through the Hudspeth County seat, **Sierra Blanca**, named for the mountain range to the northwest of town. In 1881, a transcontinental railroad was formed here, when the Texas & Pacific line met the Texas & New Orleans.

Marfa is most widely known as the filming site for the 1956 Rock Hudson–Elizabeth Taylor–James Dean epic, *Giant.* Marfa's use as a location for the film says a lot about Hollywood's version of Texas. In the eponymous novel, from which *Giant* was scripted, Edna Ferber combines the stories of a real-life ranching family from the Gulf Coast region and of an oil wildcatter from East Texas—locales that are hundreds of miles and worlds away from Marfa. Nevertheless, the ruins of the movie set, about 15 miles west of town, are still an unofficial tourist attraction, and, in an unusual twist, have themselves become a minor myth in Hollywood: the set was used for filming parts of the 1985 Kevin Costner–Sam Robards film, *Fandango.*

Most Big Bend travelers breeze through **Alpine**, seat of Brewster, a county larger than Connecticut, and head straight south on TX 118 to the western gates of Big Bend. But Texans are apt to linger awhile in town, because it's home to **Sul Ross University.** Despite an enrollment of only 2,500 students, the school's rodeo team, cowboy poetry meets, and agriculture program (specializing in ranching, of course) are unmatched anywhere else, giving the whole town a reputation as "Texas hip."

Study Butte, Terlingua, and **Lajitas** are the settlements nearest Big Bend on the west. All three are revived ghost towns. Study Butte and Terlingua were founded in the early part of the century as outposts for Mexican laborers who worked mercury mines in the area. By the end of World War II, all three communities had ceased to exist.

■ BIG BEND NATIONAL PARK

Big Bend National Park dates from 1944, when the government accumulated public land parcels and smaller tracts donated by Texans interested in the project. The name comes from its setting at the toe of the 100-mile-long dip in the Rio Grande, where it turns from a southeasterly course to run northeast. The park's nearly virgin wildland covers 801,000 acres—an area a bit larger than the state of Rhode Island. Parts of it—like 7,825-feet-high Emory Peak—are almost perpendicular. Contained within the park, the Chisos Mountains, a roughly circular range about 20 miles in diameter, are home to hundreds of protected javelina (stubby porcines with fierce tusks), coyotes, mule and whitetail deer, gray fox, jackrabbits, skunks, raccoons, and even a few black bear, who are believed to commute to Mexico.

The mountains and the valley greenery close to the Rio Grande are rich birding country: 430 species of fowl, from small desert wrens to golden eagles, gray-

Claret Cup cactus blossoms (above) in the Chisos Mountains of Big Bend National Park.

The Chisos Mountains reflected in the Rio Grande (opposite) in the Santa Elena Canyon of Big Bend National Park.

breasted jay, hummingbirds, and the Colima warbler—found within the United States only in its Chisos Mountains nests. The bird most often seen is the paisano, or road runner, a common and feisty bird that can reach land speeds of 20 mph, fueled on moisture it extracts from lizards and snakes.

More than 1,100 species of plant life also inhabit the park, mostly on the desert floor, including creosote, a dozen cactus varieties, and ceniza, a bush that grows to five feet with gray perennial leaves and purple flowers that blossom anytime it rains. Ceniza ("ashes" in Spanish) is known to most Americans as "purple sage." At higher altitudes you'll find quaking aspen shimmering in light breezes, pine juniper, and wildflowers in summer and fall.

Ten miles west of the park headquarters and just below **Casa Grande**, an imposing stack of rocks 7,325 feet high, is **Chisos Basin**. Centrally located, the only motel in the park is located here as well as a restaurant, shops, and a campground. Chisos Basin is also the base for several hiking trails including the 5.6 mile Window Trail, the 4.6-mile Lost Mine Trail, and the more arduous 14-mile South Rim hike.

From Chisos Basin, it's 34 miles through the wild to the Rio Grande at **Boquillas Canyon Overlook**, where, on the Mexican side, the river has cut its rock sides into a high cliff. The village of **Boquillas del Carmen** is just across, and can be visited without the formalities of immigration and customs checks. From the end of the paved park road, a path leads a few hundred yards down to the river, where a Mexican entrepreneur will guide you in a scramble down to the water and across in a metal fishing boat: a few dollars for the crossing, a few more for the half-mile ride up the slope to Boquillas by burro or pickup. The main attraction of the village is cold beer—not available in the park—on days when Boquillas has electricity, anyway. Authorities in both countries ignore the Boquillas crossings because it's easier to control the roads leading out than to set up a customs house. On the American side, an illegal entrant faces 54 miles of exposed, two-lane road to get out of the park, and another 40 miles through open country to reach a highway going towards urban civilization. And on the Mexican side, there are no paved roads and hence, no speedy way out.

Panther Junction Visitors Center and park headquarters are at the center of the park, about 103 miles south of Alpine on TX 118 and 68 miles south of Marathon on US 385; (915) 477-2251.

■ FOOD & LODGING

> *Restaurant prices:*
> Per person, not including drinks, tax and tips:
> $ = under $10; $$ = $10–20; $$$ = over $20
>
> *Room rates:*
> Per night, per room, double occupancy:
> $ = under $50; $$ = $50–100; $$$ = over $100

Alpine

population 5,600   elevation 4,481

X **Reata Restaurant.** 203 N. Fifth St;
(915) 837-9232 $$-$$
Upscale cowboy cuisine, served in a
turn-of-the-century adobe house. Cozy
bar in back.

🛏 **Corner House Bed & Breakfast.** 802
East Ave. E; (915) 837-7161 $$-$$$
A frendly, comfortable, and affordable
bed-and-breakfast run by a well-traveled Scotsman.

Big Bend National Park and Vicinity

X **Chisos Mountain Lodge Restaurant.**
Chisos Basin; (915) 477-2291 $-$$
The only restaurant located inside Big
Bend. The menu includes standard and
not particularly noteworthy Ameri-
can/Tex-Mex fare such as burgers and
chicken-fried steak. Stunning views of
red-rock cliffs from the restaurant's
large picture windows.

X **La Kiva Restaurant & Bar.** TX 170 W.,
Terlingua Creek; (915) 371-2250 $-$$
The entryway here is a Navajo *kiva,* and
a narrow cavelike corridor leads to the
bar. Barbecue beef, ribs, and chicken
are the specialties. Outdoor patio.

X **Starlight Dinner Theatre.** Terlingua;
(915) 371-2326 $-$$
Standard American, regional Mexican.
Not a dinner theater but a diner located
in the old Terlingua Theatre. Dinner
only.

🔺 **Big Bend National Park Campgrounds.** (915) 477-2251
Three campsites with facilities located
inside the park: **Basin** and **Cottonwood**
campgrounds are near Castolon, on the
western side of the park, and **Rio
Grande Village** (the largest of the three)
is on the eastern side of the park.
Dozens of more primitive, backcountry
campsites are scattered throughout the
park. All campgrounds are first-come,
first-served and open year-round.

Texas Trans-Pecos Food & Lodging

▭ **Chisos Mountain Lodge.** Chisos Basin; (915) 477-2291 $$
Neither historic nor fancy, but clean and comfortable. Most of the year the motel requires reservations in advance. Rooms offer splendid sunset views through a pass in the mountains known as the Window. There are 72 standard rooms and six stone cottages. Operated by the National Park Service. Reservations advised.

▭ **Lajitas on the Rio Grande.** Lajitas; (915) 424-3471 $–$$
A resort complex with 114 rooms, most in mock cavalry-outpost style. Swimming pool, golf course, and tennis courts are on the grounds. The resort also has a restaurant, RV and tent camping spaces.

El Paso

population 515,300   elevation 3,762

✕ **Avila's.** 6232 N. Mesa; (915) 584-3621 or 10600 Montana; (915) 598-3333 $
Extensive Mexican, New Mexican menu. El Paso's most well-known restaurant.

✕ **Buffalo Soldiers BBQ.** 5501 Dyer St.; (915) 566-2300 $
Texas-style barbecue.

✕ **Grigg's Gourmet Mexican Food.** 9007 Montana; (915) 598-3451 $
The Grigg family has been preparing these recipes for generations. The enchiladas and guacamole tacos are particular favorites. Chile dishes tend to be mild.

✕ **La Hacienda Cafe.** 1720 W. Paisano; (915) 532-5094 $
Housed in a historic adobe building on the banks of the Rio Grande, this Mexican/New Mexican restaurant prepares delicious chiles rellenos, steak *Tampiqueña,* and their specialty: green chile chicken enchiladas with an egg cracked on top.

✕ **La Norteña y Cafe Deluxe.** 212 W. Overland, a block south of the Civic Center; (915) 533-0533 $-$$
The in spot for border-style Mexican cuisine in El Paso, with salpicon (spicy minced meat salad), quesadillas, chilorio (venison sausage), chile-roasted corn, and a long list of other delectable botanas.

✕ **Wyngs 'n Spirits.** 100 block of S. Old Pueblo Rd. (next door to the Tigua arts and crafts center); (915) 859-3916 $-$$
A combination of Tigua and Mexican cuisine, specialties here include a savory *chile verde con carne* full of green chiles and jalapeños, *flautas,* (deep-fried enchiladas), and freshly baked Tigua bread.

▭ **Camino Real Paso del Norte Hotel.** 101 S. El Paso; (915) 534-3099/(800) 769-4300 $$$
Built in 1912 and restored in 1981, this grand old hotel has been a stopping point for Pancho Villa and Charles Linberg, Presidents Taft, Hoover, and Johnson, and Gen. John J. Pershing. Listed in the National Register of Historic Places.

Texas Trans-Pecos Food & Lodging

Texas Trans-Pecos Food & Lodging

Fort Davis

✗ **Cueva de León Cafe.** TX 17 at TX 118; (915) 426-3801 $
Legendary hole-in-the-wall with fajitas, burritos, burgers, and catfish.

✗ **The Drugstore.** Main St.; (915) 426-3118 $
Fountain soft drinks, floats and malts, sandwiches. Breakfast and lunch only.

✗ **Limpia Hotel Dining Room.** On the town square; (915) 426-3237 $-$$
Home cooking served family-style in heaping portions. Freshly baked breads and desserts.

⚐ **Davis Mountain Campgrounds.** Three miles west of Fort Davis off TX 118; (915) 426-3337
There are 94 campsites here—each one has tables and cooking grills. Hot showers, restrooms, and a trailer dump site are available.

⚐ **Indian Lodge.** Six miles north of Fort Davis off TX 118, on Park Road 3; (915) 426-3254 $$
The main facility in the park is this 39-room adobe hotel. The older rooms, constructed by the Civilian Conservation Corps, have original cedar furnishings. All guest rooms have television and air-conditioning. There is a good restaurant and a heated swimming pool.

⚐ **Limpia Hotel.** On the town square; (915) 426-3237/ (800) 662-5517 $$
Built of native pink limestone in 1912, last restored in 1990, 14 rooms fur-

nished in period reproductions. Rockers and Chinese checkers on its porches. Smoking is not permitted. Bookstore and souvenir shop.

⚐ **Prude Ranch.** 6.5 miles northwest of Fort Davis off TX 118; (800) 458-6232/ (915) 426-3202 $$
As many as 250 guests can stay in the ranch-style cottages, family cabins, and economy bunkhouses. Fifty horses, indoor pool, two lighted tennis courts.

Guadalupe Mountains National Park

⚐ **Campgrounds.** (915) 828-3251
There are two drive-in campgrounds inside the park: one on the southeast side at Pine Springs, and one on the north at Dog Canyon. First-come, first-served basis.

Van Horn

population 2,930   elevation 4,010

✗ **Smokehouse.** 905 Broadway. I-10 exit 138E, 140W; (915) 283-2453 $
The smoked meats, homemade bread, and mashed potatoes are all standouts here.

⚐ **Howard Johnson's.** One mile west on US 80 Business; (915) 283-2780 / (800) 543-8831 $-$$
Good-value 98-room hotel. Bar, entertainment, sundries. Unheated swimming pool and complimentary golf.

RECOMMENDED READING

Abbey, Edward. *Desert Solitaire: A Season in the Wilderness.* Tucson: University of Arizona Press, 1988 (reprint). Much of this book describes Arches National Monument. Originally published in 1971, this is the earliest and most treasured of Abbey's collections.

Momaday, N. Scott. *House Made of Dawn.* New York: Perennial Library, 1977. A fine Native American writer describes life on the Jémez Indian Reservation.

Castleman, Deke. *Las Vegas.* Oakland: Compass American Guides, Fodor's, 1996. A thrilling, eccentric, and scandal-drenched tour into and beyond the most flamboyant resort city on Earth.

Cather, Willa. *Death Comes for the Archbishop.* New York: Alfred A. Knopf, 1955. The story of a French bishop sent by the Pope to revitalize the Catholic Church in New Mexico during frontier times.

Cheek, Lawrence. *Arizona* and *Santa Fe.* Oakland: Compass American Guides, Fodor's, 1995, 1996. Informative, opinionated, and entertaining guides to the culture and history of the Southwest with extensive practical information.

Gregg, Josiah. *The Commerce of the Prairies.* Norman: University of Oklahoma Press, 1954. The Santa Fe Trail seen through the eyes of a 19th-century trader.

Horgan, Paul. *Great River: The Rio Grande in North American History.* New York: Holt, Rinehart, Winston, 1968. Two volumes describe the early history of New Mexico and offer a fascinating account of the region's clashing cultures.

Waters, Frank. *Book of the Hopi.* New York: Penguin Books, 1977. Waters lived among the Hopis and he writes about their religion and ceremonies with insight.

Wharton, Tom and Gayen. *Utah.* Oakland: Compass American Guides, Fodor's 1995. Tom Wharton, sports editor for the *Salt Lake City Tribune* offers this insiders' guide to the extraordinary canyonlands of southern Utah including Bryce Canyon and Zion National Park.

Thompson, Ian. *Four Corners Country.* Tucson: University of Arizona Press, 1986. Stunning and evocative photographs perfectly capture the Western landscape.

I N D E X

COMPASS AMERICAN GUIDES

Available at your local bookstore, or call (800) 733-3000 to order.

COMPASS AMERICAN GUIDES are available at special discounts for bulk purchases for sales promotions or premiums. Special editions, including personalized covers and corporate imprints, can be created in large quantities for special needs. For more information, call Special Markets at Fodor's Travel Publications, (800) 800-3246.

Arizona (4th Edition)
0-679-03388-2
$18.95 ($26.50 Can)

Chicago (2nd Edition)
1-878-86780-6
$18.95 ($26.50 Can)

Colorado (3rd Edition)
1-878-86781-4
$18.95 ($26.50 Can)

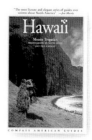

Hawaii (3rd Edition)
1-878-86791-1
$18.95 ($26.50 Can)

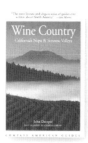

Wine Country (1st Edition)
1-878-86784-9
$18.95 ($26.50 Can)

Montana (3rd Edition)
1-878-86797-0
$18.95 ($26.50 Can)

Oregon (2nd Edition)
1-878-86788-1
$18.95 ($26.50 Can)

New Orleans (3rd Edition)
0-679-03597-4
$18.95 ($26.50 Can)

South Dakota (2nd Edition)
1-878-86747-4
$18.95 ($26,50 Can)

Southwest (2nd Edition)
0-679-00035-6
$18.95 ($26.50 Can)

Texas (2nd Edition)
1-878-86798-9
$18.95 ($26.50 Can)

Utah (4th Edition)
0-679-00030-5
$18.95 ($26.50 Can)

Boston (1st Edition)
1-878-86776-8
$18.95 ($26.50 Can)

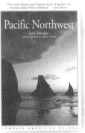

Pacific Northwest (1st Edition)
1-878-86785-7
$19.95 ($27.95 Can)

Alaska (1st Edition)
1-878-86777-6
$18.95 ($26.50 Can)

Minnesota (1st Edition)
1-878-86748-2
$18.95 ($26.50 Can)

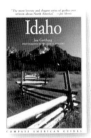

Idaho (1st Edition)
1-878-86778-4
$18.95 ($26.50 Can)

New Mexico (2nd Edition)
1-878-86783-0
$18.95 ($26.50 Can)

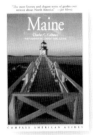

Maine (2nd Edition)
1-878-86796-2
$18.95 ($26.50 Can)

Manhattan (2nd Edition)
1-878-86794-6
$18.95 ($26.50 Can)

Las Vegas (5th Edition)
0-679-00015-1
$18.95 ($26.50 Can)

San Francisco (4th Edition)
1-878-86792-X
$18.95 ($26.50 Can)

Santa Fe (2nd Edition)
0-679-03389-0
$18.95 ($26.50 Can)

South Carolina (2nd Edition)
0-679-03599-0
$18.95 ($26.50 Can)

Virginia (2nd Edition)
1-878-86795-4
$18.95 ($26.50 Can)

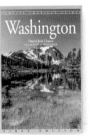

Washington (1st Edition)
1-878-86758-X
$17.95 ($25.00 Can)

Wisconsin (2nd Edition)
1-878-86749-0
$18.95 ($26.50 Can)

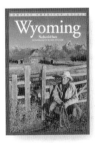

Wyoming (3rd Edition)
0-679-00034-8
$18.95 ($26.50 Can)

◼ ABOUT THE PHOTOGRAPHER

Kerrick James is well known for his photography of the American Southwest. In addition to appearing in Compass *Arizona* and Compass *Las Vegas,* his work is featured frequently in *Arizona Highways, Hemispheres,* and *National Geographic Traveler.* He lives in Mesa, Arizona, with his wife and two sons.

◼ ABOUT THE CONTRIBUTORS

Lawrence Cheek is author of Compass *Santa Fe* and Compass *Arizona,* as well as *A.D.1250: Ancient People of the Southwest,* and is also a contributing editor for *Compass Southwest.* A long-time resident of Tucson, he grew up in El Paso, Texas, and is widely traveled in the Southwest.

Tom Wharton is sports editor for the *Salt Lake City Tribune* and author of Compass *Utah* as well as other guidebooks to his home state. With his wife, Gayen, co-author of Utah, he has camped and hiked throughout the Utah Canyonlands and has run the rapids of the Colorado River through the Grand Canyon.

Nancy Harbert is author of Compass *New Mexico.* She lives in Albuquerque, New Mexico, where she reports for *Time* magazine and contributes to *New Mexico Magazine, AAA's Car & Travel,* and the *Albuquerque Journal.*

Dick J. Reavis of Dallas is author of Compass *Texas* and of *Ashes of Waco* published by Simon & Schuster. He knows Texas well, having driven every road on the state highway department map of Texas in writing his *Texas Monthly* column, "National Tour of Texas."

Deke Castleman, author of Compass *Las Vegas,* is managing editor of the *Las Vegas Advisor,* a monthly newsletter for visitors and locals. He lives in Las Vegas with his wife and children, writing articles and books on Las Vegas and Nevada in his spare time.

Jon Klusmire, author of Compass *Colorado,* reports for the *Aspen Times* and corresponds for the *Denver Post, the Rocky Mountain News,* and *Colorado Business* magazine. He lives in Glenwood Springs.